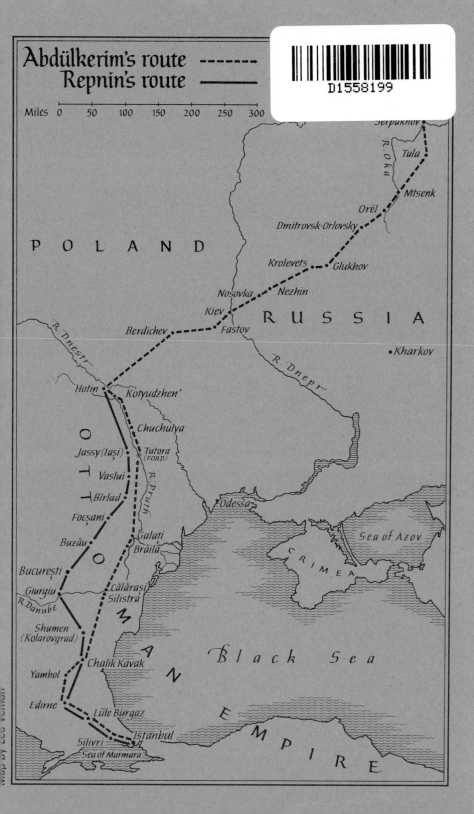

Abdülkerim's route ------
Repnin's route ———

Miles 0   50   100   150   200   250   300

POLAND

RUSSIA

R. Dnestr

R. Dnepr

Kharkov

Serpukhov

R. Oka

Tula

Mtsenk

Orël

Dmitrovsk-Orlovsky

Krolevets   Glukhov

Nosovka   Nezhin

Kiev

Berdichev   Fastov

Hotin   Kotyudzhen'

Chuchulya

Jassy (Iaşi)   Tutora
                (FORD)

Vaslui

Bîrlad

R. Pruth

Focşani

Buzău

Odessa

Galaţi

Brăila

Sea of Azov

CRIMEA

Bucureşti

Giurgiu

R. Danube

Călăraşi

Silistra

Shumen
(Kolarovgrad)

Chalik Kavak

Black   Sea

Yambol

Edirne   Lüle Burgaz

Silivri   Istanbul

Sea of Marmara

OTTOMAN

EMPIRE

Mubadele

Mubadele is the formal ceremony of exchange wherein a visiting ambassador and an Ottoman ambassador change places across the frontier.

Mubadele–

An Ottoman-Russian Exchange of Ambassadors

Annotated and Translated by
Norman Itzkowitz and Max Mote

The University of Chicago Press
Chicago and London

*The University of Chicago Press,
Chicago 60637
The University of Chicago Press,
Ltd., London*

*© 1970 by The University of
Chicago. All rights reserved
Published 1970
Printed in the United States of
America*

*International Standard Book Number:
0–226–38804-2
Library of Congress Catalog Card
Number: 77–108933*

For İsmet Parmaksızoğlu
and the late Lewis V. Thomas

Contents

Abbreviations   viii

Translator's Note   viii

Preface   ix

Introduction   1

I. The *Sefaretname* of
Abdülkerim Pasha   53

II. The Russian Embassy
to Constantinople in 1776 123

Travel Routes   205

Glossary and Biographical
Dictionary   209

Bibliography   241

Index   247

Abbreviations

BVA   Başvekâlet Arşivi, Istanbul.

Chteniia   Moscow University. I. Obshchestvo istorii i drevnostei rossiiskikh. *Chteniia.* 64 vols. Moscow, 1846–1918.

EI^2 *Encyclopaedia of Islam.* New ed. Leiden, 1954–.

İA   *İslam Ansiklopedisi.* Istanbul, 1941–.

MAE   Archives du Ministère des Affaires Étrangères, Paris.

PRO   Public Record Office, London.

PSZ   *Polnoe sobranie zakonov Rossiiskoi Imperii s 1649 goda.* 45 vols. Saint Petersburg, 1830.

RBS   *Russkii biograficheskii slovar'.* 25 vols. Saint Petersburg, 1896–1918.

S.P.   State Papers (foreign) PRO.

SRIO   *Sbornik imperatorskago Russkago istoricheskago obshchestva.* 148 vols. Saint Petersburg, 1897–1916.

TKS   Topkapı Sarayı Müze Arşivi, Istanbul.

Translator's Note

In the absence of a standardized system of transliteration for Ottoman Turkish, modern Turkish usage has been adopted for names and terms. Terms accepted into English are spelled as found in the dictionary, but vezir has been preferred to vizier.

Place Names
For the sake of consistency, place names have been given, with the exception of some generally accepted spellings, as listed in the United States Gazetteers published by the Board on Geographic Names.

Dates
The conversion tables by F. R. Unat, cited in the bibliography, were used for the basic chronology when dealing with Muslim dates. Because the Muslim day commences on the previous eve, the conversions have not always been exactly in agreement with Unat's tables. The dates given here have been carefully worked out, and represent as accurate a picture as possible.

Preface

The two translations presented in this book offer to students of Ottoman and Russian studies, and to those of diplomacy in general, the first opportunity to observe in detail an exchange of Ottoman and Russian ambassadors from the point of view of both parties. The introduction places in historical context the diplomatic moment following the peace of Küçük Kaynarca. We have not exhausted the research possibilities that this confrontation between the Ottoman and Russian empires affords, but rather we have sought to make material available to others in an area that requires special language skills, and we have ventured several hypotheses on the broader implications of the rise of Russia and the decline of the Ottoman Empire.

In a study of this kind, involving translation rather than paraphrase, researchers probably incur more debts than in any other form of historical investigation. The roster of those who willingly gave their time and knowledge would rival in length the retinues of our ambassadors. We would like, however, to offer special thanks to the directors and personnel of the Başvekâlet Arşivi and the Topkapı Sarayı Müze Arşivi. They were all most kind and helpful. Esat Fuat Tugay and Dr. Halil

Sahillioğlu graciously shared their funds of forgotten lore. Mr. Voldemars Kadikis, Father Georges Florovsky, and Professor Cyril Toumanoff also contributed their advice and special knowledge. Mrs. J. Fantova and Mr. L. Spellman, the former and the present curator of maps at Princeton University, were always most patient and knowledgeable. Professor Martin Dickson and Dr. G. L. Lewis made many helpful suggestions on knotty problems of Ottoman syntax. We are also indebted to the United States Office of Education for a Center grant to undertake the initial research, and to Professor Morroe Berger and the Princeton Program in Near Eastern Studies for timely support of this project. None of the individuals or institutions mentioned is responsible for the views expressed here, or for the shortcomings of this work.

This study grew out of readings with İsmet Parmaksızoğlu and was sustained by his constant encouragement and guidance. It also embodies an understanding of the Ottomans imparted by the late Lewis V. Thomas, professor of Ottoman history at Princeton University. Dedication of this work to the two of them only partially repays a great debt.

Introduction

Ottoman Awareness of Europe

The accepted interpretation notwithstanding, it can be argued
with much cogency that success spoiled the Ottoman Empire
in the eighteenth century. True enough, that century opened
with but bleak prospects in view. The Treaty of Karlowitz,
signed on 26 January 1699, appeared to be a betrayal of the
Ottoman raison d'être as a ghazi state.[1] Apart from such
exceptional areas as Ragusa, with which relations were governed by special treaty, the Ottoman world view classified
areas as belonging to either the abode of war (*dâr ül-harp*) or to
the abode of Islam (*dâr ül-islâm*). It was the duty of the sultan
to see that the abode of Islam expanded at the expense of the
abode of war. The reverse was catastrophe, and that was
exactly what had happened in 1699. Territory that had been
Ottoman over a long span of years was allowed, for the first
time, to fall into Christian hands. Unpopular as the Karlowitz
treaty was, it did not lack for apologists. Among their number

[1] The ghazi thesis is best stated in Paul Wittek, *The Rise of the Ottoman Empire*.

1

was the historian Naima. The preface to his chronicle embodies a deft defense of the treaty. Peace, he argued, even on unfavorable terms, was required in order to enable the empire to regroup its forces and renew its strength. Once revitalized, Ottoman arms would again be victorious. As a precedent for such seemingly un-Muslimlike behavior he cited the truce of Hudaybiyah that Muhammad had made with the Meccans in A.D. 627.[2] When necessary the Prophet himself had been willing to treat not just with infidels (as in the Ottoman case), but even with idolaters. The truce of Hudaybiyah had served its purpose, and the subsequent success of the Muslim cause bore out the Prophet's astuteness in concluding a treaty when he was not fully prepared to fight. The moral was clear.

Given the requisite breathing spell, Ottoman arms were indeed successful, as Naima had predicted. Russia was defeated on the banks of the Pruth in 1711, the Morea was reconquered from the Venetians in 1715, and the key fortress of Belgrade and parts of Walachia were regained from the Habsburgs by the treaty of Belgrade in 1739. In Ottoman circles there was talk, not all of it vainglorious, of redeeming the failures of 1529 and 1683. During the negotiations that issued in the Belgrade treaty, Hekimoğlu Ali Pasha was able to boast, as well as threaten, that the road to Vienna was open and he knew the way.[3]

After 1739 the Ottoman Empire entered upon a long period of peace on its European frontier. There was such faith in the efficacy of the empire's renewed military capabilities that no significant reforms were undertaken in the next several decades, even during the grand vezirate of Rağıp Mehmet Pasha who enjoys an unwarranted reputation as an early Westernizer. Courted by both Prussia and Denmark as they sought alliances to bolster their position in a Europe wracked by the Seven Years' War, Rağıp Mehmet Pasha held the empire to a course of nonalignment while Sultan Mustafa III busied himself with

---

[2] Mustafa Naima, *Tarih-i Naima*, 3d ed., 1:13.
[3] PRO S.P. 97/30, 4 September 1739.

the renovation of Edirne. The internal and external problems that plagued the empire were glossed over and relegated to the background amidst round after round of meaningless, but traditional, ceremonies. Soon after the steadying hand of the grand vezir was removed by his death, by natural causes, in 1763, the Ottomans found themselves at war with Russia.

The immediate cause of the conflict with Russia that broke out in 1768 was the burning of Balta in Podolia by Ukrainian irregulars in pursuit of Poles loyal to the Confederation of Bar. As with most armed conflicts, its roots were a good deal deeper. The death of Augustus III of Poland in 1763 had set in motion complicated diplomatic maneuverings to influence the election of his successor. Russia and Prussia shared a common interest in the exclusion of an Austrian candidate from the Polish throne. Russia favored the election of a Pole who would then be in no position to oppose the extension of Russian interests. Prussia feared that a French or Austrian candidate would be an obstacle to any future expansion eastward. Russian coercion in Poland and the threat of a Prussian army massed on the Polish frontier resulted in the Diet's election of their candidate, Stanislaw Poniatowski, in 1764. France sought to stem the advance of Russia and Prussia by urging the Ottomans to take a more active interest in Polish affairs. While the Ottomans hesitated, the Poles themselves resisted Russian efforts to stifle Poniatowski's attempts to reform the Polish constitution. It was during the period of the Russian attempts to suppress the Polish movement of national revival centered around the Confederation of Bar that the city of Balta was burned. The Ottomans held the Russians responsible for that raid on a city technically under Ottoman sovereignty. Torches accomplished what French diplomacy had failed to achieve; the Ottomans declared war on Russia in October 1768.

The war dragged on for four years. In 1774 the experience of 1699 was repeated. Again the Ottomans were brought up short by the stark reality of a disastrous military defeat. The treaty of Küçük Kaynarca was the jolt that awakened the empire to the

need for reform. The simplistic prescriptions of Naima would
not do; the empire was in need of more than a breathing spell.
These were different times, and different remedies would have
to be found. Success earlier in the eighteenth century had
fostered failure in 1774. The Ottomans would now turn to
Europe for access first to the military cutting edge of her
civilization, and inevitably European ideas would follow.
Ottoman awareness of Europe, which would take on new
dimensions and lead eventually to the *Tanzimat* reforms and
beyond, built up slowly and steadily after the treaty of
Küçük Kaynarca.

One channel through which information about Europe
passed into the empire was the reports of Ottoman ambassadors.
In the days of the unreformed Ottoman Empire few Ottomans
ventured beyond the confines of the *memâlik-i mahrusa*, the
divinely protected Ottoman domains, into the countries of
Christendom. Those who did were usually on official business,
particularly the business of diplomacy. Prior to the establishment of regular Ottoman diplomatic representation in European capitals, commencing with London in 1793, embassies
were dispatched on an ad hoc basis. As the need arose, Ottoman ambassadors found themselves journeying to such
Frankish centers as Paris, Vienna, Saint Petersburg, and
Moscow to announce the accession of a new sultan, or to
transmit a ratified treaty. Scribes were assigned to the embassies
to keep the mission's records, handle correspondence, and
compose the final report, the *sefaretname*. These *sefaretname*s,
over forty of which have been preserved in part or in full,
form the main literary legacy of Ottoman travel in European
lands.[4] Although neither as rich nor as varied as the Western
literature of travel in the Levant, *sefaretname*s present a unique
view of pre-*Tanzimat* Ottoman officials as they came in contact
with Europe and various material aspects of its civilization.

[4] Faik Reşit Unat, "Şehdî Osman Efendi Sefaretnamesi," in *Tarih Vesikaları*, 1:66–
70. Also, Maarif Vekilliği Kütüphaneler Müdürlüğü Tasnif Komisyonu,
"Sefaretnameler," in *İstanbul Kütüphaneleri Tarih-Coğrafya Yazmaları Katalogları*,
pp. 757–84.

The glimpses of Ottomans reacting to complex and unfamiliar situations are a welcome complement to the all too often lifeless leaves in chronicles. These reports remind us that the Ottomans were human beings and not just peculiar names frozen on the pages of antiquated annals. Moreover, when studied in conjunction with archival documents the *sefaretnames* provide insights into the workings of the state's administrative apparatus. Abdülkerim Pasha was charged with the task of conveying the letter ratifying the treaty of Küçük Kaynarca to Catherine the Second. The report of his embassy is the first *sefaretname* written after the rude awakening provoked by the defeat at the hands of the Russians. This translation and study was undertaken to determine what indications can be found in the *sefaretname* of Ottoman awareness of Europe and what details can be learned about the institution of ambassador and the organization of such an Ottoman embassy.

Treaties seldom make good reading, and that of Küçük Kaynarca signed between Russia and the Ottoman Empire on 21 July 1774 is no exception. Yet, those who have persevered in their study of the treaty beyond the now famous article dealing with Russia's relationship to the Orthodox church in Ottoman lands, may have had their imaginations stirred by article twenty-seven.

> But in order that the present peace and sincere friendship between the two Empires be so much the more strongly and authentically sealed and confirmed there shall be sent on both sides solemn and extra-ordinary Embassies with the Imperial ratifications signed confirmatory of the treaty of Peace at such times as shall be agreed upon by both the High Contracting Parties. The ambassadors shall be met on the frontiers in the same manner and they shall be received and treated with the same honors and ceremonies as are observed in the respective Embassies between the Ottoman Porte and the most respectable Powers and as a testimonial of friendship, there shall be mutually sent through the medium of the said Ambassadors presents which shall be proportionate to the dignity of their Imperial Majesties.[5]

[5] J. C. Hurewitz, *Diplomacy in the Near and Middle East*, 1:60–61.

An Ottoman embassy to Moscow in the late eighteenth
century, extraordinary in the diplomatic sense could hardly fail
to be so in the literal sense as well.

The Ottomans named Abdülkerim Efendi, a career bureaucrat, ambassador extraordinary to head the mission to Moscow.
This selection of a career bureaucrat as ambassador was in
keeping with Ottoman practice. Before 1793 most Ottoman
ambassadors were drawn from the bureaucracy and relatively
few from the ulema.[6] Like many other Ottoman ambassadors
before him, Abdülkerim bore the title of *seyyid*, which indicates a claim of descent from the Prophet. Perhaps it was
thought by some that *seyyid*hood would serve as protection
against cultural contamination by the nonbelievers. After the
round of ceremonies associated with an ambassador's departure, Abdülkerim, now elevated to the dignity of pasha, left
Istanbul with his retinue on 2 February 1775. They traveled
through Edirne, Silistra, Galaţi, Brăila, Hotin, Kiev, Orël, and
Tula, and on 18 October 1775, with full pomp, they made their
formal entry into Moscow. They left on 8 February 1776 and,
traveling by a slightly different route, reached Istanbul on 17
August 1776. It had taken them more than a year and a half
to complete their mission.

After the embassy's return to Istanbul the report, or *sefaretname*, was submitted, presumably to the sultan.[7] Although this
report has come down to us as the *sefaretname* of Abdülkerim
Pasha, it was largely the work of Nahifi Mehmet Efendi, a
scribe attached to the mission.[8] As is the case with many Ottoman figures, little is known about the life and career of either
Abdülkerim or Nahifi Mehmet. Abdülkerim was brought up
in the household of Mustafa Pasha, a man who served as grand

[6] In addition to the material given in note 4 see the charming extract from
Naima quoted in Bernard Lewis, *Istanbul and the Civilization of the Ottoman Empire*,
pp. 169–72.
[7] Mehmet Zeki Pakalın, "Sefaretname," in *Osmanlı Tarih Deyimleri ve Terimleri
Sözlüğü*, 3:138–39.
[8] Maarif Vekilliği, *Yazmalar*, p. 768. His name does not appear in the text. He
usually refers to himself as "this humble servant."

vezir. Abdülkerim was his seal-keeper. In 1756 or 1757 he
entered the ranks of the *hacegân*, the broad upper bracket of the
Ottoman bureaucracy populated mainly by bureau chiefs. His
entrance into that select group was most likely accomplished
by his patron Mustafa Pasha, for membership in the *hacegân*
was usually attained by promotion through the bureaucratic
ranks rather than by lateral integration. Before Abdülkerim
was appointed ambassador, he followed the typical *hacegân*
career pattern of rotation as chief from one bureau to another.
He was for a time chief of the bureau concerned with the pay
records of the salaried cavalry and the agas of the palace. This
position of his is mentioned in the *sefaretname*. After his Russian
experience Abdülkerim returned to the ranks of the *hacegân*,
serving as head of the cadastral archives in 1788. He died soon
after. There is no indication in the *sefaretname*, or in other
sources, why Abdülkerim was selected as ambassador, except
for the statement in the text that he was a man of reasonably
good intellect and was in the proper group—the upper stratum
of the bureaucracy. His status as a *seyyid* was perhaps a factor
in his favor.

Nahifi Mehmet Efendi was a bureaucratic efendi who had
served in the grand vezir's secretariat prior to his appointment
as secretary to Abdülkerim's diplomatic mission. After his
return to Istanbul he resumed his career in the bureaucracy
and served as chief of various bureaus until his death, also in
1788. The *sefaretname* translated here embodies many of his
own observations and comments. In the case of both these
men, therefore, we are dealing with Ottomans whose careers
were centered in Istanbul and who apparently had had no
previous first-hand knowledge of the lands beyond the Islamic
pale. We shall return to the problem of Muslim provincialism
and the outside world after considering the manuscript and the
technicalities of the translation.

This translation is based on the manuscript of the *sefaretname*
in the Esat Efendi collection, no. 2280, in the Süleymaniye
Library of Istanbul. The manuscript consists of fifty folios with

twenty-five lines to the page and is written in a fine *nesih*
script.[9] As a base it has been preferred here to the printed version which was published in Istanbul in 1898 by Ahmet Cevdet.
That "edition" is typical of many such publishing ventures of
late Ottoman times. Cevdet's text is derived from an unidentified manuscript. Some notes have been added that deal primarily with a rendition into French of place and personal
names the editor thought might present difficulties to his
readers. Ahmet Cevdet, who was a learned journalist and
founder of the newspaper *İkdam*, provided the text of the
sefaretname with some elements of Western punctuation, including paragraphs, parentheses, and periods. In addition,
several verbal forms from the late eighteenth century were
changed to those current in the late nineteenth. This may be
a reflection of Ahmet Cevdet's strong interest in simplified,
pure Turkish.

These pamphlet editions have lasted poorly. They are exceedingly difficult to find and are often difficult for librarians
to preserve. The text of the Esat Efendi manuscript, readily
available on microfilm, did not differ significantly enough from
the printed text to necessitate a critical establishment of the
text for the purposes of translation. Important differences are
few, and when they occur they are cited in the notes. Two main
differences may be noted here. The description of Moscow
given in the manuscript lacks some of the detail found in the
printed text. These details have been added to the translation
with appropriate references to the pages of the printed text.
Of greater significance, however, are the last few folios of the
manuscript which contain a section entitled "Things Seen and
Heard." That section presents information on the situation in
Poland, as well as observations on Russian history. The printed
text does not contain this material.

The language of the text is not consciously obscurantist.
With the exception of a few common Arabic sayings, the use
of Arabic is limited to items of vocabulary. What little poetry

[9] On *nesih* and other scripts see Mahmud Yazır, *Eski Yazılar Anahtarı*.

there is makes its point effectively, but without literary distinction. Although his style is far from being perspicuous, Nahifi Mehmet Efendi does not indulge in the favorite Ottoman literary pastime of sending his reader to the dictionary as often as possible. He refrains from saying the same thing three times, once in Arabic, once in Persian, and once again in Turkish, except in the few places where such a practice is almost traditional. The introduction, titles of high-ranking officials, and several lengthy, highly Persianized passages of description constitute the bulk of the decorative sections in which clarity of expression is sacrificed to the requirements of rhymed prose. A main difficulty in translating rhymed prose is finding felicitous English equivalents. One must also be aware that seemingly simple words may have several layers of meaning—religious, ethical, and mystical. An attempt has been made to remain as faithful as possible to the original Ottoman text, within the limits of the more important object of making the translation intelligible to the interested reader, specialist and nonspecialist alike. To achieve this goal certain modest liberties have been taken. Forms, usually adjectival patterns, that have been paired solely for the purposes of rhyme, or for stylistic balance, have been rendered into English as an adverb and adjective, or some combining form. Sentences in Turkish tend to be rather lengthy with few finite verbs. In the translation shorter sentences have been favored. At times this has required the repetition of the subject or some other element, in order to achieve a more readily comprehensible translation.

In the text of the *sefaretname* Abdülkerim is referred to not by name, but by the title *Elçi Paşa*, "the Pasha, Mr. Ambassador." This has been translated simply as "the ambassador." Here and there in the translation Abdülkerim is referred to as the Ottoman ambassador, although the adjective does not appear in the text. In an Ottoman sentence it can be difficult at times to determine who is speaking and who is being spoken about. Several devices are employed in the language to decrease the possibility of confusion. Consistently in this *sefaretname*

Muslims who are either speakers or objects of conversation are indicated by the expression *müşarünileyh*, and non-Muslims by the expression *mumaileyh*, both of which mean "the aforementioned." In the translation the repetitious "the aforementioned" has been dispensed with.

The tone of the *sefaretname* is subdued. There is no bombast. The superiority of the Ottoman Way is not flaunted. At times the Ottomans do become somewhat exasperated with Russian insistences upon the observance of protocol, but they hold their exasperation in check. Abdülkerim may have been provincial with respect to the world beyond the confines of the Islamic empire in which he lived, but he was fully conversant with his own Muslim tradition. That tradition places great value on *adab*—manners in the best and broadest sense.[10] He was an Ottoman gentleman, and this comes through most clearly.

This is not to say, however, that the *sefaretname* is devoid of criticism. It is there, but it is low-keyed and of inconsequential things. For example, Western singing, dancing, and music are disparaged. The music is considered to be outside the laws of harmony, the singing is likened to the creaking of doors and the buzzing of flies, and the dancing is compared to the pecking of chickens. This is not criticism of a serious nature and may even have been necessary to placate those in Ottoman society who would have been outraged by any description of Frankish life. The lengthiest descriptive passages are those devoted to the gardens and greenhouse in Kiev, the theater in Moscow, and the social events attended by men and women together in the presence of the empress. There are no direct indications in the report, other than the length of the descriptions, that anything seen or experienced might be worthy of adoption or emulation. No judgments, favorable or unfavorable, are passed. The Ottoman audience is left to draw its own conclusions.

What was the audience for such a work? Clearly, the *sefaretname* was an official rather than a literary document. It was

---

10 Clear insight into Ottoman manners is provided in the didactic poem by Nabi Efendi, *Conseils de Nabi Efendi*, trans. M. Pavet de Courteille.

intended primarily for the sultan, and then for the top administrators of the empire, that small group of professionals who
were concerned with foreign relations. It is another of the
many sources of information on the affairs of Europe available
to the Ottoman government. In many ways it can also be
considered an intelligence report, for it contains information on
roads, the location of fortresses and strongholds, and local
conditions. The Ottomans do not appear to have been planning
any trans-Danubian campaigns, but they were probably glad
to have the information. Other sources of information on
Europe available to the Porte included reports from the voi-
vodes of Moldavia and Walachia—the main Ottoman listening
posts on Europe—advices from renegades, and the steady
stream of that mixture of gossip, rumor, falsification, and fact
supplied by the community of European ambassadors resident
in Istanbul. Like all states, the Ottoman government continu-
ally gathered political and other kinds of information for its
own use. In the Ottoman Empire that knowledge and information was the monopoly of a circumscribed group of people.
It rarely filtered down into general Ottoman opinion. The
filter was clogged at both ends. The government did not really
wish to disseminate the information, and the Ottomans were
not particularly interested in obtaining it. The term Ottoman
here is used to signify those who qualified for first-class status
in that society by serving the religion (being Muslim), serving
the state (holding a position that gave them a state income and
a privileged tax status), and knowing the Ottoman Way (using
the Ottoman Turkish language and conforming to the manners and customs of the society that used Ottoman Turkish).[11]
These Ottomans were cut off from Europe by both a religious
barrier and a physical frontier.[12] Europe did not impinge on

[11] The definition of who was an Ottoman is a complicated problem. What is
offered here is only an attempt at a working definition derived from Lewis V.
Thomas. See also, Norman Itzkowitz, "Mehmed Raghib Pasha: The Making of
an Ottoman Grand Vezir," pp. 15–21.
[12] On the effects of this frontier, especially in the economic sphere, see Robert
Mantran, *Istanbul dans la seconde moitié du XVIIe siècle*, pp. 179–231.

their consciousness enough for them to have more than a vague notion that Europe was somehow inferior. This notion rested, ultimately, on the primacy of the Islamic dispensation. From the existence of several manuscript copies of a number of *sefaretname*s,[13] we may conclude that the reports did not circulate far beyond the small group of officials at the Porte. The printing of several *sefaretname*s in the late nineteenth century widened the audience, but back in 1776 the *sefaretname* of Abdülkerim Pasha, in manuscript, was no intellectual shot heard round the Ottoman world.[14]

While not an explosive document calculated to jar the Ottomans loose from their complacency, Abdülkerim's report does contain several items indicative of views perhaps somewhat less narrow than those dominant in Istanbul. The report speaks, for example, of Peter the Great's concern for the proper allocation and expenditure of military funds, and for the primacy of military matters. Firearms and other war implements of excellent quality produced in the city of Tula through the combination of technology and craftmanship are described almost with envy. Day and night, the report notes, the Russians engaged in this industry attempted to perfect their techniques in order to become superior to similar craftsmen in other countries. Was the ambassador hinting that it was time for the Ottomans to put their own military house in order and try to move ahead in technological matters? The report contains a lengthy description of a greenhouse in Kiev. Is that merely a reflection of the Turkish interest in horticulture, or is it simultaneously an indication to other Ottomans that significant things were going on in Europe and that they ought to take notice? Curiosities always attract attention, but the function of their description may also be didactic. Change in the Ottoman Empire was initiated from the top. If the sultan's interest could

---

[13] Maarif Vekilliği, *Yazmalar*, pp. 757–84.

[14] The account of Ahmet Resmi's embassy to Prussia was printed in Istanbul in 1885–86, and Ali Moralı Efendi's account of his mission to France was printed in 1891–92. For others see the material in note 4.

be attracted, then a beginning in some new direction might be made.

The open advocacy of receptivity to things European, especially so soon after a defeat, was probably neither good form nor safe. The *sefaretname* makes certain information available, but by not assuming a position overtly in favor of the adoption and emulation of things European in origin, Abdülkerim does not prejudice opinion against change by backing it too strongly, nor does he place himself in a potentially embarrassing and dangerous situation. It is important to note here, however, that Abdülkerim is not negatively disposed toward change. The report nowhere becomes a vehicle for advice to the prince, harking back to past Ottoman glories and seeing the chief cure for the empire's faltering fortunes in a return to the practices of Süleyman's golden age. What is not said, therefore, is as important as what is said.

All things considered, the report is not a particularly pro-Western document. Why, one might ask, was Abdülkerim Pasha not more favorably impressed with what he saw, more interested in society and institutions? One possible reason, in addition to the factors cited above, is that Russia, despite almost half a century of Petrine reforms, may not have appeared to him to be all that different from the Ottoman domains. Both were still sprawling agricultural empires, on the surface more alike than different. Also, the hostility between the two empires would not have predisposed the ambassador to be favorably impressed. More important, however, is the role played by Islam.

The Ottomans were a great universal, dynastic Islamic state. They had inherited the full Islamic tradition and were the prime protectors of Muslim orthodoxy. To them in 1775–76 the world of Islam was still *the* world. A sincere Islamic feeling pervades this *sefaretname*. There is a quiet, but firm sense of the righteousness of Islam, and an awareness of the intimacy between the Muslim and his God. The trust in God to see the embassy through to a successful conclusion of its mission and a safe return to Istanbul is far from being mere fatalism. The concern on the part of the ambassador for Muslim prisoners in Russian hands is real and deep. To Ottoman sultans gaining freedom for these prisoners was a sacred obligation for which they were prepared to make heavy sacrifices.[15] It is wrong to consider religiousness among the Ottomans simply affectation, and religion solely the handmaiden of politics. The virtues of self-analysis and self-criticism, however, do not appear to have been common among the Ottomans,[16] but this was not a serious problem as long as they continued to be successful in the field against the Europeans. When the tide turned before the gates of Vienna in 1683 and the dikes were breached by the treaty of Karlowitz in 1699, Ottoman reflection on the causes of those defeats and the measures necessary to avoid further disasters was strictly within the Islamic-Ottoman pattern and tradition. The remedies suggested by Naima and others had worked earlier in the eighteenth century, but their efficaciousness turned out to be illusory. This *sefaretname* was written too early in the development of a new atmosphere which would be favorable to change to expect it to be a more aware, more self-critical and analytical document than it is. One must remember that it was the product of Ottoman bureaucrats functioning as diplomats. Their training and roots were totally on the other side of the watershed represented by the treaty of Küçük Kaynarca. Although this *sefaretname* is no outspoken proponent of change, neither is it a reactionary tract in favor of cultural seclusion. Modest as it is, it is a beginning step in the process that ultimately made late Ottoman opinion, previously unconcerned with Europe, aware of both the dangers and the opportunities it presented.

[15] BVA Cevdet/hariciye, 2357. The term used is *fariza*, and the injunction is Koranic, surah 9, verse 60. "The alms are only for the poor and the needy, and those who collect them, and those whose hearts are to be reconciled, and to free the captives and the debtors and for the cause of Allah . . . ," Marmaduke Pickthall, *The Meaning of the Glorious Koran*, p. 199.
[16] Bernard Lewis, *The Middle East and the West*, p. 29.

The Ambassador as an Ottoman Institution

Little is known about the selection, organization, and procedures of ad hoc Ottoman embassies dispatched to foreign courts prior to the establishment of regular diplomatic relations with European states in 1793.[17] Professor Faik Reşit Unat, who did the most fruitful groundwork on this subject, was on the point of publishing a full-scale study of Ottoman ambassadors and their *sefaretname*s when he died in 1964. In the absence of such a synthesis it is worthwhile to present the specific information on those matters gleaned from both this *sefaretname* of Abdülkerim Pasha and archival materials related to his and other diplomatic missions.

Early in this *sefaretname* we are told of the selection of Abdülkerim as ambassador to Catherine the Second. Then we are given a description of some of the ceremonies involved in his investiture and leave-taking, and the exact time of his departure is noted. There is no further information in the *sefaretname* on his selection, nor did anything on that matter come to light in the archives. There is, however, an archival document that provides illuminating information on the arrangements for the ceremonies themselves. The information pertains specifically to the embassy of Mustafa Rasih Pasha to Russia in 1793 but appears to be valid for Abdülkerim's case as well, since it contains a review of past procedures.

The document is a memorandum to the sultan from the grand vezir.[18] Although some two inches of paper along the entire length of the right side of the document have been eroded away, most of its contents can be reconstructed: the sultan is informed that an ambassador (Rasih Pasha) is being sent to Russia and the time for his departure is drawing near. He must be entrusted with the royal gifts and letter he will

17 On the beginnings of regular Ottoman diplomatic relations with Europe see Thomas Naff, "Reform and the Conduct of Ottoman Diplomacy in the Reign of Selim III, 1789–1807," *Journal of the American Oriental Society*, 83, no. 3 (Sept. 1963): 295–315.
18 BVA Hatt-ı Hümâyun 14380.

carry to the empress. When Hatti Efendi was sent to Austria as ambassador in 1754 the gifts were brought from the royal treasury to the Porte.[19] After being checked and inspected, they were returned to the sultan's treasury to be placed in their wrappings. They were then handed over to the ambassador. When Ahmet Resmi was sent to Prussia in 1763, the gifts were brought to the Porte where they were handed over to the ambassador immediately after their inspection. Then, with the cognizance of the ambassador, they were placed in their wrappings. Since then the gifts have been handed over directly to the ambassador, in the presence of the grand vezir, without having to be returned to the treasury. The ambassador receives the royal letter during an audience with the sultan to which he is invited a few days after the ceremony for the gifts. The document states that the time for the ambassador's departure has been fixed for a day ten days away. Of those ten days one day for the gifts and one day for the letter must be set aside. A schedule is suggested, which calls for the ceremony of the gifts to take place on Wednesday and the audience with the sultan on Saturday, but the final decision, it is noted, rests as usual, with the sultan.

In the upper right-hand corner of the document is the reply in the sultan's own hand. The portion of the reply that is still legible reads, "Let the gifts be handed over on Wednesday and the audience be held on Saturday as stated in your memorandum. After that, let him depart. May God grant him a safe journey."

It is apparent from the précis of the above document that once an ambassador had been named and the preparations for his departure had progressed to the point where he was about to set out on his mission, two ceremonies were arranged, one for him to take possession of the gifts, and the other for him to receive the royal letter. Those arrangements were made

---

[19] The date given in the document for Hatti Efendi's embassy is 1167/1753–54, but according to the information in Maarif Vekilliği, *Yazmalar*, p. 772, it took place in 1748.

within the framework of the established protocol that had itself undergone a change in 1763. The timetable for those ceremonies was established after a propitious departure time had been determined. The sultan was then informed of the arrangements, and his agreement secured.

In this *sefaretname* it is noted that on 26 January 1775 Abdül-kerim took possession of the gifts in a formal ceremony carried out in the presence of the grand vezir. On Saturday, 28 January 1775, he had an audience with the sultan. At that time he received the instrument of ratification (*tasdikname*) and probably the royal letter as well. He left Istanbul with his retinue two days later, at 5:31. The time is given according to the Turkish-Muslim method of reckoning the hours. Sundown is taken as the beginning of a twenty-four-hour day divided into two twelve-hour segments. If we fix sundown in January at present-day 5 P.M., they would have left at 10:31 A.M. They spent the first night at Küçükçekmece, which is about a five- or six-hour march from Istanbul.[20] According to these calculations, they would have arrived there close to sundown. From the internal evidence in the memorandum it is reasonable to assume that the ceremonies for Abdülkerim Pasha were scheduled in the same manner as those for Rasih Pasha.

There is frequent mention in the *sefaretname* of the gifts the embassy carried to Catherine the Second. Although generous by nature, the Ottomans were also compelled by article twenty-seven of the treaty to send the gifts. Reflecting the sentiment expressed in the Turkish proverb, *veren el acı duymaz* (the giving hand feels no pain), the Ottomans prepared a varied array of costly gifts for the empress. There is no detailed description of the gifts in the *sefaretname* itself, but two lists do exist. One list is in the archives of the Topkapı Palace,[21] and the other is

---

[20] Hans Dernschwam's *Tagebuch einer Reise nach Konstantinopel und Kleinasien* (1553/55), ed. Franz Babinger, p. 29. See also R. G. Boscovich, *Giornale di un Viaggio da Constantinopoli in Polonia*, pp. 8–9. For a description of the region see Hans J. Kissling, *Beiträge zur Kenntnis Thrakiens im 17. Jahrhundert*. On telling time see Ghazi Ahmed Moukhtar Pasha, *La reforme du calendrier* (Leiden, 1893).
[21] TKS E 3957.

in a register of important state acts and papers preserved in
the Başvekâlet Arşivi.[22] Professor L. Fekete has published the
Topkapı document.[23] It is almost identical with the list in the
register, but without some of the details of cost given there.

The gifts are grouped under sixty-six headings and include
an aigrette encrusted with diamonds and emeralds, and a silver
breast collar for a horse, with head harness, studded with 385
diamonds. A large sapphire, surrounded by diamonds and
rubies, decorated the center of the collar. Another costly gift
was a gold sword in a red-velvet sheath. The handle was made
of jade worked in enamels, with diamonds and other precious
stones on the hilt and cross piece. There was also a pair of
stirrups embellished with 136 diamonds, 6 garnets, and 4
emeralds, and a saddle with a purple-velvet cloth lavishly
decorated with rubies, emeralds, and diamonds. Many of the
remaining gifts were from the vast array of horse furnishings,
and included surcingles, halters, bridles, reins, blankets, saddlecloths, tethers, and crupper straps. Over one hundred bolts of
cloth, including silks, brocades, and satins were among the
presents. The cloth came from such places as India, Aleppo,
Bursa, and Istanbul. There were also turbans, carpets, prayer
rugs, divans, and cushions. Finally, the list concludes with
perfumes, balms, and fragrances. At the bottom of the list
in the register is a total cost of 102,400 *kuruş*. The Topkapı list,
which does not contain a figure for the cost of the aigrette,
shows a total of 98,220 *kuruş*. The totals in both cases appear
to be wrong since the 10,000 *kuruş* indicated in the register list
as the cost of the aigrette is suspect. The aigrette is the first
gift described, and one would expect it to be the costliest, or
at least as costly as the next-mentioned gift. This second gift
is the horse collar, valued at 40,000 *kuruş*. In 1793 Mustafa
Rasih carried a similar array of gifts to Catherine. In a

[22] BVA Name-i hümâyun defteri no. 9, pp. 36–37. These registers are described
in Midhat Sertoğlu, *Muhteva bakımından Başvekâlet Arşivi*, p. 14.
[23] L. Fekete, "Die Geschenke des Sultans Abdulhamid I an Zarin Katharina II
im Jahre 1775," *Acta Orientalia*, 2 (1952): 1–18.

document giving the details of those gifts an aigrette is the first gift again, and a horse collar is the second. Each was valued at 75,000 *kuruş*.[24]

There is a statement at the end of the Topkapı list that Abdülkerim took possession of the gifts and, as a record of receipt, signed for them at the bottom of the list. A copy was then made of the list and the receipt in the office of the chief accountant. In accordance with a firman that was issued, another copy of the list was drawn up and given to the sultan's treasury. It is probably that additional copy which is now document E 3957 in the archives of the Topkapı Palace, and the one that formed the basis for the translation by Fekete.

In addition to the gifts prepared by the sultan's treasury, Abdülkerim took Catherine a handsome tent, complete with furnishings. There is a description of the materials involved in the manufacture of the tent and its furnishings in the same register of state papers that contains the list of gifts.[25] The materials are listed without comment on their cost or source within the governmental organization. Fortunately, another document is preserved that gives full details on the construction of a similar tent that Mustafa Rasih Pasha took to Catherine in 1793.[26]

A bureaucrat named Abdurrahman was delegated to superintend the manufacture of that tent and its furnishings. In his report to the chief financial officer (*baş defterdar*) he indicated that the tentmakers used 86 bolts of red Diyarbekrî cloth and 125 bolts of white Anatolian cloth, drawn from the supplies of the imperial tent depot (*mehterhane-i amire*).[27] Silver used for the tent-pole fittings and rings, quilting, Ankara camlets, and some other materials were bought on the open market at the going price (*rayiç*). The *rayiç* price was higher than the *mirî* price, which was the price established by the government when

[24] TKS D 10617.
[25] BVA Name-i hümâyun defteri no. 9, p. 34.
[26] BVA Cevdet/hariciye 5967.
[27] On the *mehterhane-i amire* (tents) and their furnishings see L. Fekete, *Die Siyaqat-Schrift in der türkischen Finanzverwaltung*, 1:768–87.

it preempted commodities for its own use. Remuneration for the tentmakers and ropemakers, outlay for waterproofing and the materials bought on the open market totaled 45,074 1/2 *kuruş*. Abdurrahman noted that 40,000 had been advanced previously and asked that the remaining 5,074 1/2 *kuruş* be granted from the state treasury. This sum was rounded off to 5,000 *kuruş*, and therefore the treasury gained by 74 1/2 *kuruş* (in much the same manner that race tracks gain from the principle of breakage). The chief accountant's office audited Abdurrahman's report and issued an order for the 5,000 *kuruş* and a voucher for the bolts of cloth used from stock.

From comments in the *sefaretname* it is obvious that the tent and the other gifts pleased Catherine, but she was also a person not easily upstaged. Moreover, the treaty dictated that gifts were to be exchanged mutually. There is a description of Catherine's gifts to Abdulhamit I in a dispatch sent to London by Anthony Hayes, the British representative in Constantinople.

> A very large beautiful toilet, or dressing table, in the form of an altar, inlaid, and ornamented in a most elegant manner, with crystal and some topases, and other precious stones intermixed, all from the production of the mines in Siberia, and other parts of Russia, the work remarkably well finished and polished which gave it the eclat of diamonds, the whole set in silver gilt, and said to have been the labor of years in completing. An elegant piece of Mr. Fox's invention purchas'd in England, said to have been intended for India, the upper part exhibiting 2 small elephants carv'd in gold and chests on the backs of them, in form of castles, ornamented with jewels, the interior containing various trinkets, underneath various figures, cascades and in the center a small clock ornamented with jewels, the pedestal and 4 rhinoceros silver gilt, the figures, cascades elephants etc. put in motion by clock work.
> A gold cassette the lid richly ornamented with diamonds rubys etc. the interior part containing china coffee cups, 6 gold cups set with diamonds, gold spoons, and pots for sweetmeats etc.
> A very rich diamond aigrette, for the sultans turbant, said to be worth 20 thousand roubles, and two other aigrettes, ornamented with jewels, but of no considerable value.

sultan decided in favor of the government's price, the requisite orders were issued and Abdülkerim was authorized to draw the necessary 25,460 *kuruş* from the state treasury as an advance. The preemption price represented a saving of approximately 25 percent for the government.

Detailed information on the nature of the provisions requested for the journey as far as Edirne is contained in the petition submitted to the sultan for his decision. To the gourmet this material is marginal, but to the historian it is the sweet food of knowledge and merits consideration:[34]

Provisions to be given by the controller of the imperial kitchen

Daily		*Total for Ten Days*	
rice	25 *keyl*	rice	250 *keyl*
clarified butter	50 *kıyye*	clarified butter	500 *kıyye*
honey	30 *kıyye*	honey	300 *kıyye*
coffee	6 *kıyye*	coffee	60 *kıyye*
tallow	5 *kıyye*	tallow	50 *kıyye*

From the people of the towns from Küçükçekmece to Edirne

Daily		*Daily Total*	
bread	1000 loaves	at 2½ *akçe*	2,500
meat	250 *kıyye*	at 12 *akçe*	3,000
barley	300 *keyl*	at 78 *akçe*	23,400
fodder	60 *kantar*	at 30 *akçe*	1,800
firewood	20 *çekka*	at 90 *akçe*	1,800
hay	15 wagon loads	at 155 *akçe*	2,325
			34,825 *akçe*

Provisions mean transportation problems. The imperial gifts also needed transport and, according to their description, the gifts were numerous, bulky, and weighty. Abdülkerim was authorized to obtain ten covered carriages and fifty horses from

[34] BVA Cevdet/hariciye 8941.

A Ponyarot, the sheath richly ornamented with diamonds, Rubys and emeralds, and a large fine emerald at the top of the handle of the ponyard.

Two large round gold clasps, aloops, for the sultans vest, inlaid with rose diamonds and a large emerald in the middle of each clasp.

Two sets of jasper and china coffee cups with gold cups salvers etc. Six large silver dishes gilt, and in the middle of them jasper terrines with gilt covers.

A beautiful black fox furr, said to be finest known in Russia, the nominal value reckoned above 30 thousand roubles, 3 other black fox furr said to be worth from 3 to 10 thousand roubles each.

Several furrs of red fox, *petite gris*, and ermin. A considerable number, said to exceed 100 pieces of rich gold brocade stuffs, china silks, sattins, and a large quantity of the best tea, Rhubarbdi.

The presents made to the vizir and his household, it is said consisted chiefly in a great number of valuable furrs, rich stuffs, silks etc. It is reckoned the presents in the whole amounts to about the sum of 250 thousand roubles.[28]

No Ottoman mission to a foreign court was complete without a royal letter from the sultan to the host ruler. A draft copy of the letter entrusted to Abdülkerim is preserved in the previously mentioned register of state papers. That letter is equivalent to the ambassador's credentials, and it is replete with the highly ornate phraseology usually associated with such documents. Opening with a long section that lists all the sultan's titles, the letter informs the empress that the sultan has nominated Abdülkerim Pasha as ambassador to Russia, in keeping with the requirements of the twenty-seventh article of the treaty of Küçük Kaynarca. The sultan's wish is for the continuance of peace and good relations between the two countries. The ambassador carries with him the ratified treaty, and the sultan awaits the arrival of the Russian ambassador. When both ambassadors have completed their missions they shall be given leave to return to their respective countries.[29]

The royal letter itself was prepared by a calligrapher on

28 PRO S.P. 97/51, ff. 121–22.
29 BVA Name-i hümâyun defteri no. 9, pp. 30–31.

noted, "Papers of the remotest date, if singly the year of th
transaction is known, may be found at the Porte; every co
mand granted at that time, and every regulation then mad
can be immediately produced."[32] He might also have add
that when produced those transactions would demonstrate tl
the conduct of administrative affairs was characterized m
by adherence to precedent than by innovation. It is evid
from existent documents that files were kept on the vari
embassies commissioned by the Porte. Those files were a
able for consultation by newly appointed ambassadors
studied them to determine what funds, supplies, and provis
had been granted in the past, and what precedents had
established.

Those concerns were uppermost in Abdülkerim's mind
he set about to organize his retinue and prepare for the
trip. After consulting the files, he submitted a petition t
Porte in which he requested that the provisions for the jo
to Edirne and from there to the frontier be granted to l
the same manner as they had been granted to a predec
Ümni Pasha, in 1740.[33] The records of Ümni Pasha's m
indicated that the provisions as far as Edirne had be
tained from both the controller of the imperial kitchen (*n*
amire emini) and the people of the districts along the
Abdülkerim's memorandum indicated the amount of
sions that would be required to Edirne and estimated
of provisions that would be bought from the villag
townspeople beyond Edirne as far as the frontier.
mitted two figures, one of 33,790 *kuruş*, based on th
price, and one of 25,460 *kuruş*, based on the gov
controlled price. The chief financial officer then pres
case to the sultan and requested a decision on whi
figures would be used in reimbursing the people.

---

[32] Sir James Porter, *Observations on the Religion, Law, Government, an
the Turks*, 2:131.
[33] BVA Cevdet/hariciye 8941. On Ümni Pasha's embassy see Maa
Yazmalar, p. 771.

appropriate paper with much gold leaf and special ink. The
necessary paper, gold leaf, ink, and wax for the seals were
obtained from the controller of stationery supplies by special
order of the chief financial officer. Illustrative of the procedure
is the order for the supplies needed to prepare the royal letter
that Mustafa Rasih would carry to Catherine.

> Chief Stationer
> Issue a three fold length of Sultanabadî paper, four *deste*s of
> gold leaf, fifty *dirhem*s of special ink, and fifty *dirhem*s of
> sealing wax for the royal letter to be sent to the ruler of
> Russia by means of Mustafa Rasih Pasha who has been
> entrusted with the embassy, and who is about to depart for
> Russia.[30]

From soup ladles to spare rims for wagon wheels, almost
every conceivable need of the ambassador and his retinue was
taken care of by one or another section of the governmental
organization. In Abdülkerim's case the entourage consisted of
six hundred men, twelve hundred horses, and eighty carts.[31]
Much effort and paper work went into keeping track of the
supplies and provisions needed by the mission. In the effort
to reconstruct Ottoman procedures we are the beneficiaries
of the Ottoman bureaucratic habit for committing even the
most minute transaction to paper. The documents that have
survived and are now catalogued in the various archives of
Istanbul and elsewhere are only a random, fortuitously preserved, sample of day-to-day Ottoman paper work. Because
of both the ravages of time and the role of chance, however,
not all the information one would like to have is available.
Additional details may still come to light, but until then the
material presented in the concluding pages of this section
represents as informed a view as is possible of the outfitting
of Ottoman embassies.

Commenting on Ottoman administrative practices, Sir James
Porter, British ambassador to the Porte from 1746 to 1762,

---

[30] BVA Cevdet/hariciye 7915. Sultanabadî paper was of Samarkand manufacture;
see C. Huart, *Les calligraphes et les miniaturistes de l'Orient musulman*, p. 11.
[31] *SRIO*, 5:202.

the depot of the cannon wagoners for the transportation of the gifts. He was allowed to draw spare parts, such as iron rims for the wheels, wooden spokes, axles, and connecting screws for the steering mechanisms. From that same agency he also received feed bags, water buckets, saddle cloths, ladles, leather tables, cutlery, water pitchers, rugs, and lanterns.[35]

A document related to Mustafa Rasih's embassy contains further details on transportation problems.[36] In a memorandum the chief financial officer informs the head pursuivant (*baş bakı kulu ağası*) that Mustafa Rasih is about to depart on his mission. The ambassador will rent the twenty oxcarts needed to transport his provisions as far as Edirne. The *baş bakı kulu ağası* is ordered to rent the oxcarts immediately through the chief steward of the oxcarters. At the bottom of the order there is a receipt, with the seal of Rasih Pasha. It attests to the fact that the twenty oxcarts were rented, with the cognizance of the head pursuivant, at the rate of 15 *kuruş* each. The required 300 *kuruş* were handed over to the chief steward and the head foreman, who returned a written receipt. Here we see official transportation problems being solved within the framework of the guild system.

Much of the materials, supplies, and provisions given to an embassy were consumed along the way, broke down, wore out, or were disposed of in some other way. The ambassador was responsible, however, for the return of all supplies that were still in good condition, to the governmental agency that had issued them. This was especially true of expensive items such as silver pitchers, incense burners, candlesticks, elaborate standards, tents, in short, anything of value and durability. Some of the trays, cutlery, pitchers, and utensils of various sizes, shapes, and purposes that Abdülkerim and his staff used to make life on the road a bit more comfortable were made of silver. Twenty years later Mustafa Rasih Pasha complained bitterly in a memorandum that he was being asked to have

---

[35] BVA Cevdet/hariciye 6986.
[36] BVA Cevdet/hariciye 1429.

some of those items that had to be replaced made out of copper
and brass instead of silver. This, he said, depreciated his mission, and would reflect poorly upon the grandeur of the
Ottoman state. The discussion about whether those utensils
should be made out of silver or copper and brass was carried
all the way to the sultan, Selim III. In a curtly phrased decision,
the sultan replied that the honor and glory of his state did not
depend on whether Mustafa Rasih Pasha had utensils made
out of silver. He ordered them made of copper and brass.[37]

Selim's decision is a reflection of the grave economic difficulties the Ottoman state experienced towards the end of the
eighteenth century. Silver and gold were in short supply, and
serious inflation had developed. The cost of outfitting embassies, like everything else, rose. Some indication of just how
sharp the rise was can be obtained by comparing the cost of
Abdülkerim's embassy with that of Mustafa Rasih's twenty
Muslim (or eighteen Christian) years later. According to the
totality of entries at the accountancy office, Abdülkerim had
been given 171,500 *kuruş*. In clear recognition that times had
changed, Mustafa Rasih was allowed an increase of 28,500
kuruş, a difference of close to 17 percent.[38]

Despite cost increases, the style of life remained constant.
While on the journey ambassadors and their entourages
often slept in tents. Those tents, and their furnishings, were
issued to the ambassador by the chief aga of the imperial tent
depot (*mehterhane-i amire*). That official was also responsible
for the maintenance of the tents and furnishings, but the actual
work was performed by members of various guilds. For
example, some of the tents, divans, pillows, and rugs had to be
repaired before being issued to Abdülkerim. The repairs, costing
5,007 *akçe*, were carried out with the cognizance of the aga.[39]

It was often impossible for an ambassador to anticipate all
his needs. While at Hotin, Abdülkerim decided that he had

[37] BVA Cevdet/hariciye 1402.
[38] BVA Cevdet/hariciye 2357.
[39] BVA Cevdet/hariciye 8920.

not brought with him a sufficient number of tents from Istanbul. He borrowed five additional new tents from Mehmet Pasha, the governor of Hotin. Abdülkerim sent to Istanbul a bill of transfer in which he described the tents he had received from Mehmet Pasha and requested that replacements be sent to Mehmet Pasha from the tent depot. The governor too sent a letter to Istanbul that substantiated the statements made by Abdülkerim. He also seconded the request for replacements. The Ottoman built-in system of checks and controls was still in good working order. A memorandum that embodied the request for the tents to be taken from the depot and sent to Hotin was presented to the Porte by the chief financial officer. Then, a firman granting the request was issued.[40] While the bureaucratic machinery ground away, Abdülkerim crossed the Dnestr River and was on his way to Moscow.

Once the ambassadors left their own countries—when they had crossed the Dnestr, Abdülkerim to Zhvanets and Prince Repnin to Hotin—they became the guests of their respective hosts. In addition to such things as transportation and lodgings, the host government also supplied the provisions needed for the maintenance of the ambassador and his retinue. General Repnin informed the Ottomans that the needs of his group could be met by the same amount of provisions that had been given to the Rumiantsev embassy in 1740. Repnin sent Abdülkerim a copy of the list that showed in detail the provisions that had been given to Rumiantsev. In return, the Russians requested that Abdülkerim furnish them with a list of the supplies he would need. Replying to the Russian request, Abdülkerim noted that since his and Repnin's embassies were of approximately the same size, he would be content with the same amount of provisions that would be provided to meet Repnin's needs. Abdülkerim also forwarded to Istanbul the provisions list he had received from the Russians that indicated what had been allocated in 1740. That list has survived

---

[40] BVA Cevdet/hariciye 6801.

and merits close scrutiny.[41]

> This is the translation of the letter that arrived through Abdülkerim Pasha from the Russian ambassador saying, "This is the register of provisions that were prepared by the Sublime State and given everyday to the Russian ambassador in the year A.D. 1740."

bread	2800 loaves	bitter almonds	20 *para* daily for a sufficient amount
beef	250 *kıyye*		
calves	4		
lambs	8		
lamb meat	200 *kıyye*	lemons	40
chickens	40	tallow	50 *kıyye*
turkeys (young)	16	beeswax	5 *kıyye*
capons	40	coffee	6 *kıyye*
pullets	100	rice	150 *kıyye*
goslings	12	honey	30 *kıyye*
pigeons	50	cheese (fresh)	10 *kıyye*
eggs	400	olives	5 *kıyye*
butter (clarified)	40 *kıyye*	wheat starch	5 *kıyye*
butter (fresh)	10 *kıyye*	soap	20 *kıyye*
milk	10 *kıyye*	cereals (various)	60 *kıyye*
clotted cream	5 *kıyye*	cinnamon	40 *habbe*
onions	15 *kıyye*	cardamon	25 *habbe*
garlic	15 *kıyye*	cloves	25 *habbe*
vegetables	510 *akçe* daily	pepper	20 *habbe*
ice	40 *para* daily	gum mastic	20 *habbe*
sugar (fine)	4 *kıyye*	nutmeg	30 *habbe*
sugar	40 *kıyye*	wine	500 *kıyye*
olive oil	8 *kıyye*	charcoal	200 *kıyye*
fish	40 *para* daily for fish called *sardalya* [sardines]	barley	132 *keyl*
		fodder	30 wagon loads
		firewood	a sufficient amount
almonds	3 *kıyye*	horses	1350

[41] BVA Cevdet/hariciye 6101. Two copies of this document are pinned together, but the number of horses appears on only one of them. A copy of Repnin's letter to Abdülkerim, dated 11/22 May 1775, is in *SRJO*, 5:184–85. There the fine sugar is described as Canary Island sugar, the vegetables as lentils, peas, and beans, and the wheat starch as good flour.

Obviously, Repnin and his retinue ate well, and if the reciprocity implied in the exchange of correspondence referred to was observed, so did the Ottoman embassy. There is no indication of the cost to the Ottoman government of the supplies mentioned in the list. An indication of prices is obtained from a similar list of provisions given to the Russian ambassador who came to Istanbul in 1793.[42]

bread (*farancala*)	100 *kıyye* at 4 *para*	clotted cream	5 *kıyye* at 20 *para*
bread	1000 *kıyye* at 4 *akçe*	onions	15 *kıyye* at 2 *para*
beef	200 *kıyye* at 3 *para*	vegetables	170 *para* daily
		salt	40 *para* daily
calves	2 head at 100 *para*	sugar	10 *kıyye* at 80 *para*
lambs	4 head at 50 *para*	sugar (finest)	4 *kıyye* at 140 *para*
lamb	100 *kıyye* at 4 *para*	almonds	1 *kıyye* at 40 *para*
chickens	20 at 8 *para*	fish	40 *para* daily
turkeys (young)	8 at 20 *para*	lemons	40 at 2 *para* each
capons	20 at 25 *para*		
pullets	50 at 3 *para*	tallow	15 *kıyye* at 22 *para*
pigeons	8 at 20 *para*		
eggs	400 at 20 *para* per hundred	butter (clarified)	10 *kıyye* at 16 *para*
		beeswax	5 *kıyye* at 120 *para*
butter (fresh)	5 *kıyye* at 25 *para*	coffee (Yemenî)	3 *kıyye* at 100 *para*
milk	10 *kıyye* at 1 *para*		

[42] BVA Cevdet/hariciye 8822. *Francala* today denotes a loaf similar to an Italian or French bread. *Rakı* is the contemporary form of *arak* in Turkey. Insight into money and prices is provided by the letter-books of Jeremy Bentham who traveled in the Ottoman Empire in 1785 on the way to visit his brother, a shipbuilder in the employ of the Russians. Bentham notes that four *para* was the equivalent of 2½d., and 200–300 £ equalled 2000–3000 piastres (*kuruş*). Mutton was selling for 3 farthings a pound, and bread was ½d. a loaf. British Museum, Additional Manuscripts 37520, f. 108. Professor Bernard Lewis kindly drew my attention to these valuable letter-books.

rice	30 *kıyye* at 13 *para*	vinegar	30 *kıyye* at 4 *akçe*
cheese	10 *kıyye* at 3 *para*	charcoal	200 *kıyye* at 2 *akçe*
olives	5 *kıyye* at 16 *para*	barley	42 *keyl* (Istanbul) at 10 *para*
soap	10 *kıyye* at 30 *para*	fodder	30 wagon loads at 15 *para*
cereals	60 *kıyye* at 110 *para*		
wheat starch [flour]	30 *kıyye* at 15 *para*	firewood	60 wagon loads at 15 *para*
wine	300 *kıyye* at 4 *para*	horses	1100 for 80 hours at 10 *akçe* an hour
arak	20 *kıyye* at 16 *para*		

total price of the provisions (for 41 days) 12,928 *kuruş*
total cost of the horses   7,333
                                                 20,261 *kuruş* and 13 *para*

Fascinating in themselves, the archival documents cited here give flesh and substance to the skeletal *sefaretname*. They assist in the visualization of the ambassador against the background of his own culture as he went about the business of organizing his embassy and carrying out his mission. The translation of Abdülkerim's report presents the story of his day-to-day experiences as he and the members of his train sought to serve their state and religion within the framework of the Ottoman Way. Their courage and fortitude in the face of the unknown world beyond the confines of the Ottoman domains is a fitting tribute to the great empire and civilization of which they were a part. They appear on the stage of history at a significant turning point in Ottoman affairs. At such crucial moments the historian is forced to yield to the dramatist. The words of Schiller, spoken by Wallenstein before his fateful interview with Wrangel, capture this moment best:

> Not o'er the threshold yet. So slender is the boundary that
> divides life's two paths.

Although the empire was to endure for nearly a century and a half after the mission of Abdülkerim and his train, it was to be transformed beyond their recognition, in part because of what they and their contemporaries set in motion.

Repnin's Report

The Russian text translated here records Prince Repnin's mission to Constantinople in 1775 and 1776. It appears to be a much neglected work. Published in 1777 and now a rather rare book, it has been ignored by everyone but meticulous bibliographers. Yet, it has several uses for students of eighteenth-century history.

First of all, it is valuable because it provides a comparison of Russian and Ottoman diplomacy and thus contributes to an understanding of the relations of the Ottoman Empire to Europe, and to the far-reaching question of modernization. This section of the introduction draws attention to the differences in manner and purpose of these diplomatic reports and illuminates contrasts in style of policy prosecution which are vastly interesting to students of the two political cultures.

The second and probably the most obvious contribution of the document is the basic data it provides on a period that has received only scant attention in most histories of Russia and the Ottoman Empire, the 1770s. That decade was of crucial importance in regard to Russia's physical presence in the Crimea just prior to annexation. Incidental to the main discourse is another body of data that provides detailed geographical information on the Balkans.

Paradoxically, the third major use of the document results from its lacunae. In the process of relating the text to the whole matter of the embassy and to larger issues, one comes upon an important amount of information pertaining to Russian expansion toward the Black Sea. Questions are raised that fairly beg for further investigation. It will be seen that the document is not so much an end point as an avenue leading to the problems with which the ambassadors and their governments were dealing at the time. Repnin's report serves as a framework around which to arrange the chronology and data on persons concerned with Russian foreign policy during the months in question. The most important single source for the supplementation of this outline is the private correspondence of Repnin, written before and during his mission, and published in the *Sbornik imperatorskago russkago istoricheskago obshchestva.*

Serialized at first in 1776, the account of the embassy appeared as a book in the following year. The text was written by Iakov Ivanovich Bulgakov, marshal of the embassy, and was printed in 600 copies at the expense of the Academy of Sciences.[43] At this time the press of the Academy of Sciences was one of fifteen operating in Russia, of which three were private. It was the most important single publishing house throughout the century.[44] The average number of books published in Russia (nonliturgical texts) at this time was 166,[45] and one may ask why the trouble was taken to print this bare diplomatic journal not once, but twice. The answer appears to be that it was published by the government as a tribute to the government. The victory over the Turks, recorded in the treaty of Küçük Kaynarca, had been the cause of great celebration in Russia during 1775, and this book is in a sense a contribution to the spirit of those times, for the document hardly goes further than to flatter national pride.[46] Such a deduction is supported by comparing the journal with Repnin's official papers addressed to members of his government. Those

[43] *Svodnyi katalog russkoi knigi grazhdanskoi pechati XVIII veka 1725–1800*, 3:52, 465–66. It first appeared as a supplement to the *Sankt-Peterburgskie Vedomosti* in 1776, the official newspaper published by the Academy of Sciences from 1728 to 1917.
[44] A. A. Sidorov, ed., *400 let russkogo knigopechataniia 1564–1964*, 1:161, 197.
[45] Valentin Giterman, *Geschichte Russlands*, 2:480.
[46] There are several indications of this. See, for example, "14.274. Marta 17 [28 March 1775]. Manifest: O zakliuchenii mira s Ottomanskoiu Portoiu," in *PSZ*, 20:80–82, declaring a celebration for 10–17 July of that year. Also, *SRIO*, 19:450.

papers indicate just how little has been included in the book with regard to the difficulties of the negotiations. Important and involved aspects of the mission have been filtered out of this account. In short, the book can be characterized as a Festschrift, in the most literal sense of the word, on the occasion of the glorious victory of Her Imperial Majesty over the Turks.

Article twenty-seven of the treaty of Küçük Kaynarca provided for an exchange of ambassadors and specified certain things in regard to their treatment from the time of arrival at the border of the host country. Therefore, the Russian text begins with the exchange ceremony on the Dnestr River, which took place on 13 July 1775 near Hotin.[47] Prince Repnin had been appointed by the empress as her ambassador extraordinary on 7/18 November 1774.[48] He spent the winter for the most part in Moscow, in communication with the empress, preparing for the trip which he did not begin until the following spring. Part of Repnin's preparation was to write to Russian representatives in various European capitals to ask for their appraisal of local opinion on the diplomatic climate in Constantinople.[49]

Repnin's embassy consisted of between six and seven hundred persons. Only a limited number of them have been identified. The edict that appointed Repnin to his ambassadorship mentions the list of ranks and salaries for those appointed to the embassy, but the list was not published with the edict.[50] The officers were mainly from the ranks of the nobility, and many had served with Repnin during the war.[51] Repnin devoted considerable energy to assembling the most qualified personnel for his entourage. On 10/21 December 1774 he sent various requests for men and equipment to the commander

[47] Although many works indicate that Hotin was in Russian hands at this time, it is clear that the Ottomans held the city.
[48] *SRIO*, 5:159–60.
[49] The list is in *SRIO*, 5:167–70, but no replies are recorded.
[50] *SRIO*, 5:159–60.
[51] *SRIO*, 5:162–65, 175.

in chief of the First Army, Field Marshal Rumiantsev, and asked that the persons in the detachment be given double pay, and that the lower ranks receive new uniforms. The grenadiers, hussars, and cuirassiers were to come from various regiments, among them the First Grenadier (Petersburg Grenadier) Regiment, the Sumskii Hussar Regiment, and the Kievskii Cuirassier Regiment.[52]

In a subsequent letter to Rumiantsev Repnin mentioned the need for supporting personnel, including tailors, carpenters, smiths, saddlers, and shoemakers. He asked that these masters be selected from the best regiments. He also expressed concern about the appearance of the entourage and asked that the regimental commanders send the trumpeters, kettledrummers, and other musicians in "rich dress."[53]

Repnin was not the only one involved in making decisions concerning the embassy and their implementation. After Catherine herself, the others included Field Marshal Petr Aleksandrovich Rumiantsev, commander of the First Army (on the southern front) and Repnin's immediate military superior, Khristofor Ivanovich Peterson, the chargé d'affaires in Constantinople, Aleksandr Stakhievich Stakhiev, the envoy to Constantinople from the fall of 1775, and Count Nikita Ivanovich Panin, the prime minister and Catherine's closest adviser. Many of the instructions issued to Repnin were drawn up after discussions in the newly created war council, the Imperial Council, composed of Catherine and her advisers.[54]

Repnin left Moscow in the spring and arrived at Kiev by 15 May 1775, where he held discussions with Rumiantsev and others.[55] Only in July did he arrive at the frontier. The narrative begins with the exchange ceremony on the Dnestr River. It goes on to describe his trip through Moldavia and Walachia to Constantinople, his audiences with the grand vezir and the

[52] *SRIO*, 5:162–63.
[53] *SRIO*, 5:163–65.
[54] For the council membership see *SRIO*, 5:185, n 2.
[55] *SRIO*, 5:177.

sultan, and the ceremonial dinners, and finally his return to
Hotin in 1776.

Although the text provides a useful chronology of Repnin's
mission, it does not mention the serious issues involved in the
final settlement of the treaty. Thus, the omissions lead one to
an investigation of the sources of contention which at times
threatened to break relations and cause a renewal of the war.
The most important gap in the narrative occurs on page 46 of
the Russian text (page 163 of the translation), where the journal
skips from 19 October to 9 December 1775, that is, from the
ceremonies connected with Repnin's arrival in Constantinople
to his first visit with the grand vezir. The absence of any
record during those weeks suggests that the conflict between
the Russians and the Ottomans was still unresolved. An
explanation of the conflict leads eventually to a discussion
of three topics: (1) Russia's war aims, (2) the treaty of
Küçük Kaynarca, and (3) the continued struggle for the
Crimea.

Although these three matters can be isolated for the purpose
of discussion, such a device should not deflect attention from
their close connection, or to put the case more strongly, the
linear development from one to the other. These three subjects may be treated as steps in Russia's move into the Crimea.
War aims included the plan to force an entrance onto the
peninsula, and the treaty represented formal success. Seizure
of the objective, which was the third stage, was of sufficient
difficulty to nearly negate the earlier successes. Of course, this
is to describe the events from the Russian point of view, the
more familiar one in the literature. The unfortunate thing here
is that the notion of a plan unfolding in stages may influence
the reader toward an idea of some inevitable development.
Surely, the Ottomans were not likely to see historical inevita-
bility at work in the surrender of the Crimea. For them it was
a great loss, but just barely. If Prince Repnin's journal served
no other purpose, it would be important for drawing closer
attention to this episode.

A discussion of the three points raised by the text will serve
as a convenient introduction to the text itself.

1. *Russia's War Aims.* The treaty of Küçük Kaynarca can
hardly be separated from the whole course of Russian-Ottoman
relations in the eighteenth century. At the risk of finding causes
for a given event in subsequent developments, one is inclined
to say that 1774 marked an enormous step forward in Russian
plans to extend their empire to the shores of the Black Sea.
B. H. Sumner has drawn attention to the similarity of Russian
aims in the reigns of Peter the Great, Anna, and Catherine II.
The goals were essentially those set by Peter, advanced by
Ostermann during the negotiations of 1737, and brought to
completion by Catherine in her two wars with the Ottomans.
Those goals were: acquisition of ports on the Black Sea, a
more favorable position vis-à-vis the Crimean Tatars, and certain plans to use and extend Russian influence among the
Christian subjects of the Porte.[56] The continuity suggested
here is perceptible in the comments of a contemporary English
observer, Richard Tooke, who wrote of Repnin's mission in
the following way:

> Marshall Romantzoff [Rumiantsev] had already received
> orders to collect an army on the banks of the Borysthenes
> [Dnepr]. Every thing seemed to indicate an approaching
> rupture between Russia and the Porte: but prince Repnin,
> being sent ambassador extraordinary from the empress to
> Constantinople, succeeded in calming, for some time, the
> resentment of the Divan. This was all Catharine wished for.
> She only desired to gain time for preparing to enter the lists
> with advantage; as the war was necessary to her schemes of
> invasion.[57]

On the other hand, Catherine's wars with the Ottomans
need not be regarded as only the continuation of her predecessors' policies. Kliuchevskii, for example, suggests that one
reason she undertook the wars was to demonstrate her personal
abilities to Europe.[58] Gitermann ascribes commercial causes to

[56] B. H. Sumner, *Peter the Great and the Ottoman Empire*, pp. 15, n 2, 75–79.
[57] William Tooke, *The Life of Catharine II. Empress of Russia*, 2:415.
[58] Vasilii O. Kliuchevskii, *Sochineniia*, 5:46.

the war of 1768–74 and points to the need for ports from which grain could be shipped to Europe. The tendency to see it as a "commercial war" is not limited to him alone.[59] Also, there was a shift in attention from the unsuccessful Northern Accord to the southern frontier by the late 1760s, but for an immediate cause one may refer to the hostilities in Poland in 1768.[60]

Although a war of some five years may well have many causes and results, there is no denying that one of the objectives was to gain a footing in the Crimea, and this was accomplished by the successes of Rumiantsev's armies. The story of Russia's relations with the Crimea is still largely an untold historical tale.

2. *The Treaty of Küçük Kaynarca.* The drafting and signing of the articles of the treaty put an official stamp of success on the aims of the war and gave the Russians as much as they had hoped for.[61] The peace was also welcomed because Catherine was anxious to end the annual campaigns, at least for a time, so that internal order could be restored within her empire. When the treaty was concluded, Pugachev had not yet been captured, a large section of the country was in revolt, the harvest of 1774 was poor, and the 1774 levy of recruits for the army had not been carried out.[62] It is possible that the Russians were in a better position than the Ottomans to put troops into the field; nevertheless, an advantageous peace seemed preferable to continued hostilities at that moment.[63]

The treaty itself was drafted and signed in the field within five days after considerable military pressure forced the grand vezir to negotiate. In March 1774 Rumiantsev had been negotiating for some time with the grand vezir who was at Shumen. The Russians had been willing to make certain conces-

[59] Giterman, *Geschichte*, 2:268–70. See also Hans Auerbach, *Die Besiedlung der Südukraine in den Jahren 1774–1787*, p. 22.
[60] See Herbert H. Kaplan, *The First Partition of Poland.*
[61] For a Soviet view of the literature and sources see the introduction to E. I. Druzhinina, *Kiuchuk-Kainardzhiiskii mir 1774 goda*, pp. 3–28.
[62] L. G. Beskrovnyi, *Russkaia armiia i flot v XVIII veke*, (*Ocherki*), pp. 295–96. See also Johann W. Zinkeisen, *Geschichte des osmanischen Reiches in Europa*, 6:80.
[63] Zinkeisen, *Geschichte*, 6:136.

sions, since previous negotiations held at Focşani and Bucureşti had broken down, largely over the Crimean question. Aware of Russia's internal difficulties, the Ottomans became intransigent. Thereupon, the Russians sought a military exit from the impasse. Generals Kamenskii and Suvorov pressed on toward Shumen, defeating an Ottoman army of some forty thousand men on the way and threatening the grand vezir himself.[64] Discussions were begun at Küçük Kaynarca and the articles were drafted and signed within a five day period, ending on 10/21 July 1774.[65] Repnin carried the articles to Saint Petersburg and the empress signed them in August.[66] Colonel Peterson, the Russian chargé d'affaires in Constantinople, had another copy signed by the Porte. The exchange or ratification was then carried out by Peterson on 13/24 January 1775. The document, to use Catherine's words, secured "precious fruits" for Russia.[67]

Perhaps the greatest advantage secured by the Russians in the treaty is in article three, which declared the Crimea free and independent. In addition to gaining the ports of Kinburn, Kerch' and Yenikale, Russia removed the areas surrounding them from Ottoman influence and prepared for its own further advance into the region. A Crimea not under Ottoman suzerainty meant to the Russians, to the Ottomans, and to Europe, a Crimea under Russian influence. The balance of power in the Balkans had been altered now that the Russians had gained ports, and a position for both trade with Europe and further military operations against the Ottomans. Catherine expressed this clearly in a communication to Field Marshal Rumiantsev

[64] Sergei M. Solov'ev, *Istoriia Rossii s drevneishikh vremen*, 29:78–80.
[65] A record of the negotiations was kept by Khristofor Ivanovich Peterson, "Zhurnal, vedennyi s pribytiia gg. upolnomochennykh Verkhovnym Vizirem, Akhmeta-Resmi, kegaiia-bei nishandzhi-efendiia i Ibragima-muniba, Reisefendiia, na kongres, v derevniu Buiu-kainardzhi, do ot'ezda ikh, polkovnikom i kavalerom Petersonom," *Chteniia*, 1865, vol. 2, pt. 2, pp. 311–30. For an Ottoman view of the war and the various negotiations see Ahmet Resmi, *Hülâsat ül-İtibar*.
[66] Druzhinina, *1774*, p. 308.
[67] Nikolai F. Dubrovin, *Prisoedinenie Kryma k Rossii 1775–1782*, 1:1.

dated 12 August 1774: should the Porte attempt at some future
time to deprive the Crimea and the Tatars of their complete
freedom and independence, Russia would be in a position to
use the new outlets on the Black Sea to "harm the Porte in its
most sensitive places."[68] Thugut, the Austrian ambassador in
Constantinople, was concerned over Russia's ability to attack
Constantinople within thirty-six hours.[69] Although Russia
did not in fact put such an ambitious plan into action, she was
most insistent that the treaty be ratified without the alteration
of a single word in any of its clauses. The true meaning of
Kerch' and Yenikale was political rather than military. In them
the Russians saw a guarantee of Crimean independence from
the Ottomans.[70]

Repnin's task in Constantinople was to complete the arrangements of the treaty, a matter about which Catherine's instructions, again, were crystal clear. She wrote to him late in 1774,
saying, "the aim of carrying out this ceremonial exchange of
embassies between the two empires is nothing other than the
last act of the treaty of peace, putting the seal on fulfillment
of its other provisions."[71] He succeeded in doing that much.

On the other hand, Repnin had several specific points to
negotiate in Constantinople. He was to represent the interests
of Moldavia, Walachia, and Poland, to investigate the possibilities of expanding Russian trade via Turkey, to discuss the
exchange of prisoners, and to arrange for the payment of
Ottoman reparations to Russia.[72] In addition, Repnin was
given thirty thousand rubles for "extraordinary expenses, and
especially for establishing in Constantinople new, reliable
channels for official matters."[73]

In most of these matters Repnin was unsuccessful. Writing
to Count Panin on 26 December 1775, Repnin mentioned that

[68] *SRIO*, 135:159.
[69] Zinkeisen, *Geschichte*, 6:82–84.
[70] Solov'ev, *Istoriia Rossii*, 29:62–63.
[71] *SRIO*, 15:606.
[72] Druzhinina, *1774*, p. 318.
[73] *SRIO*, 5:159–60.

he had not been able to discuss matters relating to Moldavia and Walachia, the Polish embassy, and trade, nor had he been able to solve the Tatar issue.[74]

Perhaps the only success he had in these secondary issues concerned reparations, but negotiation was slow and difficult. The subject comes up repeatedly in his correspondence from Constantinople, especially that with Prince Viazemskii on the means of transferring the first year's installment.[75] The total reparations of 4,500,000 rubles were to be paid in three equal parts, due on the first day (o. s.) of 1775, 1776, and 1777. The amount of 5,000 *kese* was due each year.[76] The major concern of the Russians was how to transfer the sums to bankers in Amsterdam without suffering a loss of some 20 percent in the transactions. The matter was handled by the English banker, George Abbot,[77] and by the firm of Hibsch and Timoni. Repnin wrote to Catherine in December 1775 that he had to remind the *defterdar* and the *reis efendi* almost daily of the matter.[78] On 7 January 1776, he wrote to Panin that of the 2,500,000 *levok*s due in the first installment, all but 75,000 had been paid.[79] The *levok* was equal to the Ottoman *kuruş*, and each purse consisted of 500 *kuruş*.[80]

From the Ottoman point of view, the treaty of Küçük Kaynarca was calamitous. The hurried conclusion of the negotiations in the field, under military pressure, has been described above. The *reis efendi* referred to the undesirability of these conditions in his discussions with the Russians in Repnin's

[74] *SRIO*, 15:580.
[75] *SRIO*, 5:209–10.
[76] *SRIO*, 15:578.
[77] *SRIO*, 5:216.
[78] *SRIO*, 15:566.
[79] In Rumiantsev's correspondence with Repnin on finances the term *lev* is used. *Levok* appears to be the term preferred by the editor of the documents. See *SRIO*, 5:171.
[80] In the 1770s the Russian army command issued copper money, made from captured cannon, for use in Moldavia and Walachia. One *para* equalled 3 *den'gi*, 2 *para* equalled 3 *kopeki*, and 40 *para* equalled one *lev* (40 *para* equals one *kuruş*). This coin was produced by Gartenberg in his mint near Rogozhna, Ivan G. Spasskii, *Russkaia monetnaia sistema*, 3d ed., p. 191.

entourage. It is possible that the Ottomans realized the full significance of the provisions only after the grand vezir had returned from the negotiations to Istanbul.[81] In a conversation that took place on 17 December 1775 between the *reis efendi* and the Russians, the former expressed his dissatisfaction with the negotiations. He said, "we are aware of the conditions under which and the people by whom the treaty was concluded. The latter, repressing all our demands to the point of absurdity, suggested, on their own, indemnities for war expenses, and did many other preposterous things."[82]

Almost from the beginning the Ottomans attempted to bring about a revision of the articles, primarily those by which the Ottoman Empire surrendered its position in the Crimea.[83] An independent Crimea meant the loss, in the first place, of an army which had been maintained at practically no expense to the Porte.[84] More than that, the caliph of the Muslim world was asked to surrender a host of subjects to a Christian ruler, an act which was intolerable to the more religious Muslims of the capital. Moreover, the hans of the Crimea, descendants of Genghis Han, were regarded by the Ottomans as successors to the Ottoman throne should a catastrophe ever destroy their line.[85] Finally, loss of the Crimea to the Porte implied eventual subjugation by the Russians, a fact that was as clear to the Ottomans as it was to the European diplomats in general, even though the overt arguments advanced at the time centered around the religious rather than the military issue.

Faced with this difficult situation, the Ottomans sought a revision of the treaty. Since the balance of power in southeastern Europe was involved, the countries of the continent tended to align themselves with one or the other of the two parties. France, represented in Constantinople by Saint Priest, supported the Ottomans. Both the Russians and the Ottomans

[81] Zinkeisen, *Geschichte*, 6:86.
[82] *SRIO*, 15:577.
[83] Druzhinina, *1774*, p. 312; also Zinkeisen, *Geschichte*, 6:86–87.
[84] Solov'ev, *Istoriia Rossii*, 29:81, and *SRIO*, 135:159–62.
[85] *EI²*, "Giray" by Halil Inalcık, 2:1112–14.

used Prussian diplomatic channels, Solms in Saint Petersburg, and Zegelin and later Gaffron in Constantinople, whereas the Dutch and the English leaned more toward the Ottomans than toward the Russians.[86]

Austria was a special case. In September 1774, Austrian troops occupied Bukovina, an area lying south and west of Hotin.[87] Backing up their occupation with a threat of further use of force, the Austrians let it be known that if the Ottomans wished to go to war over the matter, there were sixty thousand more troops ready in Hungary, waiting to be sent into battle. The Ottomans could not afford to resume the war at this time. Instead, they applied pressure through various diplomatic channels, including French, Prussian, and even Russian representatives at the Austrian court, but to no avail. Russia responded in two ways. On the one hand, Rumiantsev let it be said confidentially through Peterson that Russia was displeased by the Austrian move.[88] At the same time, the Ottomans felt that the Russians were trying to promote an Austro-Ottoman war by other means. In the end, a treaty was signed on 7 May 1775 and a convention on 12 May 1775 that ceded the area to Austria. The *reis efendi*'s wrath, aroused over the hopeless situation in Bukovina, was turned partly against the Russians and resulted in his taking an adamant position in regard to revisions of the treaty and the future of the Crimean Tatars.

3. *The Struggle over the Crimea.* The issues of the war and the terms of the settlement have been mentioned, and both of them point to the heart of the difficulties which slowed down the final negotiations in Constantinople, namely, the question of

[86] For information on diplomats and diplomacy in Constantinople at this time see the series of articles by Bertold Spuler, "Die europäische Diplomatie in Konstantinopel bis zum Frieden von Belgrad (1739)," *Jahrbücher für Kultur und Geschichte der Slaven*, 11 (1935), no. 1, 53–115, no. 2, 171–222, nos. 3–4, 313–66. This article was continued under the same title the following year in *Jahrbücher für Geschichte Osteuropas*, 1 (1936), Hft. 2, 229–62, Hft. 3, 383–440. The articles carry the subject far beyond 1739.
[87] Zinkeisen, *Geschichte*, 6:101–18.
[88] Solov'ev, *Istoriia Rossii*, 29:82.

the future of the Crimea. By the time Repnin arrived in Constantinople it appeared possible that the Ottomans, fully aware that they were now about to lose the Crimea for good, and hard pressed on other issues, were ready to resume the war rather than conclude it. The problem for the Ottomans was how to bring about a revision of the treaty that would save the Crimea, while they were threatened by Russia, by the Austrians, by a war in Persia, and by the possibility of mob uprisings in Istanbul. In Zinkeisen's view, the *reis efendi*, opposed by internal factions, convinced the sultan that they had to accept the Austrian occupation of Bukovina since any other course meant war, but they must also attempt to avoid fulfilling all the provisions of the Russian treaty.[89]

Ottoman hostility is only obliquely evident in the text, where it appears as a delay Repnin encountered in securing a meeting with the grand vezir. Soon after his arrival, Repnin reported to Panin that he saw "remnants of the past war" in the behavior of the Ottomans. Three times a date had been set for his visit with the grand vezir, and three times it had been postponed on one pretext or another. It was finally scheduled after *Ramazan* and the holiday (*bayram*) that followed it.[90] Repnin's visit was a ceremonial function, and therefore, any postponement of the ceremonies was a sign of strained relations.

The source of the difficulty, to return to our main theme, was the Crimea. Battles over that territory represented the second most important campaigns of the war, the major ones having been fought in Moldavia and Walachia. The diplomatic struggle continued throughout Repnin's stay in Constantinople and was not finally resolved until the area was incorporated into the Russian empire several years later.

Unfortunately, it is precisely in regard to the question of the Crimea during 1775 that a definitive account is missing in the histories of the Russian and Ottoman empires. A brief digression into the salient facts of Crimean political affairs,

---

[89] Zinkeisen, *Geschichte*, 6:131.
[90] *SRIO*, 15:434.

based on the work of Halil Inalcık, may help to clarify some of the complicated data which appear to be the stuff of Crimean history.[91]

One of the basic political factors in the Crimea at this time is the existence of two factions among the Tatars, one inclined toward the Porte and the other toward the Russians. The outcome of the struggle for the peninsula revolved around and depended on which of those factions gained the upper hand. Changes in political fortunes, and the shifting of allegiances, positions, and leaders complicate the story. The episode drags on from the beginning of the war through the negotiations discussed here, and ends, in a sense, only with incorporation of the region into the Russian empire in 1783.

The Girays were the ruling dynasty in the Crimea. They were descendants of the line from Genghiz Han through Tokay Timur, a son of Couci. In 1454 Hacı Giray made an alliance with the Ottoman sultan, Mehmet II. Acting on this alliance, the Ottomans came to the aid of the Girays against the Genoese and drove the Italians from their strongholds in the southern Crimea. As a result of this episode the Ottomans placed their protégé, Mengli Giray, on the throne in 1475. He, in turn, recognized the sovereignty of the Ottomans. In order to regulate succession to the throne the hans designated an heir apparent, known as the *kalkay*. After 1584 a second heir apparent, known as the *nuradin*, was also designated. According to Mongol tradition, the *kalkay* should be the han's brother. He would succeed to the throne, and the *nuradin* would become the *kalkay*. Some hans sought to designate their sons in those capacities and at times, as a result, caused internal strife of a serious nature. The Ottoman sultan could depose the reigning han, and the Ottomans usually kept one of the han's brothers in Istanbul as a hostage and pledge for good behavior. Actually, the Ottomans sought to placate the Crimea by selecting a han acceptable to the Crimean tribal aristocracy. This was not always possible and often the result was Ottoman interference.

[91] *İA*, "Kırım," 6:746–56. *EI²*, "Giray," 2:1112–14.

The *mirza*s, who formed the tribal aristocracy, constituted a third political force in the Crimea. Free-agents, the *mirza*s tended to be anti-Ottoman and hoped for independence from the Ottoman sultan. This internal political division was the factor that gave the Russians an opportunity to conquer the country by other than purely military means.

After an initial Tatar campaign led by Kırım Giray in 1769, the Russians, under Prince Dolgorukii, invaded the Crimea in 1770 and 1771 and forced Han Selim Giray to flee to Istanbul. In 1772 a new *kurultay* (tribal assembly) was summoned at which the *mirza*s refused to recognize the han appointed by the Ottomans, Maksud Giray. Instead, they succeeded in the selection of their own candidate, Sahip Giray. They chose the han's brother, Şahin Giray, to be *kalkay*. During the course of the war, Sahip Giray placed himself under Russian protection and ceded to them Kerch', Yenikale, and Kinburn.

At least by this time, the Russians were working to deepen the division between the Tatar factions and to win over to their side larger numbers. Şahin Giray was invited to Moscow together with a number of anti-Ottoman *mirza*s. The alignments, however, proved to be somewhat unstable. Han Sahip Giray, by the time the treaty was signed, if not earlier, had become disenchanted with the increasing Russian influence and aligned himself with the pro-Ottoman group of Tatars. One of the reasons for this is found in article three of the 1774 treaty itself: whereas the Crimea was declared to be independent, Kerch', Yenikale, and Kinburn were ceded to the Russians. As long as the Russians held those fortresses on either side of the mouth of the Sea of Azov and on the Dnepr, independence in fact was clearly impossible.

At this juncture, Şahin Giray, with the support of the Russians, was in the ascendancy in the Crimea, although he was not elected han until 1777. His brother, Han Sahip Giray had been driven from the Crimea and had fled to Istanbul. The Ottomans sent Devlet Giray to take the title of han. At the

time of the negotiations discussed in Repnin's report the issue
was whether the Russian-backed Şahin Giray or the pro-
Ottoman Devlet Giray would win out, and the question was
still in the balance. Each side felt it could gain the upper hand,
and in such a situation negotiations were bound to be bitter
and inconclusive.

Another complication that impeded a settlement was a
distinction being drawn among the various Tatar peoples. The
Yedisan, Camboyluk, and Yediçkul of the Nogay tribes had
migrated to regions north of the Black Sea from the Kuban
basin early in the eighteenth century. Conflict characterized
their relations with the hans of the Crimea who sought to bring
them under their control. These Nogays were extremely anti-
Ottoman and cooperated with the Russians in the 1768–74 war.
The importance of all this for the negotiations discussed here
was whether the term "Crimean Tatar" used in the Küçük
Kaynarca treaty included the Nogays. The Ottomans claimed
that it did not include them. This interpretation was to their
advantage since the Ottomans sought to retain sovereign rights
over the regions along the northern shores of the Black Sea.
The Russians, for their part, insisted that the Nogays were
included by the treaty, the reason being that they could use
this to support their aim of an independent Crimea. They could
produce evidence of actions and sentiments among the Nogays
indicative of their hostility toward the Ottomans, and then
claim that this was reason enough for severing the Crimea from
the Ottoman Empire, since the people themselves willed it.

The result is, of course, well known. During the first few
years after the signing of Küçük Kaynarca, the Crimea was
decimated by civil war. Thousands of Tatars fled to the Ottoman domains, and thousands of settlers were brought in by
the Russians to replace them. The region was gradually
Russianized.

Repnin's mission was encumbered by these intricate developments. Each side continued to maintain its position from
the standpoint of legality and right at the discussions, while

pressing for a military victory in the field that would decide the matter in fact.

On 25 October/5 November 1775 Repnin advised his court that there were three possible solutions to the Crimean question: (1) abandon all efforts, (2) prepare for a resumption of the war, or (3) win over Devlet Giray, who had the support of the tribal leaders in the Crimea. His recommendation was to send gold to buy Devlet Giray.[92] At the same time, he presented to the Ottomans an unyielding position as far as the revision of the treaty was concerned, on the repeated instructions of Catherine.

A record of some of the negotiations that were held shortly after Repnin's arrival in Istanbul is available from Russian sources, and a summary of them is presented here. The first of those conversations lasted for four hours on the evening of 2 November 1775. Prince Repnin sent his representatives, Major Markov and the interpreters Tamara and Pizani, to confer with the *reis efendi*. The principal points of the discussions have been referred to already and are reproduced here from the contemporary record both to fill out the gap in the journal and to add detail and precision to these important aspects of Repnin's mission. The material has been condensed from Repnin's private papers.[93]

The Russians opened the discussions by noting that instead of making the arrangements for Prince Repnin's ceremonial audiences, the Ottomans preferred to talk about revisions in the treaty with respect to the independence of the Crimea. Through his interpreter, the *reis efendi* countered that the Ottomans had not hesitated in confirming Sahip Giray as han, but he was driven out by his own people because he had agreed to the article on Crimean independence. The Tatars sent a delegation to Constantinople to seek a return to their former status, and they were continuing to stir up the people and the ulema in support of their cause. Markov replied that Russia

[92] *SRIO*, 15:446, 470, 476–77.
[93] *SRIO*, 15:446–64.

wished to maintain good relations with the Porte, but that any attempt to alter the terms agreed upon would destroy the existing amity. The *reis efendi* said that he too wished for good relations, but he could not refrain from dwelling on the articles of the treaty. The Porte did not wish to violate the treaty, but those articles placed the Porte in an embarrassing position. The Porte had agreed on independence in the belief that it was the wish of all the Tatars, but now that did not appear to be the case. Out of regard for their religion, the Tatars wished a return to their former condition, and the Porte was seeking Russia's aid in the attempt to extricate itself from a difficult position.

Markov neatly parried the *reis efendi*'s thrust. He pointed out that the independence of the Crimea was called for by the treaty. Russia was being faithful to the treaty and expected the Porte to do the same. Crimean independence was agreed to, the *reis efendi* said, on assurances given by Orlov and Obreskov at the congress of Focşani and Bucureşti that it was universally desired by the Tatars. To this, Markov replied that the two years of war that followed those congresses had cancelled that, and what mattered was the treaty agreed to at Kaynarca. The *reis efendi* replied that the Porte wished it could carry out the articles, but it could not because their religion opposed it. Markov snapped that when the Porte signed the treaty it knew whether it could carry out the articles. Hard pressed, the *reis efendi* asked whether it was possible to propose some amelioration of a treaty when things were written in haste and then proved too severe for one of the parties. He noted that the treaty of Belgrade (1739) had been altered. Countering, Markov replied that anything could be suggested, but the proposition put forward by the Porte could not be entertained, and Prince Repnin would not be able to present it to his court.

The *reis efendi* took a new tack. He stated that the Porte always regarded Prince Repnin as one of the most important figures of his state, an enlightened man of influence. If he did not wish to oblige the Porte by transmitting their views to his court, some other means would have to be found. Markov defended his superior by noting that Repnin would not do so because he knew how firmly his court would reject the views of the Porte and any notion of a revision in the treaty. The *reis efendi* replied that it made no difference, the Porte must attempt it.

Next, the *reis efendi* sought to shift the ground by accusing the Russians of duplicity in allowing the Austrians to seize part of Moldavia and Walachia, but Markov insisted that Russia was not responsible for Austria's actions. The *reis efendi* closed the meeting, after touching on several other matters, by saying that he could only report the content of these discussions to all the vezirs and to the ulema.

In Repnin's view that was bound to be unfavorable. His information led him to believe that while the sultan and the *reis efendi* were advocates of peace and would be willing to abandon the Tatars, the religious fanaticism of the ulema, who had the support of the mob and could threaten the internal order of the state, would prevent them from doing so.[94]

A second major discussion recorded in Repnin's papers centered around the question of the Crimean and Nogay Tatars. That conference, held on 17 December 1775, was attended by the *reis efendi* and the Russians Markov and Tamara. On that occasion Markov handed the *reis efendi* letters from various Nogay leaders. Those documents supposedly declare that an important segment of the Tatars accepted Şahin Giray as han and rejected Ottoman suzerainty.[95] The Porte sent a formal reply to Repnin early in 1776, suggesting that the Russians were confusing the Nogay Tatars with the Crimeans, and further, that the missives were false documents.[96] The Russian reply to this was that the Ottoman communication was an

[94] *SRIO*, 15:484. The Russian interpreter Pinii was able to meet and speak confidentially with a member of the ulema, and his information provides the basis for Repnin's report and assumption that the ulema would not abandon the Tatars. See *SRIO*, 15:498–99.
[95] *SRIO*, 15:567–77.
[96] *SRIO*, 15:593–97.

insult to the empress.[97] It is on this strained note that Repnin's correspondence closes.

Within a few weeks Repnin was relieved of his post. There are various indications that he never had, or else quickly lost, the ability to negotiate with the Ottomans and was unable to produce any sort of accord on those difficult issues. On the one hand, Catherine insisted on ratification of the treaty without alteration of a single word. On the other, the Ottomans were increasingly reluctant to agree to an "independent" Crimea, which obviously meant abandoning the area to Russian influence. It is possible that even the most skilled negotiator could not have reconciled the parties. It is almost certain that Repnin lacked the delicacy of maneuver to attempt it. Repnin's biographer writes that Count Panin decided late in 1775 to recall him, feeling that it would be better to "transfer the diplomatic part of the embassy, under the conditions which had arisen, to an ordinary envoy . . . genuinely wishing to lead him [Repnin] out of the abyss there."[98] Stakhiev, who had thirty years in the diplomatic service, and who was considered to be an accomplished negotiator, was transferred from Stockholm to replace him.[99]

The recent work by the Soviet historian Druzhinina indicates too that Repnin had not completed the mission assigned to him, and older sources furnish the reasons.[100] Zinkeisen writes, "Prince Repnin, who . . . ruined much through his gruff, brutal, and yet inconsistent manner, still had accomplished practically nothing as he left Constantinople in April 1776 and was replaced by Herr von Stakhieff as the regular ambassador at the Porte."[101]

As was pointed out earlier, the war and the treaty raised the issue of the Crimea, they did not settle it. In a sense the text, and

[97] *SRIO*, 15:598.
[98] *RBS*, 16:108.
[99] Zinkeisen, *Geschichte*, 6:133, based on Solms's report of 2 November 1775.
[100] Druzhinina, *1774*, p. 322.
[101] Zinkeisen, *Geschichte*, 6:131, and the summary and appraisal of comments by Gaffron on pp. 131–32.

this introduction to it, must end on the same unfinished note, which may be interpreted as a plea for further research into these complex problems subsumed under the heading of the Crimean question.

Reception of an Ottoman ambassador by
Catherine II. (Alexander Brückner,
Katharina die Zweite [Berlin, 1883], p. 241.)

I

The *Sefaretname*
of Abdülkerim Pasha

Praise without end to the eternal Lord of the realm, and invocations to and benedictions on the Holy Prophet, the Companions, and the Holy Family!

Now, our lord, His Excellency, the adorner of the Ottoman throne, and the embellisher of the custodianship of the world, the caliph on the face of the earth, the justly acting padishah, our majestic, august, powerful benefactor, the *şahinşah* in whom the world seeks asylum, is the esteemed sultan, the illustrious *hakan*, Sultan Abdülhamit Han, son of Sultan Ahmet Han. May God perpetuate his caliphate and cause his sultanate to endure forever so long as the heavenly spheres rotate and night succeeds day.

It is a duty of faithful obedience to proffer at the beginning of the pages of a work and in the preface of what is said a prayer that one hopes will be answered. May the stretching shadow of the sultan's grandeur and authority be extended and prolonged from the reaches of the width and breadth of the world to the highest heaven, and may the cordons of the tent of his prosperity and majesty be firmly tied to the God-given tent pegs.

In 1768 during the sultanate of His Excellency, the former emperor, the late, God's pardon-marked sultan Mustafa Han whose abode is paradise, war broke out between the eternal Sublime State and the state of Russia. In 1774 the great and the low, the young and the aged were extremely upset, suffering from the maladies of anxiety and distress that were universal because of the prolongation of the disagreement and dispute with Russia. At that juncture, when by the grace of God who be exalted, our Lord of sterling qualities, that *şahinşah* in whom the world seeks asylum, that monarch who is the chief seat of kindness, that august personage who is the luminary of the sphere of justice, with felicity and fortune, became the glow-increaser of the zodiacal house of place and position and the radiant one of the zodiacal house of royalty and glory, the effects of his auspicious accession to the throne was a bounteous gift of spring to the rose garden of the world.

Signs of readiness to accept measures for peace and tranquility were apparent daily among the public. Much thought was
given to the effective medication for the conditions and temper
of the time through a choice draft based on the precept that
peace is the noblest of judgments. Resmi Ahmet Efendi, the
grand vezir's *kethuda* [adjutant] with the imperial army, was
appointed first delegate. İbrahim Münip Efendi, a former *reis
ül-küttâp* [head of the secretaries], was appointed second
delegate. They arrived and began conversations with Field
Marshal General Rumiantsev at the Russian headquarters in a
place named Kaynarca situated in the region of Silistra. Since
most of the articles had been decided on earlier in repeated
discussions and conversations, the business of the conference
was finished speedily within a week. Upon the exchange of the
written document, the chain of enmity was cut and broken.
Through the auspicious effect of the felicitious accession of
His Excellency, the asylum of the caliphate, the face of the
earth began to resemble the gardens of paradise. The gentle
breezes of God's kindness began to blow in all directions. With
the warm, blessing breeze of tranquility, the distraught hearts
of mankind opened and smiled like roses. Night and day the
tongues of the great and the low, like nightingales, made the
nine strata of the rotating firmament resound in praise of God
the Protector, and with prayers for the endurance of the sultanate of the beneficent sovereign. Praise, again, praise, again
praise unto God.

Verse

Oh Lord, lengthen the life and good fortune of the present
    world-adorning padishah on the throne of the sultanate.
In whatever direction he turns the reins of his charger of
    determination, set the Hizir of thy guidance before him to
    lead him and show the way.[1]
Let the resplendent rays of his glory, sun-like, light up the
    world. Just as shadows everywhere set, so too let his
    enemies be up-ended.

---

[1] Hizir is recognized among the Muslim people as a prophet, and considered to
be the patron saint of travelers. On this colorful figure see F. W. Hasluck,
Christianity and Islam under the Sultans, 1:319–36.

As written above, the work of the treaty was completed. At the end of *Recep* 1188 [6 October 1774], the imperial army arrived and settled down in Istanbul. It was an established practice of the Sublime State to commission and send as ambassador someone from among the men of practiced good intellect, a man of good standing and esteem. Therefore, *Seyyid* Abdülkerim Efendi, who had been rotated from the *mukabele-i süvari* [control bureau for the cavalry], was chosen and selected from among his equals. On Monday, 26 *Recep* [3 October], this important duty was delegated and committed to the responsibility of his care.[2] The simulated rank of *Rumeli beylerbeyi* [governor-general of Rumeli] and the grade of *mir-i mirân* [bey of the beys] were conferred on him.[3] His authority and esteem were raised and advanced. He was clothed with a robe of honour, and all his provisions were granted him in the same manner as they had been granted to his predecessors.

I, this humble servant [Nahifi Mehmet Efendi], through exalted royal kindness and sublime regal favor, was appointed chief of the *silâhdar* [imperial cavalry] bureau, an assignment that would begin upon return, and I was appointed and detailed to the ambassador's suite for the purpose of writing down and recording the events connected with the embassy.

On 24 *Zilkade* [26 January 1775] the regal gifts that the sultan had ordered prepared, according to custom, for the empress of Russia were consigned to the ambassador against a checklist. This was done in the presence of the grand vezir.[4]

On Saturday, 26 *Zilkade* [28 January], the ambassador went to the grand vezir's residence on invitation. Together with the

[2] The British ambassador in Constantinople reported on 17 October 1774 that Abdülkerim had been named as ambassador. PRO S.P. 97/50 no. 22, dated 17 October 1774.

[3] Ottomans on special assignments of this sort were often given temporary high ranks in order to facilitate their mission. As a pasha of three horsetails, Abdülkerim would be higher in rank than almost every Ottoman official he would have to deal with along his route and the equivalent of the very few to whom he was not superior. This procedure also had the advantage of not placing a permanent strain on finances, since he reverted to his bureaucratic rank upon return.

[4] The grand vezir at the time was İzzet Mehmet Pasha. İsmail Hami Danişmend, *İzahlı Osmanlı Tarihi Kronolojisi*, 4:485.

grand vezir and the sheikh ul Islam,[5] he humbly departed for the formal audience with His Excellency, the shadow of God. In a place of refreshment called *Ağa Bahçesi* that might be mistaken for paradise,[6] they — the grand vezir and the sheikh ul Islam, and after them the ambassador — had their justly proud eyes treated with the great kindness and favor of the sultan's presence. He decorated their ears with an elegant speech, employing expressions that were jewels worth the world. After it was commanded that their proud shoulders be draped with a happiness-producing robe of honor, the *tasdik-name* [instrument of ratification] was presented to the grand vezir by the blessed, and divinely aided royal hands. The grand vezir in turn surrendered it to the ambassador, present-ing it with the full meed of reverence. The ambassador, observing the prescribed forms of reverence, and performing a respectful salutation, departed from that place which is as majestic as the heavenly sphere, with servitors for stars. He committed the *tasdikname* reverently to the hands of his *divan katibi* [council secretary] and then returned to his home.[7]

Later, on Monday, 28 *Zilkade* [30 January], the grand vezir and the sheikh ul Islam Efendi and high officials of the Porte came to bid farewell. After that, on Thursday, 1 *Zilhicce* [2 February], at the auspicious time of 5:31 on that felicitious day, the procession set out from the ambassador's home in parade formation as follows: the *divanegân* and *gönüllüyân* con-tingents, then the horsetail and the standard, and then the fast horses and caparisoned reserve horses. After them came the carriages carrying the imperial gifts, then the *kapıcılar kethudası* [adjutant of the gate-keepers], and the *selam ağası* [master of ceremonies], then I [Nahifi Mehmet Efendi], and the ambas-sador's son-in-law, who was from among the *hacegân* of the

---

[5] The sheikh ul Islam was İvaz-Pashazade Ibrahim Bey Efendi. Danişmend, *Kronolojisi*, 4:541.
[6] *Ağa Bahçesi* is located on the grounds of Topkapı Sarayı. See Ekrem Hakkı Ayverdi, *19. Asırda İstanbul Haritası*.
[7] The printed text (p. 6) differs from the manuscript (f. 3b) here. In the printed text the ambassador raises the document to his forehead in reverence.

imperial divan.[8] Then came the carriage for the *tasdikname*, and
after it the *şatiran* [footmen] and *çuhadar*s [valets] together with
the ambassador. His *gedik* agas [household attendants] were
behind him. After them came his *divan katibi*, his *kethuda*
[household steward], and then his *enderun* agas [attendants of the
inside service]. Behind them came the *mehterhane* [military band]
and the *karakullukçu* detachment [janissaries]. Passing the
Şengul bathhouse[9] and the grand vezir's residence, they arrived
in front of the Alay kiosk which is the majestic golden tower,
the lofty prospect where the sultan sits as though in a phoenix's
nest.[10] The Ambassador descended from the saddle of his horse
to the ground of obeisance, and his justly proud eyes were
anointed with the dust of abasement. As he lifted his eyes from
the supplicant's position, they were anointed by the presence
of the sultan, and he was again clothed with a sable robe of
honor as a mark of the beneficent sultan's favor, king of kings.
After withdrawing from the radiant, world-illuminating gaze,
he got back on his horse and together with the procession
passed through Silivri gate.[11] That night they bedded down at
Küçükçekmece.

On the morrow the horses were urged in the assigned direction. At Kınıklı, which was the fourth stage, we had some snow,
rain, and extreme cold. Upon our arrival at [Lüle] Burgaz, the
weather, by the grace of God, the Almighty, and the felicitous
favor of the beneficent Lord, improved. The countryside
became like a picture of spring, and in the fine weather we
arrived at Edirne on 10 *Zilhicce* [11 February], the feast of
sacrifices. The day after our arrival at Edirne two letters were

[8] His son-in-law remains unidentified. His rank indicates that he would have
been among the high-ranking bureau chiefs of the central bureaucracy.
[9] For its location see Ayverdi, *Harita*.
[10] The Alay kiosk was built into the walls of Topkapı Sarayı, close to the grand
vezir's offices. See Ernest Mamboury, *The Tourists' Istanbul*, trans. Malcolm Burr,
p. 451; and Ayverdi, *Harita*.
[11] The Silivri gate is the third one from the Sea of Marmara side (Ayverdi,
Harita). In a short entry on Abdülkerim's mission in his chronicle Cevdet Pasha
has the procession leaving by the Edirne gate, the sixth gate ([Ahmet] Cevdet
Pasha, *Tarih-i Cevdet*, 2:7).

written, one to the Russian ambassador, and one to Field
Marshal Rumiantsev, notifying them of the time of our
departure from Istanbul. Another kindly phrased letter was
sent to the voivode of Moldavia, in connection with his pur-
chasing supplies that would be needed from the time of our
crossing the boundary into Moldavia.[12] This was sent with the
kapıcılar kethudası. Afterward, because we heard rumors from
the mouths of the people to the effect that the Russian ambassador was close to the frontier, it was not deemed expedient
to wait any longer. Immediately, on Friday 16 *Zilhicce* [17
February], we set out from Edirne. We stayed in Yambol one
day, and, traveling by way of Chalik Kavak pass, we arrived
at Shumen on 26 *Zilhicce* [27 February].[13]

During our stay there a letter arrived from the voivode of
Moldavia. He indicated a route for us by way of Isaccea and
Timarabad.[14] That region, however, had just escaped from the
fetters of the occupation. Since it had not yet returned to its
original state, there would be great obstacles in the way of pro-
curing supplies, and in other matters. We wrote again to the
voivode explaining that in comparison with other regions,
Moldavia would be easier to pass through. It would be necessary, therefore, to travel to Hotin by way of Galaţi, along the
Pruth River. After writing the letter, we set out from Shumen
on Monday, 4 *Muharrem* 1189 [6 March 1775].

We set up camp in Silistra on Friday the 8th [10 March]. The
intention was to stay until the arrival of an answer from the
Russian ambassador that would give information on his move-
ments and progress. In the region of Silistra, however, there
was a scarcity of meat and other provisions. It was clear that
if we stayed too long, our neediness and indigence, and that of

[12] The voivode was Gregory Ghika II.
[13] For a description of this area see Felix P. Kanitz, *Donau-Bulgarien und der
Balkan*, 3:49–117. This pass is now Karnobatski Prokhod. With the exception of
some common usages, place names have been indicated as given in the gazetteers
of the United States Board on Geographic Names: *Bulgaria*, no. 44; *Rumania*,
no. 48; *Russia*, no. 42; and *Turkey*, no. 46. Shumen is now Kolarovgrad.
[14] Timarabad has been difficult to locate. One possibility is Timareşti.

the people of Silistra would increase daily. Also, the fact that
the Russian ambassador was close to the frontier was public
gossip. Moreover, there was a good possibility that the former
kaimakam [deputy] of the grand vezir, His Excellency Melek
Mehmet Pasha, that vezir who was like Aristotle in measures,
who had been appointed to the exchange of the ambassadors,
would be delayed because of the distance from Lepanto, the
seat of his jurisdiction. In addition, in the grand vezir's letter
that arrived from the capital, it was explained that the ambassadors of the other states resident in Istanbul had communicated [to the Porte] that carrying out the exchange ceremony
with the participation of only the official escorts [*mihmandars*]
and the officers on the frontier had a precedent and conformed
to the law of nations. The ambassador was ordered not to
delay, in expectation of Melek Mehmet Pasha's arrival, but to
depart for the frontier.

It was decided, therefore, to depart from Silistra on Monday,
25 *Muharrem* [27 March]. The people of Silistra expressed
doubts and reservations, however, about having the imperial
gifts loaded on boats and shipped from Silistra to Galaţi
by way of the Danube River. After investigating the condition
of the route with the idea of sending the gifts to Măcin by land
and from there to Galaţi by the river, people who knew the
area well reported that the distance overland to Măcin was
twelve stages. That area, however, had just begun resettlement.
Since they were busy with the repair of homes and dwellings
and were bringing food from distant places, it would not be
possible to find a grain of provisions during the course of the
journey. Since it would be exceedingly difficult to acquire a
sufficient amount of supplies in Silistra, it would be necessary,
there being no other possible route, to cross over to a place
called Călăraşi situated on the Walachian bank opposite
Silistra, and to proceed from the Walachian boundary to
Brăila, and from there to Galaţi. A letter was written to the
voivode of Walachia asking him to purchase the provisions
necessary for the three-day trip from the afore-mentioned place

to Brăila.[15] Five hundred *kuruş* were sent on account. The
itinerary register that we had prepared, indicating that we
would cross the Pruth River at a place called Tutora, beyond
Galaţi, was given to the *portar başı* [protocol officer] of the
voivode of Moldavia who had arrived at that time. After a
robe of honor had been bestowed upon him, he was given
leave.

In the reply that arrived from the voivode of Walachia, he
made lame excuses about the procurement of the requested
supplies and sent back the five hundred *kuruş*. Therefore, there
was nothing to do but buy and acquire in Silistra the three-days'
worth of supplies needed to reach Brăila. On the Monday that
had been agreed on as explained above, we set about to move
the heavy baggage and loads across to Călăraşi by means of
three or four small boats [*kayık*] that were available and known
locally as *karla*. Kara Hisarî Ahmet Bey of the chief gatekeepers [*kapıcıbaşıs*] of the Imperial Palace, who had been
appointed from Istanbul as a *mihmandar* [official escort] for the
Russian ambassador showed up at this time, and therefore he
too was ferried across to the Walachian bank. On Thursday, 28
Muharrem [30 March], the ambassador and his personal retainers boarded two Danubian river-crafts called *şayke*. On that
day, by the felicitous favor of the Lord, the page of the sky was
polished by the burnishing-stone of the world-illuminating sun
and became clean and bare of the traces of cloud. With the
approach of the auspicious festival of spring, field and plain
were emerald-hued with a carpet of greenery, and every tree,
with multicolored blossoms, was the very picture of a wedding
garland. Taking pleasure in the view of the surrounding
scenery, and delighting in the gracious shadow of the sovereign, we crossed over to Călăraşi under the enduring mantle of
God's protection.

At the three stopping places situated in the territory of
Walachia from Călăraşi to Brăila not a pin was asked for or
taken from the people of Walachia. Moreover, such things as

15 The voivode was Alexander Ypsilanti.

poultry that were brought by a servant of the voivode of Walachia were not accepted. Making do with our supplies that were on hand, we moved on. We crossed to and settled in at Galați on Wednesday, 4 *Safer* [5 April]. Previously, in the course of the war, Galați had been completely destroyed, and except for two dyeing establishments, all traces of the buildings were destroyed and nonexistent. As a result of the felicitous, thoughtful endeavor of the sultan, who is the fount of justice, as many as several hundred houses and a number of shops have been built, and many *reaya* [subjects] have been settled and domiciled. It is fervently hoped that by their increase and multiplication Galați will acquire its original aspect in the near future. We spent the next day in Galați.

We set out on Friday. We reached and spent the night in a village four hours from Galați. There, a communication arrived from the Russian field marshal. He requested that we send ahead the register of whatever we would require in the way of supplies after the exchange of ambassadors. Abdülkerim Pasha replied in amicable terms to the effect that it was contrary to the laws of hospitality to impose burdens on one's host. He left the matter of provisions to the dignity of the Russian state.

At that point, Mehmet Pasha's letter arrived by his *çuhadar*s [valets]. It stated that he had arrived at Turnovo. The ambassador dispatched an answer, also by those *çuhadar*s, containing gracious discourses to the effect that Mehmet Pasha should arrive at Hotin as quickly as possible. The next day we set out from the town, and we arrived at a village called Izburuga,[16] six hours from Jassy [Yaş], on Thursday 12 *Safer* [13 April]. Upon our arrival at Izburuga a messenger delivered a letter from the field marshal to the Russian chargé d'affaires resident in Istanbul. The letter stated that the arrival of the Russian ambassador, General Repnin, at the frontier would be delayed until the latter part of June or early July because of the overflowing of the rivers and the harshness and prolongation of the

---

16 Unidentified, possibly Izvor.

winter in Russia. Since it would be a long wait until that time, the ambassador wrote to Istanbul about the situation. He indicated that he awaited the issuance of orders on this matter. He gave the letter that had arrived, and the exposition of his views, to a *tatar* [courier] and sent him to Istanbul, accompanying the afore-mentioned messenger.

When the ambassador wrote the voivode of Moldavia about the Russian apologies and explained that he would have to wait within the territory of Moldavia for the arrival of the sultan's orders, he requested that the voivode place at his disposal a village suitable for his residence until that time. The voivode indicated a village from among the villages of Moldavia by the name of Chuchulya, close to the Hotin frontier. The next day we set out. Crossing the Pruth River at the Tutora ford, we arrived at the village on Tuesday, 17 *Safer* [18 April]. We set up camp and settled in. Afterwards, on Saturday, 28 *Safer* [29 April], we received news that Mehmet Pasha was close to the village. The ambassador himself, together with his personal retainers, mounted and went out to meet him. He performed *istikbal* at a distance of one hour's ride and invited Mehmet Pasha to the village.[17] They conversed as they rode side by side into the village. After all due signs of deference had been shown His Excellency by a few hours of quiet conversation, and by the serving of trays of food and the presentation of a caparisoned horse, Mehmet Pasha left and set out in the direction of Hotin. While we awaited the arrival of orders, the horses, with the approach of Saint Hizir's Day, were put out to graze in the fields along the banks of the Pruth River.[18]

The courier who had been sent earlier from Izburuga to Istanbul returned on Saturday, 20 *Rebiyülevvel* [20 May]. He delivered the valuable gift of fifteen thousand *kuruş* that he

[17] *İstikbal* is the act of showing deference to a high-ranking official who is approaching a town or camp by riding out to meet him and escort him back. Usually, the higher the rank of the official, the farther out one rode to greet him.
[18] In the Islamic folk tradition, especially in Anatolia, Hizir was identified with Saint George. The feast of Lydda for Hizir coincides with St George's day, 23 April (o.s.) (Hasluck, *Christianity*, 1:320). The date here would be 4 May.

brought from the sultan, His Imperial Highness, he who
scatters kindness broadcast. He also brought the orders and
firman of the beneficent sultan. The tenor of the royal order
was as follows:

> The ambassador should compute the price of the provisions
> provided for and overseen by the voivode of Moldavia
> according to the prices requested by him. He should then
> return immediately the sum that remains after deducting the
> amount paid out, and send the voivode's own written receipt
> to Istanbul. The ambassador should remain within the Hotin
> border until the agreed upon time.

Immediately afterward, the ambassador wrote to His
Excellency Mehmet Pasha. He requested that a suitable village
from among the villages of Hotin be set aside for him. Mehmet
Pasha suggested that he stay in the village of Kotyudzhen'.

On Thursday, 2 *Rebiyülâhır* [1 June], we received a letter
from the Russian ambassador while we were on the road after
having moved from Chuchulya. He wrote that his own rank
was superior to the rank of Ambassador Rumiantsev who had
been sent by the Russians at the time of the Belgrade peace
[1739]. Nevertheless, he was satisfied with the treatment that
had been accorded Rumiantsev and with the daily allowances
that had been prepared for him. In addition to a *kapıcıbaşı*, one
of *mir-i mirân* had been assigned as *mihmandar*s for Rumiantsev.[19]

19 Repnin was extremely sensitive about protocol. From documents in his
possession he knew that in 1740 Count Aleksandr I. Rumiantsev (father of the
field marshal) was assigned a pasha of two horsetails and a *kapıcıbaşı* as *mihmandar*s. In May 1775 he wrote to Catherine from Kiev that if he were not
assigned *mihmandar*s of equal rank he would not travel any further (*SRIO*, 5:177–
78). The letter mentioned here was sent from Kiev on 22 May (*SRIO*, 5:183–84).
Peterson, the Russian chargé d'affaires in Constantinople, wrote to Repnin that
he had requested the assignment of a pasha of two horsetails as official escort,
following the precedent of 1740. Ahmet Pasha, who met that requirement, had
been assigned (*SRIO*, 5:179). The Ottomans were already angry over the delay
in Repnin's arrival. Mehmet Pasha wrote Repnin that the first *mihmandar*, Ahmet
Pasha, was a pasha of two horsetails, and that the second *mihmandar*, Ahmet Bey,
was a *kapıcıbaşı*. He noted that Ahmet Pasha was "one of the most renowned of
the *mir-i mirân*." He closed the letter with a flourish, saying that although they
had not yet met, their friendship was already so perfect that he anxiously awaited
his arrival and "could not take his eyes from the road by which he was to arrive"
(*SRIO*, 5:203–4). Repnin apparently was satisfied, and a colonel, the equivalent
rank of *kapıcıbaşı*, was assigned to be Abdülkerim's second official escort.

This time, the Russian state had appointed a colonel and a general as official escorts for the Ottoman ambassador. General Repnin sent a copy of the list of provisions that had been given to the afore-mentioned Rumiantsev.[20] He requested that in addition to the *kapıcıbaşı* one of the *mir-i mirân* should be appointed as official escort too, and the provisions should be prepared with that change in mind. General Repnin also suggested that the ambassador send a list of the provisions he would need. Our ambassador immediately sent a reply saying, "in addition to the *kapıcıbaşı* of the Imperial Palace, Kara Hisarî Ahmet Bey, who had been appointed earlier as *mihmandar*, *mütesellim* [high ranking officer in the provincial administration] Ahmet Pasha, the former *mutasarrıf* [administrator] of the *sancak* [provincial subdivision] of Beyşehir, and one of the noble *mir-i mirân*, has also been appointed. At present, they are expecting the Russian ambassador's arrival at Hotin. Other necessities too are in perfect readiness. On the matter of provisions, since the size of the retinues on both sides are similar, the amount of provisions that will be prepared for the Russian ambassador will suffice for us. There is no necessity to prepare another register." A copy of the Russian ambassador's communication was sent to Istanbul, and the situation was explained as described above.

After that, on Sunday, 5 *Rebiyülâhır* [4 June], we arrived at Kotyudzhen' village. When we had settled down and were awaiting the arrival of the appointed time, a further communication arrived from the Russian ambassador on Saturday, 3 *Cemaziyelevvel* [1 July]. He explained that he was about to arrive at a place that was one hour from Hotin, after proceeding from a station eight hours outside of Hotin. Our ambassador too should advance and take up residence in a place one hour's march from Hotin. They would then begin discussions on whether the *mubadele* should be carried out on land or on the river. Also [the Russian ambassador] wished to be told how many boats had been prepared for the crossing of the Dnestr River.

20 BVA Cevdet/hariciye 6101.

Our ambassador wrote in reply to the Russian ambassador
that His Excellency Mehmet Pasha had been appointed to deal
with the *mubadele*. Therefore, answers on these matters would
come from him. Our ambassador then communicated the situation to Mehmet Pasha. His Excellency Mehmet Pasha wrote
to the Russian ambassador that the necessities had been arranged for performance of the *mubadele* on the Dnestr River
according to precedents, and that the other requisites had been
completed. Later, letters arrived from His Excellency Mehmet
Pasha, explaining that the Russian ambassador had arrived at
Zhvanets. Therefore, our ambassador should arrive at a point
on the opposite bank of the Dnestr. On Wednesday, 7 *Cemaziyelevvel* [5 July], the ambassador left Kotyudzhen'. With his
procession he passed through the outskirts of Hotin and made
camp in a tent that had been pitched on the plains of Hotin
opposite the Russian ambassador's headquarters.

The next day, His Excellency Mehmet Pasha summoned me
[Nahifi Mehmet Efendi]. He explained that the Russian ambassador expected our ambassador to ask after his health first.
After someone had been sent by the ambassador, the Russians
would reciprocate in a like manner. He further explained to me
that since I had been assigned to and was taking part in this
venture and was familiar with the reports given by the officers
who had called on the ambassador, he [Mehmet Pasha] would
be pleased if I called on the Russian ambassador. When I
returned to our ambassador with Mehmet Pasha's request and
explained the situation to him, he prepared several gifts of
such things as dates, tobacco, and Yemen coffee, saying, "This
is the produce of the Ottoman realm." He also assigned his
translator to my suite out of consideration for the fact that this
was the first interview with the Russians, and with the intention of facilitating other formalities. I arrived at the Russian
headquarters. I delivered the aforementioned gifts and completed the social amenities of spending some time and inquiring
after the health of the Russian ambassador.

When I returned I found that the ambassador had gone to pay a visit to His Excellency Mehmet Pasha. I went straight over. While I was describing the situation to them in a lofty castle that looked out on the Dnestr River, the Russian ambassador's personal secretary and some of his men crossed the Dnestr River. When we saw that they were making for the ambassador's headquarters, there was no more standing around. Immediately, the gathering was ended and the tables of food were cleared away. The ambassador departed on a caparisoned horse of pleasing gait that had been presented to him by His Excellency Mehmet Pasha. The ambassador returned to his encampment. He granted an audience to the personal secretary of the Russian ambassador, and they passed a pleasant time in the necessary display of niceties.

When I went to call on the Russian ambassador, the six men who accompanied me rode on horseback and were neatly dressed, and the translator's two grooms walked. The [Russian] personal secretary's six men rode and were wearing new clothes and his translator's two grooms walked, and in addition, the gifts that he brought, when compared with the gifts the ambassador had sent, were of equal value. This indicated at the very start that the Russians were adherents of a policy of reciprocal treatment.

Discussion on the Form of the Mubadele

His Excellency Mehmet Pasha appointed and assigned his *divan katibi* to the discussions concerned with the *mubadele*. Arriving at the scene, they began to discuss the exchange. The Russian ambassador laid the preliminary groundwork on the subject saying, "It is fitting to carry out this time, exactly as before, the ceremony that was carried out during the *mubadele* at Bender in 1740 on the occasion of the Belgrade peace treaty. Back then, at the time of the exchange ceremony after the formal exchange of the ambassadors, Numan Pasha, as courtesy demanded and choice accorded, accompanied Rumiantsev on

Rumiantsev's left from the scene of the ceremony to his own
tent and then from his own tent as far as the ambassador's
quarters. Now, this time my rank is superior to that of Rumiantsev's. His Excellency Mehmet Pasha most certainly will usher
me to my quarters in the same fashion, after the *mubadele*. Also,
the chair that will be placed for me on the other raft assigned
to transport me to the riverbank from the exchange raft must
be covered in gold brocade."

His Excellency Mehmet Pasha's *divan katibi* began to answer
according to Mehmet Pasha's insistent instructions, "It is
true that Numan Pasha was of lofty veziral rank. Mehmet
Pasha, however, in addition to possessing that eminent rank
is also the sultan's brother-in-law. Moreover, he remained for
a number of years the grand vezir's *kaimakam*. Distinguished
from among the other great vezirs by the mark of the sultan's
favor, his rank and his station are more exalted than those of
Numan Pasha."

In the following way the secretary also answered the proposals on the protocol of right and left.[21] "The arrival of ambassadors from both countries uniquely evidences the desire to
strengthen the ties of friendship and amity. Such obstinacies
with regard to right and left [in 1740] resulted in Numan Pasha's
not escorting Rumiantsev after the *mubadele*. It is evident that
forbearance to such petty matters would have consolidated
the ties of friendship. Because of this break in good relations,
the formality of accompaniment was not carried out at that
time. Since there is no precedent, similar unprecedented proposals are burdensome, and because they are unseemly, they
cannot possibly be accepted."

After a couple of days passed in this way, the Russian ambassador spoke on this subject. "Now then, the reception tent that
will be set up on the bank of the river will be Mehmet Pasha's.
I shall arrive at that tent after the *mubadele*. In this way I shall

---

[21] For an interesting view of this right hand, left hand protocol see W. H. Lewis,
Levantine Adventurer, p. 26.

have arrived at Mehmet Pasha's tent alone. Consequently, since he will not have escorted me to my quarters, the next day, out of respect for the rule of equable treatment, he must call on me with full veziral pomp at the quarters set aside for me.''

After the Russian had made this proposal of his, Mehmet Pasha replied in a friendly manner. "We are perfectly willing to meet and have a pleasant conversation with you every day when our guest the ambassador has crossed over to this side. But this is contrary to the custom of our frontier. The soldiers attach great importance to seeing the governors on this type of frontier act in accordance with custom. If there should now be behavior contrary to custom, we can expect the appearance of a state of affairs embarrassing and vexatious for you and for us. Therefore, it is needless to explain that we regret the impossibility of our having such an interview."

The following answer was given to the proposal for an upholstered chair mentioned above. "The people of the Sublime State have been on familiar terms with horse and saddle for a very long time. Since we are not accustomed to chairs, disposing of an upholstered chair in this area is difficult. This time, however, it has been arranged. The chair that will be placed on the exchange ceremony raft has been brought from the voivode of Moldavia on condition that it be returned after the *mubadele*. When you get to Jassy you will see the chair as cordial proof of our claim." During the course of some ten days of coming and going, and discussions and talks between Mehmet Pasha's *divan katibi* and the Russian ambassador's translator, these proposals of his were not close to being accepted by the Russian ambassador. When it was clear that this meant there would be no crossing of the river, His Excellency Mehmet Pasha stood his ground with the reply, "My appointment as *muhafız* [governor] of Hotin is not related to my assignment to assist in the *mubadele* of the ambassadors. It is more likely [the other way around,] that my assignment to the exchange stems from my being the governor of Hotin. Since I have no idea of going back to Istanbul after the ex-

change, whatever time they desire to cross to this side is of no
consequence to me. It is up to them."
In the end, the Russians retreated from their demands for
an upholstered chair and formal escort, and for [Mehmet
Pasha's] calling at the Russian ambassador's tent the day after
the *mubadele*. It was also decided that we would stand up from
the time the Russian ambassador left the reception tent until
he mounted his horse. A sealed letter then arrived for His
Excellency Mehmet Pasha from the Kiev general, General in
Chief Voeikov, who had been assigned to the *mubadele* of the
ambassadors by the Russians. The letter described the form
of the ceremony as it would be carried out. The Russians requested a written answer agreeing to how the ceremonies
would be carried out in conformity with the details as they had
been discussed.[22] His Excellency Mehmet Pasha, on the dictates of his innate intelligence, hesitated to give a written
answer. Although he made counterproposals, it was not possible to mollify the Russians in any way. When they insisted,
he necessarily reflected on the matter and consulted with men
well versed in protocol. The local garrison people related that
formerly when the Russian ambassador appeared, a forty-five-
gun salute was fired from the Hotin fortress. In the *mubadele*
that took place earlier at Bender, the Russian ambassador
entered the reception tent. After that he walked and sat at
Numan Pasha's right until he departed. Therefore, of the
articles contained in the letter sent by the general, all had
precedents except the proposal that the official escort walk in
the procession unaccompanied. His Excellency Mehmet Pasha

22 The fine points of protocol had been a matter of serious dispute up to the time
of the exchange on the Dnestr. Each ambassador felt compelled to defend his
sovereign's honor, and his own competence to that sovereign. Both sides claimed
to be following the precedents set at Bender in 1740. Repnin, for example, wrote
to Mehmet Pasha on 1 July 1775 that he had a copy of the proceedings at
Bender and hoped that they had one also (*SRIO*, 5:215). On the matter of the
right hand, the Ottomans said that their records contained no specific information on it. In fact, Abdülkerim maintained that no precedent had been set on
that issue. The Russians appear to have been extremely sensitive on minor points
that the Ottomans were willing to leave for settlement on the spot by capable
officials.

begged to differ with the Russians on this article. He pointed out that since one of the official escorts had the rank of *mir-i mirân*, and the other was one of the *kapıcıbaşı*s their marching in the procession with their suites was among the ancient usages of the state. With the exception of the *divan çavuşları* [pursuivants of the imperial divan], no one marches in processions unaccompanied. It was now understood what our guest the Russian ambassador had meant earlier. In a previous *mubadele*, a couple of *divan çavuşları* had taken part in the ceremony, and they had walked unaccompanied.

After it was decided that the *mihmandar*s would march in the procession together with their suites and equipage, Mehmet Pasha sent a written reply that conformed to the requirements of hospitality and was worthy of the honor of his state. Since Thursday, 15 *Cemaziyelevvel* [13 July], had been designated as the time for the exchange, on Wednesday they set about transporting the heavy baggage from both sides.

Description of the Mubadele

They carefully selected two boats that were riding on the Dnestr River and were known locally as *acek*. The boats were gotten ready several days in advance. Progress was made on the preparation of the furnishings that would be constructed and placed on board. Two rafts were covered over with green cloth fashioned into a very ornate canopy. One of the rafts was designated for the *mubadele* itself, and, moored by a dropped anchor in the middle of the river, it was aligned with Zhvanets. The other one was stationed on the [Ottoman] bank in order to effect the passage of His Excellency Mehmet Pasha, together with the ambassador, to the *mubadele* raft. Another raft, prepared by the Russians and canopied in red in the same manner, stood ready on the shore on the Russian side to bring the Kiev general and the Russian ambassador to the *mubadele* raft. At a short distance of about forty or fifty paces from the river on the [Ottoman] bank across from the *mubadele* raft a large brocade

çerge [tent] was set aside for the profferment of hospitality to
the Russian ambassador after the exchange. A decorated *oba*
[another form of tent] was set up for Mehmet Pasha to rest and
take his ease in prior to the exchange. A number of *şemsiye*s
[awnings] and plain tents were set up for the *mihmandar*s and
other attendants. On the opposite shore a number of tents
were set up by the Russians. At three o'clock [11:30 A.M.] of
the next day, Thursday, which was the appointed day, His
Excellency Mehmet Pasha, with his full equipage, and in
parade with the military band playing, arrived at the previously
mentioned tent. Afterwards, at 4:30 [1 P.M.] a cannon shot was
fired from the Russian side in order to communicate that they
were ready to proceed. When a cannon shot responded from
this side, the ambassador departed from his headquarters on
horseback. The Russian ambassador set out from his headquarters toward the place of the exchange and marched with
his procession. When they arrived at the opposite banks, ten
cannon shots were fired from each side. The ambassador rested
in Mehmet Pasha's tent until the rest of both ambassadors'
few retainers who would be at the place of the exchange were
transported with their baggage across the river. A little earlier,
ten of His Excellency's *enderun* agas had gone over to the
mubadele raft. After they had boarded a cannon shot was fired
from the Russian side to announce that they were ready. After
the response from this side, there was activity on both sides.
Abdülkerim Pasha arrived at the bank with the two *mihmandar*s and a certain number of his attendants. They boarded the
transfer raft that had been prepared and moored at the bank as
described above. The Russian ambassador boarded his own
raft that had been prepared in a similar fashion on the opposite
bank. They arrived at the *mubadele* raft slowly with matching
strokes, while on the two banks the military bands of both
ambassadors beat their drums. Each party boarded the *mubadele* raft through the entry that faced them. Earlier, Mehmet
Pasha, with subtle theses, logical answers, and graceful re-
marks, had not been able to overcome the Russian ambassa-

dor's insistence that the Russian sit on his right. It was obvious that if it were not done that way there would be extreme distress, annoyance, and clamor. Out of necessity, His Excellency Mehmet Pasha, with the assistance of innate skill, designed a subtle procedure by which outwardly there would be no perception of left and right, and thereby the Russian ambassador would not be disabused of his belief that [Mehmet Pasha] had yielded to his view in the matter of right and left. When the *mubadele* raft was boarded from the Russian side, the area reserved for the Russians was on the right. They would sit on chairs which Mehmet Pasha had arranged so that to those entering from the [Ottoman] side it appeared that the Russian side was on the left. At the completion of the ceremony of welcome, the Kiev general, for the Russians, took a position on his own ambassador's right-hand side. Mehmet Pasha, in the same way, took a position on his ambassador's right-hand side. They completed the formal *mubadele* ceremony by presenting each to the other. When the completion of this ceremony was signaled from the *mubadele* raft, ten cannon shots were fired immediately from each side. The body of five hundred infantry troops lined up in formation on both banks fired three rounds in succession. After some delay, Mehmet Pasha took the Russian ambassador onto his raft. They sat on chairs facing each other and set out for the Hotin bank. The Kiev general took our ambassador onto his raft, and as they set out for the Zhvanets shore ten cannon shots were fired from each side.

When they got to the bank of the river, the janissary aga of Hotin took a position on Mehmet Pasha's right side, and his *kethuda* [steward] took a position on his left. Mehmet Pasha had ordered this because he had foreseen that if the Russian did not somehow or other walk on the right, or if it be suggested that he walk on the left, there would be hesitation and dispute. They walked toward the reception tent. Because the janissary aga was between Mehmet Pasha and the ambassador, whenever conversation was begun, the latter was obliged, in

order not to speak over the janissary aga's head, to take several
steps forward and turn and face them. Whenever he held back
and got in line with them, Mehmet Pasha stopped on the pretext of greeting the onlookers. The Russian [therefore] was
again out in front. In short, whereas the Russian ambassador
would not consent at all to the left-hand position, Mehmet
Pasha, by this clever maneuver and smooth arrangement, did
not let the Russian enjoy the fruits of his labor.[23]

With Mehmet Pasha letting the Russian ambassador walk in
front, they entered the reception tent, and they sat awhile face
to face inside the tent on spread carpets and divans. When the
Russian ambassador was ready to leave, a caparisoned horse
was prepared for him in accordance with the precedent set in
Numan Pasha's time. At that moment, again according to
Mehmet Pasha's orders, the janissary aga entered the tent and
informed them that the procession and the horse were ready.
When the janissary aga went to kiss the hem of Mehmet
Pasha's robe, the Pasha stood up, as well-established protocol
dictated in relation to the aga. Thereupon, the Russian ambassador stood up too. After the Russian ambassador had
mounted the caparisoned horse, Mehmet Pasha did not sit
down again. He visited the other tent and carefully explained
that he had stood up only to facilitate the janissary aga's kissing
his hem, and not out of respect for the Russian ambassador.

Description of the Russian Ambassador's Procession

The flags of Mehmet Pasha's *divanegân* and *gönüllüyân* were the
van of the procession. Behind them came the *kapıcılar kethudası*

[23] Peterson was attempting to work out an arrangement on the right-hand
protocol. On 21 May he reported a conversation with the *reis efendi*, who maintained that his notes did not indicate that Rumiantsev had been granted the
right hand in 1740. Moreover, Mehmet Pasha could hardly be expected to offer
his right hand to Repnin, for Mehmet Pasha had long been the grand vezir's
deputy. He was a man in the presence of whom other pashas of three horsetails
would not dare to be seated without his order. The *reis efendi* was of the opinion
that a solution would be found at the scene by Mehmet Pasha, a man of sufficient
knowledge to deal with protocol matters (*SRIO*, 5:179). Catherine placed the
blame for the problem on the Turks who, "in accordance with their characteristic indelicacy, have to haggle over every point of ceremony" (*SRIO*, 5:211–13).

and his *selam ağası*. After that came the *mihmandar*s and their attendants. A little behind them followed the Russian ambassador with his own attendants and servants. Behind them were Mehmet Pasha's *kethuda* and his *divan katibi*. Behind them marched the *mehterhane*. A twenty-five-gun salute was fired when the Russian ambassador arrived with the procession in the described order opposite the fortress. They then conducted the ambassador to his quarters that had been prepared in the outskirts of Hotin.

Description of the Equivalent Ceremonies for the Ambassador

The ambassador, after crossing over to the Russian side by means of the raft, entered his tent set up on the bank of the river. The ambassador sat on a chair to the right of the chairs that the Russians had arranged in rows according to their usual custom. Next to him was Nahifi Mehmet Efendi, then the ambassador's *kethuda*, and next to him his *divan katibi*. On the left, seated on chairs were first of all the Kiev general, next to him our official escort, a major general named Igel'strom, next to him the full colonel assigned to the aforementioned general's suite, and further down a number of distinguished officers. Russian-style sweets, coffee, and sherbet were served. After that, the Kiev general addressed himself to the ambassador. "His Excellency Mehmet Pasha will present a caparisoned horse to our ambassador. Therefore, it is incumbent upon our side to reciprocate in a like manner. But, since the saddle and stirrups on our horses are not like those to which you are accustomed, our failure to reciprocate is excusable." After the Russian had made excuses in this way, the ambassador replied, "My carriage is ready. I'll ride in that." Thereupon, the Russian responded, "If you ride in your carriage, let us send word to our ambassador that he should ride in his carriage from the reception tent and go to his quarters by carriage."

The ambassador immediately replied, "If my riding my horse will please you, then I am prepared to do so. I shall ride my horse." When they replied, "That would please us," the ambassador's horse was brought and he mounted. Immediately, the five hundred infantry soldiers, ready and in formation as described earlier, began to present arms. In parade formation, we set off for our headquarters which had been set up previously on the plains before Zhvanets. We arrived and settled in.

Digression

The clamor from the arguments that had occurred earlier over proposals on the matters of accompaniment and positions of honor at the time of the *mubadele* that had taken place in connection with the Belgrade peace treaty still rings in the ears of man to this day. If the two occasions are compared, a tremendous difference is evident. Because the proposals made this time were more unwelcome than those of the other occasion, there was hesitation and dispute. His Excellency Mehmet Pasha, who is a veritable Aristotle in his reasoned counsels, was appointed to the *mubadele*. In matters of contention and forbearance he mirrored the wisdom of the sages. His employment of subtle measures and his display of penetrating intellect, in addition to the ambassador's [Abdülkerim's] acting with sagacity, softened the unyielding arrogance of the Russians which was evident from the very beginning. Their judicious, fitting treatment of matters put right some of the unseemly Russian proposals. This important matter was carried out and completed more easily and amicably than in 1740 and is clearly due to the felicitous good fortune of the sultan and to the bounty of God.

This is a copy of the official itinerary through Poland to the Russian frontier at Kiev fortress. It was prepared during our stay on the plains of Zhvanets by the general who was our official escort.

After leaving Zhvanets

Dolzhok	three hours	Nastana Karşı	three and one-quarter hours[24]
Negin	three hours		
Tynna	four hours, stayed one day	Chudnov	four hours, stayed one day
Yarmolintsy	three and one-quarter hours	Pyatki	four hours
		Berdichev	four hours, stayed one day
Shumovtsy	four hours		
Masivtsy	four hours	Belopol'ye	four hours
Medzhibozh	four hours, stayed one day	Utaşrahina	four hours[25]
		Pavoloch'	four hours, stayed two days
Buzticnu	five hours		
Severiny	five hours	Fastov	three and one-quarter hours
Polonnoye	four hours, stayed four days		
		Motovilovka	three and one-quarter hours
Miropol'	three and one-quarter hours		

After that, on Wednesday, 21 *Cemaziyelevvel* [15 July], when the necessities had been taken care of, we departed from the aforementioned plains. After the tents had been pitched and we had settled in near Dolzhok village situated before the fortress of Kamanice [Kamenets-Podolsky], I [Nahifi Mehmet Efendi], with the permission of the ambassador, went to Kamanice with some of my men to visit that fortress.

It is a medium-sized fortress finished off in cut stone. It is in the midst of a plain that extends in all directions. It has no towers, but is encircled by a running stream and moat about thirty *arşın*/deep and wide.[26] Facing it on the other side of the moat are a small fort and bastions. They are joined to each other by a masonry bridge as tall as a minaret. The bastions

[24] The manuscript (f. 18b) gives Nāstana qarshī 3¼ hours. The printed text gives Nāstana 3 hours, qarshī ¼ hour. This could mean they stopped at a station ¼ hour's march from Nāstana, which is unidentified.

[25] In the printed text (p. 26) Bilopillya and Utaşrahina are given as one location, 4 hours. Utaşrahina remains unidentified, and is not listed, alone or in combination, in any of the itineraries given in J. Tournier, *Postguide through Russia*.

[26] A measure of length, approximately 68 centimeters.

were equipped with long-range cannon placed row after row.
In this way the path of easy access was barred to its enemies.
Most of the buildings were of masonry, and many of its districts
were in ruins at this time. They had begun to make repairs.
Earlier, after Kamanice had been conquered, on the date that is
given in the chronogram—"The light of Muhammad fell on
the fortress of Kamanice"[27]—two churches were converted
into mosques for the community of Muslims and places of
prayer for the body of true believers. Today the minaret of one
of them and the *minbar* [pulpit] of the other are still intact. The
words of the *şehadet* [profession of faith], which are on the
minbar, a memento of the pen of Islam, face the door of the
church, silent witness as it were, affirming to those who enter
the unity of God. The *lam* of absolute negation, by the raising of
the fingertip, gives warning against worshipping any but Him.[28]

The next day we broke camp and set out from the aforementioned place. We arrived at Tynna on Friday, 23 *Cemaziyelevvel* [21 July]. We stayed there the next day, Saturday, and
set out on Sunday. On Wednesday we entered Medzhibozh.
We spent the next day there. Because the area east of the town
for a distance equal to a fifteen-minute march is swampy and
full of reeds, travelers cross over a bridge made of wood. There
is a rather small fortress, more like a medium-sized mansion,
and it has no weapons or ammunition. On the western flank
there is a river that drives a number of mills. There is a bridge
over the river. We departed from there on Friday, the last day
of the month of *Cemaziyelevvel* [28 July].

[27] The chronogram is from Nabi Efendi's *Tarih-i Kamanice*, p. 64. Kamanice fell
to the forces of Sultan Mehmet IV in A.H. 1083 (1672–73). As given in both the
manuscript (f. 18b) and the printed text (p. 27), the chronogram is defective, and
inaccurately rendered. The play on words concerns the sultan's name, Mehmet
which is Muhammad in the Arabic script, and Muhammadî in the adjectival
form. This gives two meanings, Muhammadan light fell on Kamanice fortress,
or (Sultan) Mehmet's light fell on the fortress. Nabi's dates are 1642–1712.
[28] In the Muslim profession of faith the negative particle *lā* occurs, there is *no*
God but Allah. That particle is the *lam* of absolute negation. In the course of his
prayers the Muslim raises the first finger of the right hand and utters the full
profession of faith. The illusion here is to that part of the prayer. See Edward W.
Lane, *An Account of the Manners and Customs of the Modern Egyptians*, pp. 65–66.

We arrived at Polonnoye on Sunday, 2 *Cemaziyelâhır* [30 July]. In the course of our four-day stay there a holiday very popular among the Russians was celebrated.[29] On this occasion they all make merry and divert themselves. In addition, since news had arrived that the [major] general who was our official escort had been promoted to the rank of lieutenant general, he gave a party for his fellow countrymen in order to express his pleasure and joy. Since he was the official escort, he invited the ambassador, who accepted, thus conforming to the dictates of the [Arabic] saying, "Do what pleases them while in their country."[30]

The Russian men and women who gathered in the banquet hall amused themselves for a couple of hours with Frankish song and music, and with songs and dances of their own. At present there is in the town a rather tall earthen fortress. In the bastions that go all the way around it there are cannon in position. In a vast, rather dilapidated stone monastery-like boyar's mansion situated within the fortress there is a good deal of Russian ammunition, war requisites and material, and other supplies. There are a number of troops and their officers who guard these supplies. A river that drives several mills flows through the edge of the town. We left there on Thursday, 6 *Cemaziyelâhır* [3 August]. On Saturday we arrived at Chudnov and stayed there the next day. We departed on Monday and settled in at Berdichev on Tuesday, 11 *Cemaziyelâhır* [8 August]. We stayed there the next day and on Thursday we packed up and left. The town is situated on a height at the edge of a vast lake. In lieu of a fort there is a strong and impregnable monastery surrounded by a moat and a stockade.[31] Earlier, some of Poland's allies entrenched themselves in the monastery. For

[29] 20/31 July is the feast day of Saint Elijah in the Russian church calendar. The celebration might also have been in connection with festivities decreed in honor of the treaty. Such festivities were held in Moscow on 1 August (*RBS*, 17:548).
[30] *Dārihim mā dumta fī dārihim.*
[31] The Carmelite monastery in Berdichev was founded in 1627. It was looted by Khmel'nitskii in 1647, and rebuilt in 1663. It was famous for its fairs, schools, library, and printing press. The area was acquired by Russia after the second partition of Poland.

several days they fought with the Russian troops who attacked
them. The effects of two cannon balls that hit the dome of the
monastery in the course of the action are still visible. Afterward,
on Saturday, 15 *Cemaziyelâhır* [12 August], we arrived at
Pavoloch' and rested there for two days. We set out on Tuesday. On Friday, 21 *Cemaziyelâhır* [18 August], we quit Poland.
We arrived safely at the quarantine station situated about half
an hour's march from the town of Vasil'kov which is dependent
on the province of Kiev, the Russian frontier.

Description of the Polish Lands

The villages that are one hour, or at most two hours, apart in
the territory of Poland between Zhvanets and the Russian
frontier are flourishing and well cultivated. At the edges of each
of them there are rather extensive lakes and a considerable
number of water-driven mills. On the plains and fields one can
see from one village to the next. The villages have many
orchards. The land, except for the pathways for people, is
plowed and sown entirely with various cereals. On the occasion
of our passage it was harvest time. When one looked about, the
fully ripe crops made waves of motion with the incitement of
the winds, and each level steppe appeared to be a boundless sea
of tumultuous waves.

Description of the Quarantine Station[32]

The station is situated on a wide plain and consists of about
fifteen or twenty separate sections. Each one of its sections is
composed of a garden, entrance hall, and numerous rooms, like
a separate house. The walls, roofs, and furnishings made are of
pine wood. In every room there is a stove made of porcelain-
like baked brick. The surfaces of walls of a number of rooms

[32] The word used in the text is nezarethane. William Macmichael, *Journey from
Moscow to Constantinople in the Years 1817, 1818*, pp. 76–77, describes a later
quarantine station and indicates that quarantine was then fixed at eighteen days.
Dr. Geoffrey Lewis suggests that the Ottomans confused lazareto with nezaret
after the Venetian quarantine island of Santa Maria di Nazaret.

set aside for more notable guests are embellished with decorated papers, resembling cloth. A goodly number of soldiers and
officers have been detailed to see that arrivals carry out fully the
formalities of the quarantine and to superintend the defense of
the station. Its four sides were encircled and protected by beams
with outwardly protruding spikes, and sentry boxes. The
general, our official escort, wanted to write to his empress
before our arrival in Moscow to inform her of the value and
nature of the imperial gifts the ambassador was bringing with
him. Sometimes he would brag about the preciousness and
delicacy of the empress's gifts that had been entrusted to their
ambassador. He would try different tactics and abase himself
and grovel in quest of information.

As his desire for some clue met with no fulfillment from His
Excellency the ambassador, at length, in order to attain his
desired objective the general even took his chances with the
following ploy. He said, "In conformity with our regulations
on quarantine, one must stay in this place for many days. But,
since you are the ambassador extraordinary of the Sublime
State, I do not see it fitting that you should be detained in this
place like the others. If you would display all the things you
and those who are in your train have with them, after inspect-
ing and fumigating them one by one we would be able to leave
this place in a day or two. To distinguish you from the others
we would be most happy with your doing this much in carrying
out the quarantine procedures." The ambassador replied,
"From those who have been on embassies, and from a number
of documents presently in my possession, it is clear that up to
now there has been no precedent for the proposal that ministers
plenipotentiary sent by the Sublime State either to Russia or to
other states should be detained in a place for the purpose of
quarantine, or for their goods to be fumigated. On behalf of my
state I cannot accede to or accept your unprecedented proposals." Thereupon, the general replied, "My intention in this
matter is not to be overly insistent, but I speak out of real
affection for you. Our empress is extremely horrified at the

thought of disease. Your acquiescence in the procedures would please her. I am sure that she would be well disposed toward you." He terminated his words with some Frankish cliché such as, "My friendship for you is joined to faithfulness and is beyond description." He was unable to achieve his aim.

It will be recalled that after the *mubadele* Mehmet Pasha presented General Repnin with a caparisoned horse. He also sent several dishes of excellent food to the general's quarters that evening.[33] Moreover, when he passed in front of the fortress with his procession, Mehmet Pasha gave the Russian ambassador a twenty-five-gun salute. Consequently, on a reciprocal basis, the Kiev general who was assigned by the Russians to the *mubadele*, sent a carriage for our ambassador during the course of our five-day stay at the quarantine station.

On Wednesday, 26 *Cemaziyelâhır* [23 August], we set out and spent the night three or four hours up the road. The next day, Thursday, when we arrived at the city of Kiev, the Kiev general had a twenty-five-gun salute fired from the fortress. After we settled in at the guest house they had made ready, they wanted to prepare and send food to the ambassador. Although the ambassador showed proper disdain in a friendly way, saying, "It isn't necessary to go to so much trouble. Praise be to God, we have our own food to which we are daily accustomed. There is really no need for your taking such trouble," it was not possible to prevent it. At the time of afternoon prayer a huge amount of food was prepared and sent. The next day the ambassador got together gifts of costly Indian cloths and other expensive goods, and some estimable oils of a value in excess of seven or eight hundred *kuruş*, and sent them to the Kiev general by means of his *kethuda*. The ambassador was not off by a hair's breadth in repayment of the kindness.

Description of Kiev Fortress

This fortress is the celebrated Russian march contiguous to the Polish frontier. It is a medium-sized earthen fortress. The

[33] Dinner was sent for fifty people.

fort had been destroyed earlier. Peter the Great constructed a
new fort of earth on its western flank in a place about one hour
away. Inside it he constructed stone cells for the Christian
monks and students and built a rather large atelier and mon-
asteries for the printing of books in their language and regulated its provisions and duties. They have set aside a sombre
place underground to deposit skeletons of men considered
distinguished among them. Today each of the forts has its
suburbs surrounding it, each as large as a town. The new part
is named Pechersky. It is replete with implements and instruments of war. It itself is more important than its suburb. The
old fort, since it has been allowed to go to ruin, has a suburb
which is more flourishing and populated. It is now known by
the name of Podol. There are many soldiers and officers assigned
to its defense. The great river called the Dnepr, a little bigger
than the Dnestr, flows before it on its eastern side. At present
travelers cross it on a bridge made of pontoons.

Description of the Ambassador's Quarters

The ambassador's quarters are situated between the suburbs of
the fortresses that were mentioned. It is a palace containing
more than fifty rooms, large and small, and possessing a garden
in excess of one hundred *dönüm*s.[34] Its lower story and foundation are of stone, its upper story is of wood. The surfaces of
the walls of the upper story are decorated with fabriclike wall-
paper, and with gilt moulding. Its ceilings are decorated with
white-colored cloth used like plaster. The wooden parts of the
upholstery are highly polished, and the material resembles
Egyptian matting. In every corner there is set up a stove of
baked brick that resembles porcelain.

On the approximately three *dönüm*s of land of the garden that
were within view from the drawing room there is a lawn devoid
of shrubs or trees. Special attendants clip the grass over four
inches in height with scissors. It comes out level, looking like

[34] A measure of land about 1600 square *arşın*, or 939.3 square meters, according
to James W. Redhouse, *A Turkish and English Lexicon*, p. 928.

a rug. The four sides and center of the aforementioned lawn
are defined by a white gravel footpath and decorated all the
way around with flowers such as lilacs, passion flowers, and
violets. Separate lawns of one hundred or two hundred *zira*
[one *zira* is about three-fourths of a meter] each were set aside
in several places to the right and left of, as well as behind, this
lawn. They were separated from each other by wall-like, green,
level, and equal partitions formed by such plants as lime and
bryony. Within the sections are planted young fruit trees such
as apple, pear, and plum. Each section takes on the appearance
of an individual orchard. In a number of places between the
sections, covered pathways are created by foliage entwined
from both sides. Where the paths cross each other there are
domed wooden-latticed buildings resembling summer houses.
In a number of places there are pavilions. Behind them one
ascends to a hill by means of a stairway of seventy broad,
permanent steps cut into the earth. On top there is a rectangular-
shaped building eight or ten *zira* in width, and thirty or forty
in length. Its right side and top open and shut. It is enclosed
with glass frames. Under it is a row of ovenlike stoves. In the
area contiguous to the building they have built a raised bed of
the same dimensions. The building's particular function is to
make the fruits and flowers peculiar to warm countries bloom.
In hot weather they are moved to the bed, and in winter they
are moved to the glass-enclosed building. They are watered and
fed with care, and they produce a variety of fruits and flowers
such as pomegranate, fig, lemon, sweet lemon, and carnation.
A number of species of apple, pear, and plum from the orchards,
being ripe and abundant, were received and eaten daily. In the
back of the aforementioned place a number of *dönüm*s on the
slope have been set out in vineyards. Their grapes were still
unripe at the time, but some of them had ripened a good deal.
The palace is considered extremely remarkable among the
Russians.[35] With its strange plan and organization, described

[35] For a description of the palace and gardens see Karl Baedeker, *Russia*, pp. 376–
86. See also Kiev, Akademiia nauk, Institut istorii, *Istoriia Kieva*, vol. 1, chap. 9,
and the map facing p. 265.

above, it appears very pretty when seen from afar. On closer scrutiny, however, it is clear that the structure is not so costly as a solid structure with the surfaces of its walls painted and decorated in various colors by the minute work of the hair-fine brush of the artists.

In the course of our stay, the general who was our official escort prepared this itinerary as far as our arrival at the Great Russian frontier. This copy of it was inscribed in the journal.

From Kiev

Brovary	two hours	Gorodishche	[no time recorded]
Semipolki	six hours		
Kozelets	five hours, stay one day	Baturin	three hours, stay one day
Nosovka	three hours	Altynovka	five hours
Nezhin	six hours, stay two days	Krolevets	three hours
		Tuligolovo	four hours
Komarovka	six hours	Glukhov	stay two days
Borzna	four hours		

From Kiev to Moscow posts were set up on the side of the road at a distance of every twelve-minute journey. On each post there was written in Russian letters and numbers indicating how many posts it was from Kiev. They call the distance between every two posts a *vers* [verst]. They calculate that one travels at the rate of five versts an hour.

We left Kiev on Sunday, 8 *Recep* [3 September], crossing the Dnepr River on a bridge made of pontoons. We stopped at the prepared stations and spent the night. We arrived at the town of Kozelets on Tuesday, 10 *Recep* [5 September], and rested there the next day. We started on the road again on Thursday. On Sunday, 15 *Recep* [10 September], we arrived at Nezhin and stayed there for two days. The city was vast and crowded, its market and bazaar flourishing, and its homes rather ostentatious. It has numerous wealthy merchants and shopkeepers, and various wares. It has a smallish earthen fort, encircled by a moat, which is renowned among the Russians, and a goodly

number of soldiers for its defense. At the time of our entrance
into the city they shot off a fifteen-gun-salute in honor of the
ambassador. On Thursday, 18 *Recep* [14 September], we
departed and made our way to Baturin, where we arrived on
Sunday. We stayed there the next day and left on Tuesday. We
crossed a river that resembled the Pruth.[36] It flows at the edge
of the town. On Friday, 26 *Recep* [22 September], we arrived at
Glukhov and rested there for two days. The town has a
medium-sized earthen fortress on a high place. Within the
fortress there are several small and large houses, places of wor-
ship, and various stores. A rather large lake has been made by
means of damming up and blocking the course of the river that
flows on the western side of the town. Over it they have built a
firm, wide, long bridge of wood. On one side of it a water mill
has been erected. On the west side of the bridge, in front of the
fortress, on the shore of the lake the Russian empress has had
constructed a new summer residence that resembles a summer
home on the Bosphorus. It is charming in appearance, but
worth little, and contains a large garden. In accordance with
their accepted practice it also contains several Frankish buildings. It was presented recently to Rumiantsev who is now her
field marshal. Apart from this, inside the fortress she has had
construction started on a large and spacious stone winter house
for Rumiantsev. At the time we passed through there it was not
completed. They hoped that with increased effort to have it
finished by wintertime. The designation of the town as a site of
buildings for the field marshal, being a sign of favor, stimulates
construction everywhere of such things as shops, and the
repair and construction of houses.

    From the Polish frontier as far as a village named Yesman,
which is situated four hours ahead and is one of the dependents
of Glukhov, the term "Little Russia" is used. All of its people
are cossacks. From here on is Great Russia, and its people are
called muzhiks. The costumes of the two groups are completely
different from each other.

[36] The Seim River.

From Glukhov

Tolstodubovo	seven hours	Solova	four hours, two versts
Sevsk	eight hours		
Asmon'	eight hours	Tula	eight hours, stay one day
Dmitrovsk-Orlovsky	four hours, stay one day	Vashana	seven hours
Chuvardino	three versts[37]	Savino	four hours
Kromy	four hours and two versts	Serpukhov	four hours, two versts, stay one day
Orël	stay one day	Lupasnya	five hours, three versts
Sergiyevskoye	six hours		
Mtsensk	four hours	Bahary	seven hours, two versts
Nikol'skoye	seven hours, one verst, stay one day	Moscow	six hours, three versts
Seriryovski	seven hours, one verst[38]		

Afterward, on Sunday, 29 *Recep* [24 September], we set out from Glukhov. At the time of our crossing the bridge a number of cannon were fired in our honor from within the fort. We set off in the intended direction. After stopping at the arranged stations, we arrived at the town of Dmitrovsk-Orlovsky on Tuesday, the first of *Şaban* [26 September]. We stayed there for one day and set out on Thursday. We arrived at Orël on Saturday. That town is rather large with a flourishing market and bazaar. It contains homes of its men of wealth and esteem. A river courses through it.[39] The next day we rested there. Setting out on Monday, we arrived at Nikol'skoye on Wednesday. That place is situated on a high mountain, and it consists of the homes of about five or ten poor people. Inside it and in the nearby neighborhood there was not a single drop of good water. Save for its police station and church, it was a desolate, poorly looked after place. We only stayed there

[37] The number of versts is not given for any location in the printed text, p. 38.
[38] Seriryovski is not given in the printed text, p. 38, and is unidentified.
[39] The Oka River.

to avoid disrupting the arranged program of stations. The
ambassador and I [Nahifi Mehmet Efendi] each took refuge in
a corner of the police station, and the ambassador's other
retainers and attendants camped out in the open in tents. The
next day, too, we rested there and set out on Friday. On Sunday, 13 Şaban [8 October], we entered Tula. The town is
famous among the Russians: It has wealthy merchants. Its
people, craftsmen, trades, and assorted wares are numerous.
There are richly adorned and showy houses, and well-arranged
and well-stocked stores and shops. On the bank of the large
river flowing through it are several water mills.[40] In a large
factory situated on the river, they manufacture instruments of
war such as rifles, pistols, pikes, rapiers, and other iron
implements. By using the water of the river in such services as
working the water wheels for forging iron, they ease their
labors. They want to be superior to their fellow craftsmen and
artisans in other countries in that industry. By paying attention
to detail and by being careful, they get more skilled and versed
in the process day by day and produce very pleasing and good
firearms. Because the gun factory is there, most of the townspeople do something related to the iron industry. At the time
of our arrival in Tula many rifle barrels manufactured in the
factory had been piled up and made ready. Upon our departure
from Tula at daybreak on Tuesday, they had moved the rifles
to their special place close to where we would pass, and according to their technique for testing, they fired the rifles all at
once. With the firing of a number of cannon as well, they
carried out both the proving of the rifles and the demonstration
of respect for the ambassador.

On Thursday, 17 Şaban [12 October], we crossed a great
river similar to the Dnestr River, known as the Oka, about
nineteen hours from Moscow. The ambassador and his personal

---

[40] For a description of the city in 1775 see Tula, *Materialy dlia istorii goroda XVI–
XVIII stoletii,* pp. 236–39. A bibliography is available in Vadim N. Ashurkov,
Gorod masterov; Ocherki po istorii Tuly c XVI veka do ustanovleniia vlasti Sovetov,
pp. 139–41.

retinue went across in a *zevrak*-like boat.[41] The rest of the party and the baggage went across on rafts. They were sent to Serpukhov about one hour ahead. We stayed there the next day. On Saturday, 19 *Şaban* [14 October], we set out. Upon our arrival at Lupasnya we received polite replies to the friendly letters that the ambassador had sent earlier from Tula to the prime minister and to the field marshal. The next day we left the village and on Monday, 21 *Şaban* [16 October], we arrived at a guest house situated in a suburb on the western side of Moscow. They had emptied and prepared the mansion for our rest and relaxation for a couple of days. They gave grace and charm to the mansion by means of red broadcloth-covered cushions, and beribboned, smooth, velvet pillows, and upholstered chairs, full-length mirrors, and cut-glass chandeliers. In order to pay attention to the daily requirements of hospitality, they appointed two generals whom they call chamberlains, corresponding to the *kapıcılar kethudası*, to rotate in the ambassador's service. This [appointment] was in addition to the various kinds of servants and officers from among the empress's private staff. They also sent cooks, with kitchen equipment, and vocalists and instrumentalists, with an organ and other Frankish musical instruments. All was prepared beforehand. Every day when the general on duty spread a banquet, the instrumentalists played tunes that had no time, and were outside the pale of the laws of music. The vocalists warbled without melody, sounding like the creaking of doors and the buzzing of flies, and the organ player played.

Afterward, they sent the ambassador a copy of the register that contained the procession procedure that had been carried out earlier in the time of Ümni Pasha, and that would be followed at the time of our departure for the residence they had prepared in another part of the city for our stay until the time of our departure for Istanbul. They requested that the ceremony be carried out in that manner. On Wednesday, 23 *Şaban*

41 *Zevrak-kayık* (caique).

[18 October], General Ibershukov[42] was sent with the invitation from the empress. As in the time of Ümni Pasha, in addition to a sufficient quantity of attendants for the mounts, he presented to the ambassador a horse with foreign saddle and stirrups and one horse each for five or ten personal retainers. Only the saddle, bridle, and reins of some of the horses were Ottoman, and only the stirrups, saddle, and horse armor of the others were Ottoman. The missing furnishings were made up from our own supplies. Two men were assigned to each rider as special attendants. The ambassador rested with the general for two hours until the procession was ready, and this time was spent in pleasant conversation.

When they were ready to leave, after refreshments had been served to the general, the ambassador offered his apologies. He said he would not be able to ride the horse prepared for him because he was not familiar with that type of saddle and stirrup arrangement. He mounted his own horse. Some of the others mounted their own horses, and some of them got on the horses that had been brought. The general, and general who was our official escort, as well as the general called a chamberlain, mounted and fell in in front of the ambassador. They set off with the parade organized as it had been at the time of our departure from Istanbul.

Description of the Procession

Not a single person among the men and women, the young and old, the high and low, the healthy and infirm, of the city of Moscow held back from viewing the procession. All of them locked up their houses and stores, and poured into the streets. They crowded into the houses and stores that lined both sides of the route along which the procession would pass. So many people had crowded onto the streets to see our procession that it looked like the day of judgment. The people of this region have not seen anything in the way of pomp among their own men of state other than the special wheeled-vehicle drawn by

42 Unidentified.

eight horses and called a *hanto*. When they saw in the procession
the ambassador's *enderun* agas walking and riding in front and
behind him as well as on his right and left, dressed in their
sable-lined flowing robes, and the showy horses two-by-two
decked out with saddles, the spare horses decorated with gold-
gilt saddlecloths, saddles, and expensive trappings, the *çuhadar*s
with silver-inlaid, decorated rifles, and wearing excellent new
cloths, the *şatiran* and other servants with gilded belts, silvered
battle-axes, red broadcloth *şalvar* [pantaloons], and leopard
skins around their shoulders, and several *enderun* agas in
crimson coats with silver embellishments, and at the rear of the
procession, following his *kethuda*, the *mehterhane*, shaking the
heavens with the crash and roar of their drums and trumpets,
they watched approvingly. They were struck speechless and
were amazed.

The route to the residence that they had prepared for the
ambassador on the edge of the city of Moscow was lined on
both sides by companies of infantry and military cavalry.[43] At
the end of each group its officers and trumpeters stood at
attention. When the ambassador came opposite each group of
soldiers they stood at attention, which, according to their
custom, is a great mark of honor. With the trumpets sounding
off unmelodiously, making a noise that offended the ear, the
procession entered by one of the gates of the fortress of the
city and exited by another of its gates. We arrived at the
residence that had been set aside, after walking for about three
hours slowly over the roads they had indicated.

The residence contained about fifteen or twenty rooms and a
number of courts.[44] In one of the number of rooms set aside
for the ambassador the sides were decorated with divan bolsters
of smooth velvet, in another [room] they were of orange satin,
and in the other they were of light-blue satin. In each of the

[43] Grand Duke Paul's regiment was among them. MAE, Russie [1775], vol. 98,
f. 530.
[44] The house belonged to Countess Boutourlin; see Marie Daniel Boureé,
Baron de Corberon, *Un diplomate français à la cour de Catherine II, 1775–1780*,
1:95.

rooms there were draperies of satin in the same color as the bolsters. In addition, the surface of the walls and several chairs were decorated in material of the same color. All the cushions were covered in red broadcloth. The rooms had full-length mirrors and cut-glass chandeliers. The other rooms had bolsters and cushions of the same red broadcloth. With the ambassador in the mansion they billeted his *divan katibi* and his *enderun* agas. I [Nahifi Mehmet Efendi], and the *kethuda*, and other agas and members of the retinue were housed in another rather vast furnished building in the neighborhood of the mansion. At this time they sent the register that indicated the ceremony customarily carried out in an audience with the empress. Since these ceremonies had a precedent from the time of Ümni Pasha, it was decided to do it again in the desired manner.

On Tuesday, 24 *Şaban*, General Ibershukov arrived.[45] The ambassador, having been invited by the prime minister, set out with the procession in the usual order. He rode together with the general in the carriage he had brought, and he arrived at his destination. He talked with the prime minister, and, with great respect, personally delivered two letters for the empress and the prime minister from the grand vezir.[46] After duly completing the ceremony of the audience, he returned with the procession. The next day, Wednesday,[47] a general in chief by the name of Bruce came from the empress in a carriage. Upon being invited, the ambassador outfitted the horses there were among the imperial gifts with saddles and ornamented trappings. He handed over the lead-reins to the senior groom and other grooms appointed from the sultan's own stables. The other imperial gifts and their carriages were arranged. The *tasdikname* was committed to the respectful hands of his *divan katibi* who rode behind them in a carriage that had arrived

---

[45] The text is clearly in error here. The day of the week should be Thursday, not Tuesday, corresponding to 19 October.

[46] Corberon, *Un diplomate*, 1:96.

[47] The text indeed says Wednesday, but Corberon, who describes the reception, indicates that it took place on Saturday, 21 October (Corberon, *Un diplomate*, 1:96–97).

especially for this. As a mark of respect, *çuhadar*s in regalia were
assigned to go along, on foot, three each on the right and left
of the carriage. Behind it rode the ambassador, sitting opposite
the general in a carriage that he had brought. The procession
arrived with pomp at the empress's palace. First of all, we
waited in a special place and unloaded the imperial gifts from
their carriage. They were arranged and placed in sets on hand-
worked trays. As was mentioned and precedented in the
journals of the previous ambassadors, the magnificent aigrette
was given to his *kethuda*, the register listing the imperial gifts
was placed in a pouch sewn from brilliantly sparkling gold
brocade and given to his *hazinedar* [treasurer], and the trays
containing the other imperial gifts were given one each to his
gedik agas. The ambassador, moreover, at that place was
turbaned in a *kalavi* [sugar-loaf turban] and wore a splendid
garment of black material that was a beautiful royal gift. When
he was informed that the empress was ready for the audience
and that he had been summoned, the ambassador set off. He
entered the reception room where she was sitting. When he got
to the place where he could be observed, he took the *tasdikname*
from the hands of his *divan katibi*, and reverencing it three times
with a kiss of the lips, and showing it deference by touching it
to his forehead, he stood at the side of the dais on which her
throne was set. In a sonorous voice he recited an eloquent
speech. He communicated the mission of his embassy. Their
empress, according to the custom of the Russians, was wearing
splendid raiment adorned with gold and had placed a small
jeweled crown on her head. In her right hand she held a carved
piece of wood about a *zira* in length on one end of which was a
jeweled crucifix. In her left hand she held a golden jewel-girded
sphere about as big as an ostrich egg. She sat alone in her
special place situated in a corner of the dais. On her left her
generals and high officers were present, and on her right stood
the wives of the men and generals. All of them listened in-
tently. After that, one of the men whom they call the chancellor
began to read the Frankish translation of the speech that they

had taken down earlier.[48] He sat on the edge of a rather large
gold-brocade-covered chair placed on the right of the dais. The
empress communicated by a sign her complete pleasure and
satisfaction with the honor-producing royal *tasdikname*, and
with His Excellency the Sultan's evidences of kind treatment
and compliments.

The Speech

"Sultan Abdülhamit Han, servitor of Mecca the highly
honored, Medina the highly enlightened, and of the honored,
blessed Jerusalem, the greatest padishah and most intelligent
ruler, the *hakan* of exalted station and the justice-dispensing
sultan, my majestic, powerful, august, just, benefactor, my
lord, from the seat of his government and capital whose orbit
is glory, this time in order to make firm the ties of mutual
confidence that have been newly compacted, has sent to you
who are the object of affection, the one regarded with pure love,
our royal, powerful, highly placed friend who are the Empress
of the Russian domains and their reigning sovereign, his
ambassador extraordinary, with kingly gifts weighted with
benevolent feelings, and with the royal *tasdikname*, to inquire
after your health as befits true friendship."

When he had finished the speech, the chancellor came up to
the ambassador. With the required deference, the ambassador
presented the royal *tasdikname*. After the chancellor had placed
it reverently on the chair, the *gedik* agas brought in the imperial
gifts, one by one in order. When they had placed and arranged
them with their trays on the dais, everyone inspected them.
Led by the grooms, the horses among the imperial gifts
strutted like gold-gilted peacocks in the spaciousness of the
empress's courtyard. Their jeweled and gilded trappings
sparkled like stars, and their saddles and stirrups flashed. To
those who looked on from afar, the glittering rays from adorn-
ments and embellishments of the horses were dazzling. Taking

[48] Corberon, *Un diplomate*, 1:97, indicates that the speech was translated into
Russian.

precautions for their eyes, they drew near. Upon careful
scrutiny, everyone uttered the expression *ochen khorosho*, indicating great approbation in their language. These too were
handed over to an official. They also pointed out a great tent
that was among the imperial gifts, and with the assistance of
tentpitchers they moved it to a vast field, and set it up. It was
spread with a carpet worked with silver thread, and decorated
with other furnishings of glittering ornamentation. The gold-
worked cloth of the interior surface was of envy-inducing
satin. Those who saw the height and radiance of the walls and
pillars, resembling the shaft of light from the sun of a spring
morning, were dazzled. After the ambassador had returned,
the chief tentpitcher came back and said that the descriptions
given by those who had viewed the imperial gifts made the
empress curious. She herself arrived. She looked at everything, and because she was thoroughly pleased, she gave two
hundred gold pieces as *bahşiş* [a gratuity] to the tentpitchers
and sent the horses to her master of the horse, and the beautiful
tent to her treasury.

The day after the ambassador's return in procession from the
imperial palace to his residence, he prepared the gift of a horse
with saddle and costly trappings, one each for the prime
minister, the field marshal, the empress's son the crown
prince,[49] and for General in Chief Potemkin,[50] who is employed
in the personal service of the empress, and who is the favorite
in good repute. All in all, there were four horses. He also
prepared gifts, increasing according to their rank, from fine
presents such as Indian cloths, ambergris, aloes wood, and
cologne. He sent them by means of high ranking *birun* agas
[agas of the outside service] and pleased them all.

As the Russian emperors and empresses have lived in Saint
Petersburg for a long time, the old palace in the city of Moscow
had become dilapidated. Its repair and renovation entailed a

---

[49] Grand Duke Paul is referred to in the text as the *veli-i ahd*, the term used to
designate the heir apparent. Here it has been translated as crown prince.
[50] The famous Potemkin's name is consistently rendered as Potemki in the text.

great deal of expense and required much time. At present, when the Russian empress wished to come to Moscow after the peace, they emptied two large houses next to each other, one for her and one for the crown prince. They joined the mansions to each other with the construction between them of two large halls and a couple of places for guards and watchmen.[51] She kept the rather large drawing room for herself for official functions and gatherings and assigned the other room as a salon for high ranking people. The halls were decorated with cut-glass chandeliers, and artistically made Frankish chairs. Most Sunday nights they burn a good many candles.[52] A good crowd of generals, officials, officers, and women gathers. The empress, together with the crown prince and his wife, emerges from her chambers. At that moment the men present separate to the left, and the women in attendance to the right. After she exchanges pleasantries and compliments with the notables among the people assembled in the hall, she sits on her chair. While she plays cards with whom she wishes from among the ambassadors of the other states and her leading generals, her son and his wife, and five or ten other people, generals and officers, dance with women, in couples, like pecking chickens. They dance and sway in the midst of the gathering to the sound of Frankish music. In a number of places mixed groups of men and women in fours and fives sit on chairs and play cards. Her gatherings last in this manner until three or four o'clock [Turkish time]. After this, their empress would suddenly rise and leave the room with the same slow gait as when she had entered. She takes leave of the group of notables, bestowing flattering glances on them, and departs for her chambers. Thereupon, it is the custom for the gathering to disperse and go home.

The Sunday after the audience, the general who was our official escort arrived. He invited the ambassador on behalf of the empress. Together with eight of his retinue they got into three carriages that had arrived and went to the palace. They

---

[51] Corberon, *Un diplomate*, 1:80–81, gives a similar, but more detailed description.
[52] Corberon, *Un diplomate*, 1:98–99 is in agreement.

sat on chairs in the drawing room especially placed there for
rest and repose. After they had been served coffee and sweets,
it was announced that the empress had left her apartments for
the drawing room. They went to meet her. As they waited at
the head of the reception line, the empress appeared. When she
drew opposite the ambassador she stopped and lavished
especially friendly attention and flatteries on him. With all
deference, she inquired after the health of the sultan. The
appropriate answer which the ambassador gave pleased the
empress. After voicing her faithfulness, she entered the hall in
the usual way. She sat on her chair and occupied herself with
card playing. After she had requested the ambassador to sit
down, they set chairs to one side of her and he was seated to
play chess with a high-ranking general. Having spent some
time in this fashion, the empress left her place as previously
described. She said good-night, in particular to the ambassador,
and in general to the other officials. She left for her chambers,
and the gathering dispersed. The ambassador got into his
carriage, the same one he had arrived in, and returned home.

Ferreting out and freeing the people of Islam who wore the
fetters of captivity was one of the main thoughts of the ambassador, but it was in no way possible to fulfill or carry out
[this duty] during the course of the journey. For example, in
the city of Polonnoye, situated in Poland, a lad from Bender
came to the ambassador of his own free will saying, "I am a
Muslim." While he took refuge, and after discussions and conversations were held with the general who was our official
escort, the lad was allowed to stay in the ambassador's retinue
until the article of the treaty dealing with prisoners was
regulated after the audience with the empress. When he
arrived at Moscow with the help of God's grace, and when he
had taken the occasion in the drawing room to pass on orally
to the empress the sultan's kindest regards, the ambassador
remained alone after the evening meal and made a rough draft
of a note with his own pen. A précis of its contents follows:

Paying attention to the necessary sequels of treaties and

oaths and to the required execution of sincerity-marked treaties with respect to friendly states, are among the natural accompaniments of my lord's noble and generous nature. Therefore, according to the conditions of the articles of the peace treaty that has been concluded between the two states this time, prisoners who are in Istanbul are to be presented in person at the grand vezir's offices. After interrogation in the presence of your chargé d'affaires's translator, and in the presence of the officials of the Sublime State assigned to this matter, those who declare acceptance of the Islamic faith will be detained. Those who persist in Christianity will be handed over to the translator.[53] Upon certification, a just price on an equitable basis will be paid to their possessors from the royal treasury. In order for this to be carried out in other areas of the well-protected domains too, firmans will be sent to all areas and regions by special agents. In this way both the articles of the imperial treaty will be carried out, and the possessors of the captives, receiving payment for their prisoners, will be rendered content. Similar action being taken concerning Muslim prisoners who are either in Moscow itself or in other areas of Russia is part of the requirements of the conditions of the treaty. Therefore, imperial orders should be sent and transmitted to all parts of Russia. When this is done we shall see that you have faith in this treaty. I sincerely request the appointment by your empress of a just person to discuss some of these particulars.

After that, at daybreak, he gave the draft to his *divan katibi* to make a fair copy, and after having the translator assigned to the staff from Istanbul translate it, he handed it over to the prime minister for the purpose of having him present it to the empress.[54] When an answer to the note was requested a number of times by the prime minister, they put him off saying, "Today

---

[53] Repnin complained from Constantinople to Panin that the Ottomans were not being completely honest in this matter, taking refuge in the niceties of Islamic law (*SRIO*, 15:547).

[54] Panin sent Repnin the French translation of Abdülkerim Pasha's memorandum on 6 November. It is available in *SRIO*, 15:485–87.

or tomorrow." After the passage of a couple of days, the prime
minister and other ministers traveled to a place seven or eight
hours from the city, ostensibly for an outing. They stayed there
for several days and most likely discussed things. When they
returned, and when the ambassador either sent a delegate, or
when in an interview he requested an oral answer to the note,
they put it off with expressions of regret and hope. Moreover,
in some interviews both the prime minister and the field
marshal began to spout clichés saying, "Our empress's devotion and faithfulness to the Sublime State and her regard and
affection for you are complete. Your being made happy and
comfortable in every way is desired." The ambassador replied,
"I shall surely be reprimanded by my government on this
matter of the article relating to the prisoners. This makes me
thoroughly unhappy. I shall not be satisfied or content with
anything other than your or the empress's doing something for
the regulation of this article." Reiterating his demand, he
persevered and persisted. Thereupon, again with the two-
bladed scissors of "yes" and "no," not cutting off hope
completely, they put him off, and delayed the matter until the
end of December. After that, because of the ambassador's
insisting to a degree that would have required the severance of
the bonds of friendship, the prime minister wanted to present
his views on the subject.

> Those Muslims who were captured and made prisoner during
> the course of the war have been freed universally. After the
> peace, for the purposes of sending them to the Islamic
> frontiers that adjoin and neighbor Russia, our empress sent
> numerous royal letters all over the empire and appointed
> special agents. As they warned those who concealed
> prisoners who were firm and constant in their Islamic faith,
> droves of Islamic prisoners have been sent to Muslim
> countries since the date of the treaty. As a matter of fact,
> recently Islamic prisoners have been loaded onto three ships
> on the shores near the Crimea. Several days ago news was
> received of their arrival at Islamic shores. Several of those
> who were taken prisoner earlier, however, became Christians
> of their own free will and have been inscribed in the registers
> of the priests. Those people called muzhiks, who live in our

city of Moscow, and around and near it, are firmly attached
to their faith and rite. Their obedience to our empress and to
our other officials is based on our dissimulation and our
treating them with kindness. Now, as means of saving
themselves, these captives have already demonstrated lack
of firmness in religious matters. It is clear that upon
interrogation they will claim to be Muslims. In that case,
we shall be required to hand them over to you. If they are
handed over, the muzhiks will assemble. They will take
those people from you and after punishing you and us, they
will occasion a great upheaval. Your setting free Georgian
and other types of prisoners, and the construction of a
church in Galata are among the articles of the treaty, but
these articles were postponed after careful consideration of
the likelihood of the occurrence of uproar and riot among
the people of Istanbul. Since the same fear has been
anticipated by us too, the method of interrogation and
detention is not acceptable. Nevertheless, we know that no
one from among the captives who was steadfast in his
Islamic faith has remained in the Russian domains. In
addition, although several days ago that article was insisted
on in orders sent to all parts by our empress, hereafter, too,
it will not cease to be insisted on. This matter is important
to all of us. In your note it was requested that someone be
appointed for the discussion of some particulars. All affairs
of the Russian state are committed to my complete charge.
Therefore, the discussion of every particular is my obligation.
Now, if the matters that you will discuss concern the articles
of the treaty, if they be discussed again, the alteration of
even a single letter is not possible, for we agreed upon those
articles in repeated discussions.

When the situation was explained to the field marshal, he
replied, "Do you have written authorization [from Istanbul] to
discuss these matters relating to the treaty?"[55] No matter how
much the ambassador persevered and insisted, it was no use.

In the final analysis, because they indicated their consent by
keeping quiet and winking at the situation, those who seized

[55] From the document BVA Hatt-ı Hümâyun 13343, it appears that Ottoman
ambassadors were briefed at the Porte about possible responses if certain topics
were discussed in negotiations. In 1793 Mustafa Rasih was given certain guide-
lines by the grand vezir, who informed the sultan of his actions. Selim III
replied that he approved of the vezir's reasoning, but "*evdeki pazar, çarşıya
uymaz*" "bargaining done at home doesn't pass in the market, wishful arrangements in advance can be disappointed". In this case, Abdülkerim Pasha had no
written authorization.

the opportunity attached themselves to the ambassador's
retinue, claiming to be Muslims. They were able to flee and
escape. The escapees amounted to seventy or eighty people.
The ambassador designated twenty-five particular men and
sent them to Bender. He kept the rest with him in order to take
them along when he departed from Moscow.

As was explained above, the daily banquet in the ambassador's residence tendered at the time of our entrance into
Moscow on behalf of the empress by the general who was on
duty was not discontinued during the eight days that remained
until the beginning of *Ramazan* [began 26 October]. After that,
with the arrival of the fast days, the cooks and other servants
received gifts and *bahşiş*, according to their rank, and were sent
back. Their pots, pans, and dishes were returned to their places.

Description of the Komadiyehane *(Theater)*

In the middle of the city of Moscow there is a theater[56] in the
shape of a large, roofed hall, containing about eighty little
boxes[57] in three tiers on three of its sides. On its other side
there is a rather vast, raised stage. In the middle of the hall
there was a large, empty ground-floor. On winter nights the
rich and influential Russians come, each to his own box, on
performance nights that take place in that location once every
five or ten days. They hire each of the boxes at a monthly rate
of seventy or eighty *kuruş*. Standees and the spectators down-
stairs pay a ruble each. They assemble in the empty space in the
center. In front of the stage there is suspended a decorated
curtain of waxed oilcloth. The curtain is lifted when they are
ready for the various entertainments that will appear behind it.

[56] The only large theater in operation in Moscow during 1775 was the Golovin
Theater near the Golovin Palace. There was a small theater operating in the
home of Count Vorontsov on the Znamenka, and the wooden theater of Locatelli
may have been operating. Malcolm Burgess, "A Survey of the Stage in Russia
from 1741 to 1783, with Special Reference to the Development of the Russian
Theater," pp. 348–406, indicates that the Golovin Theater had fallen into a state
of acute disrepair, but was remodelled for the return of the court to Moscow in
1775.
[57] The word used in the text is *oda*, meaning room, and translated here as box.

The players appear behind it. They imitate the droll actions of some humorous people of bygone eras who are famous and celebrated and act out some of the situations that occur between lovers, and the deceptions of women practiced upon men. The conversations that take place are performed in Frankish language to the sounds of musical instruments arranged in a place below the players. They put on curious plays. The performance ends at five or six o'clock [Turkish time]. Everyone goes home.

During the first ten days of *Ramazan* another performance was arranged. The general who was our official escort came from the crown prince and invited the ambassador. They reached the hall after sunset by means of carriages that had arrived. They sat on chairs in one of the boxes. The actors reappeared [on stage] in scenes and spectacles.

Later, with the arrival of reception night that was customary at the empress's palace, as described earlier, the ambassador went as before. After the empress had entered the drawing room in the palace, and after she had been very polite to the ambassador, asking after his health, she explained that she had ordered the arrangement of a masquerade. She said, "Because of my complete friendship for you and sincerity toward the Sublime State, I have had costumes made for myself in material that comes from there. I have ordered my household and servants to dress in the same manner." She invited the ambassador, orally, to the party. She then left for her chambers. The ambassador returned to his residence.

Description of the Masquerade

When Sunday evening, the third day of the feast following the end of *Ramazan* [26 November] had been designated for the ball, the number of people who would come was announced. To prevent entrance without authorization, anyone [of those invited] who comes during the day is given a printed invitation. After sunset several officials are stationed at the door of the drawing room and permission to enter is given to those who have the invitations in their hands. To those who do not have them, they show the face of prohibition. To facilitate the merrymaking, everyone attending the ball wears an unseemly black and white mask associated with his main characteristic. They wear cloaklike costumes of red and black silken material. They change their dress so that their identity will not be discerned. With these costumes they assemble in the evening in the drawing room of the imperial palace. Each of them finds his partner by the character of the disguise. After acquiring their companions, they promenade among the gathering, making conversation. Some of them sit on the side or in corners, and some of them dance in the center of the gathering. Some of them also sit in groups of three and four and gamble.

After sunset on that evening, our official escort, the general, arrived as usual.[58] He invited the ambassador who, together with several of his retinue, got into the carriages that had arrived. They got to the drawing room. After they had waited a little while, word was given that the empress was proceeding to the hall. They took up a position facing the passageway. As they waited, the empress, her son, and his wife appeared. They had those black masks on their faces, and they had changed their usual dress. In front of them walked Generals in Chief Potemkin and Bruce, and other officers of similar high rank. On their heads they wore pink-colored caps around which they had wrapped turbans. They adorned their heads and chests with pendants and flowers with diamonds, like women. [The empress] came up to the ambassador in this strange outfit. After she had greeted him as formerly and exchanged pleasant-ries with him, asking, "Did you recognize me?" she entered the drawing room. She sat on her special chair and played cards. A general whom we have called a chamberlain came up to the ambassador. He said, "Our empress has had some special food prepared for you. Please come this way." He took him to a vacant room in her apartments. After sitting

[58] It was Sunday, 26 November. Corberon, *Un diplomate*, 1:111.

down together with the field marshal,[59] our official escort, and
the chamberlain, at the buffet that had been prepared, the
ambassador offered his apologies. He explained that he had not
been informed earlier about the preparation of the buffet and
had eaten in his residence before his arrival. In consequence of
this, the field marshal explained that he had decided to give
another masquerade in a few days, and with the desire of
leaving no room for apologies on the matter of the food that
would be prepared and served at that time, he invited the
ambassador as of that night. After sitting and exchanging
pleasantries for a time, they returned [to the ball]. After the
passage of several days it was time for the party they had
decided on. As in the last instance, the ambassador arrived.
He watched the masquerade, and the buffet was set in the
aforementioned room.

Three Russian regiments that consisted usually of a thousand
men each, called the Preobrazhenskii, the Izmailovskii, and the
Semenovskii, had been the cause of Russian victories over the
Swedes by manifestations of constancy in their battles that had
taken place earlier against the Swedes.[60] Therefore, their
empress esteemed them more than the others. They conferred
on her a colonelcy, which consists of being the head of a
regiment, and conferred on General Potemkin a lieutenant-
colonelcy. As it was her custom to give a party in her own
palace one day a year each for the officers of these regiments
and for the men who had earned the decoration of the Order of
Saint Andrew, and the Order of Saint George, 26 *Teşrin-i
sani* [7 December] was chosen as the time for the reception given
for the holders of the Order of Saint George.[61] The ambassador

---

[59] The biography of Rumiantsev in *RBS*, 17:549, indicates that he attended the
ball and sat next to Abdülkerim Pasha at dinner.
[60] The Semenovskii and Preobrazhenskii regiments were founded in 1687, and
the Izmailovskii regiment in 1730.
[61] The Military Order of Saint George the Great Martyr and Conqueror was
instituted by Catherine II on 26 November 1769; see I. I. Vorontsov-Dashkov,
Istoricheskii ocherk rossiiskikh ordenov i sbornik osnovnykh orderskikh statutov, pp. 37–
45.

was invited to attend the reception and to visit the empress's jewel collection afterward.

He departed and arrived at the palace. While we waited in the drawing room, it was announced that the empress had left her chambers. She emerged and, having arrived at the passageway, she took one by one with her own hand crystal glasses filled with four or five drinks that resembled *rakı*. The glasses had been placed on silver trays held by fifteen smooth-cheeked young waiters who were standing on duty at the door to the drawing room. She distributed the drinks. After exchanging pleasantries with everyone, and being gracious to the officers who were present and around her on both sides, she entered the drawing room. She sat on a chair at the end of a table set up in the middle of the hall. The officers who held the previously mentioned decoration sat according to rank on chairs arranged on her right and left. After watching them eat and drink to the accompaniment of music and song, they reached their destination with General Potemkin's guidance.

They visited the jewelry collection in her apartments.

Description of the Collection of Jewels

In the corner of one room there were four display cases covered with plate-glass lids to protect the contents from dust. Since there were numerous specimens of female ornaments such as earrings, necklaces, fans, brooches, and watches in them, there is no need to go into detailed description of them. They said that one diamond, about the size of a walnut, that was rather celebrated, was worth thirteen hundred *kese*.[62] A crown encrusted with jewels was the supreme object of pride and was worth two hundred and eighty *kese*. They were proud too of about ten pearls shaped like pears and bigger than hazel nuts.

After that, the time for the holders of the Order of Saint Andrew arrived on 30 *Teşrin-i sani* [11 December].[63] They

---

[62] A *kese* contained five hundred *kuruş*.
[63] Corberon, *Un diplomate*, 1:115.

prepared a reception at the imperial palace as before. The ambassador was invited and went. He was kindly asked by the officers present to partake of the buffet.

Later, in order to demonstrate her complete satisfaction with the treaty newly concluded with the Sublime State, the empress ordered the arrangement of a fireworks display in a spacious courtyard for 29 *Kanun-i evvel* and invited the ambassador.[64] Riding in the carriage that had been sent for him, he arrived at a vast, tall palace looking onto the courtyard. He spoke with the field marshal and General Potemkin, and with other generals. He returned after watching the various pyrotechnics and outpouring of sparks until three o'clock [9 P.M.]. The next night, Friday night, upon invitation, he went to the theater.[65] He watched for several hours and returned.

At this time the empress and the crown prince proposed to go to Saint Petersburg. When the Russians travel, their entourage consists of their servants, attendants, their baggage and luggage, several carriage drivers, and carriages pulled by six or eight horses each. In a day they can do the distance [usually] covered by twenty or thirty hours of travel. For the empress's trip five stations sufficed, but for the crown prince whose wife was three or four months pregnant, the speed of the trip on the road had to be such as not to cause damage to the expected child.[66] Fifteen stopping places were prepared for the crown prince and his wife. The crown prince resolved to depart with his wife on Monday, 25 *Şevval* [18 December].[67] The ambassador, according to the [Arabic] saying, "Make them content while in their country,"[68] and out of consideration for the empress's wish, went to the palace and spoke with and said

---

[64] The manuscript (f. 40a) gives the date as stated, but the printed text gives 9 *Kanun-i evvel* (p. 60). Corberon, *Un diplomate*, 1:121, indicates that the fireworks party was held on 21 December.

[65] Corberon speaks of having called on Abdülkerim Pasha earlier that day, *Un diplomate*, 1:122.

[66] The French ambassador, M. de Juigne, mentions in a dispatch of 4 December that the Grand Duchess was pregnant (MAE, Russie [1775], vol. 98, f. 583).

[67] Corberon, *Un diplomate*, 1:118.

[68] *'Arḍihim mā dumta fī 'arḍihim.*

good-bye to the crown prince and his wife. The next day, being
the appointed day, the crown prince and his wife left for Saint
Petersburg. Later, on Sunday, the last day of *Şevval* [24 Dec-
ember], the empress departed for Tula, thirty-six hours away
on the other side of Moscow. She stayed there for one or two
days and then returned, entering Moscow on Friday, 6 *Zilkade*
[29 December]. The next day, Saturday, General Bruce, who
had come earlier to invite the ambassador for the transmission
of the *tasdikname*, arrived again with two carriages and many
attendants. He invited the ambassador, and they arrived at the
imperial palace in the same manner as before. After putting on
his splendid *kalavi* and sable-lined robe, he entered the empress's
presence. He stood at the side of the dais on which she sat and
delivered a gracious speech.

Copy of the Speech

> There is no need to explain that I was sent as ambassador
> extraordinary from His Excellency's sublime threshold that
> brushes the heavenly spheres to your friendly presence that
> is kindred to loving affection by he who adorns the seat of
> the dominion's royal metropolis, he who is diadem-illuminator
> of glory's throne, the sultan of the two lands and the two
> seas, the servitor of the two Holy Places, my majestic,
> august, powerful benefactor, the exalted padishah and the
> *şahinşah* in whom the world seeks asylum, my Lord, my
> Sultan, Abdülhamit *Han*, son of the sultan Ahmet *Han*,
> may God who be exalted perpetuate his caliphate until the
> end of time, to you who are exalted in station, the honorable,
> the great friend, and empress and padishah of the Russian
> domains. We are very pleased and satisfied with the kind
> treatment and hospitality that you have extended to us
> during the days of our visit. After ambassadors have
> acquitted themselves of their duty and have completed their
> embassies the grant of permission for them to return home
> is part of ancient practice. As befits the honor of your state,
> permission for us to return is requested.

Then, after her chancellor had read the translation, he took
the reply from the gold-brocade-covered chair placed at the
side of her dais. It was handed over to the ambassador, who
then retired and returned to his residence as he had come. The

next day, Sunday, the ambassador on his own initiative, sent the *mehterhane*, on the occasion of her departure for Saint Petersburg. He had them see her off with trumpets, drums, and kettledrums.

After the conclusion of the peace there was [the matter of] a group of cossacks. The empress had been successful, through the help of one of the hetman's aides, in doing away with Pugachev who had distressed the Russians for a long time by throwing off the fetters of submission and obedience, and by increasing his followers. In order both to drive away the cares due to this rebel and to celebrate the tying tighter of the bond of friendship with the Sublime State, she had ordered the fireworks display described above. In addition, when the empress had two richly decorated mansions, for summer and winter, constructed and given to the field marshal in the town of Glukhov, on the limits of the frontier of Little Russia, as described earlier during our journey, she changed the name of one of the villages from among the villages and peasants she had given him, and named it Kaynarca.[69] This village was four hours from Moscow. The field marshal went to that village after the empress had left for Saint Petersburg. He stayed there and in the course of a few days he invited the ambassador. He arrived there one day in the afternoon. He dined there and rested until nightfall and then returned.

After that, on 10 *Zilhicce*, the feast of sacrifices [1 February 1776], General Ibershukov arrived from the prime minister. He invited the ambassador to receive and accept the reply to the grand vezir's letter sent earlier according to ancient custom. The ambassador arrived as before. After going through the necessary politenesses and formalities, and conversing for awhile, he received and accepted the reply and returned.

Earlier, at the time of the empress's departure for Saint Petersburg, our official escort, the general, arrived from the prime minister. He communicated to the ambassador their

---

[69] Corberon, *Un diplomate*, 1:86, speaks of this fact, but the name is blank in his text.

desire that he leave and set out from Moscow after the end of January. The ambassador put forward the contentions that, apart from the fact that winter was not yet over, according to the requirements of the rules regarding the *mubadele* at the time of the return of the ambassadors of the two states, if he were to set out from Moscow before word of the Russian ambassador's time of departure from Istanbul, there was the possibility of having to stop in the course of his journey for a long time to no purpose. The prime minister explained that the waters of the several great rivers from Moscow to Kiev were frozen over and would melt during the month of March. The waters over-flowing their banks at that time would necessitate his stopping during the journey. Since these answers of his fit the heart of the matter exactly, it was resolved to set out after the end of January. Because of the harshness of the winter, and the fact that we would sometimes have to live in tents out on the open steppe as when we had come, and since most of our stopping places were villages that were too small for all of us to be sheltered in, of necessity therefore, we divided up into three caravans for travel as far as the Polish frontier. The separate caravans were to depart one by one with an interval of two or three days between each. He appointed one of his *selam* agas as head of the first caravan.[70] They set out on the road on Friday, 12 *Zilhicce* [2 February]. The next day the ambassador was invited to a party given for him by the prime minister. He stayed there until three in the evening [Turkish time]. The ambassador appointed his *kethuda* as head of the second caravan. They left on 15 *Zilhicce* [5 February]. On Thursday, 18 *Zilhicce* [8 February], the ambassador, seeking the aid of God on high who be exalted, the trusted guide of the padishah, packed up and, together with the remainder of his retinue and household, set out for the capital of the Sublime State. Several days after the departure, the ambassador wrote a friendly letter, on the request made earlier in an approved manner by the prime

[70] The printed text (p. 63) gives a bit more information on the makeup of the first group. It included the muleteers and carriage drivers.

minister, to the empress, expressing his satisfaction with the hospitality and treatment he had received. In order to have it reach her after she had departed from Moscow, he sent it to the prime minister.

Description of the City of Moscow

The length and width of the city's populated district amounts to about the distance of an hour and a half. It is a large, vast city. Most of its buildings are of pine wood, and are built far apart because of the fear of conflagration. Many of its quarters are vacant lots, great gardens, and waste lands. Most of its buildings are churches and chapels. In the middle of the city there is a medium-sized masonry fortress made of baked brick, but they have not looked after it with such things as patches and repairs.[71] It has become a ruin. They make and weave velvet and other materials in their factories and bring together workers and artisans in various goods that appear in other regions. Therefore, every type of thing is available in their market and bazaar. They take 30 percent customs on things coming from the outside; thus, the prices of these things are outrageous. Alongside of them, things made in Moscow are cheap, although lower in quality. Most people prefer the cheap things. [The Russians] seize upon this point both as a means to promote their own goods, and to increase their imperial revenues.

On one side of the city they have reserved a vast stone mansion for orphans.[72] They pay for the feeding, upbringing,

---

[71] The lines following are missing in the manuscript (f. 43a), and have been translated from the printed texts, pp. 65–66.

[72] This is a reference to the Moscow Foundling Home (Vospitatel'nyi Dom). It was founded by Catherine in 1763. For the law establishing the institution see "11.908.—Sentiabria 1 [12 September 1763]. Manifest, s prilozheniem Vysochaishe utverzhdennago proekta General-Poruchika Betskago: Ob uchrezhdenii v Moskve Vospitatel'nago Doma, so osoblivym goshpitalem dlia neimushchikh rodil'nits," *PSZ*, 16:363. The home was supported by donations from wealthy patrons as well as the tax mentioned. Paragraph 16 of the General Plan, found on page 363, reads, "From public performances, that is, comedies, operas, balls and all games for money, take one fourth of the income for the Foundling Home." For information on the location of the home, and for a picture of it, see Leningrad, Akademiia nauk, Institut istorii, *Istoriia Moskvy*, 2:472, 485.

and education of the orphans by collecting one-third of the revenues received by the theaters, and by doubling the cost of playing cards. They have regulations that allow those orphans who are past their childhood and are capable of military training to be enrolled in the military upon completion of their education. That is why sometimes children of the poor, and often boys who have no fathers, are brought to the orphanage right after their birth. They give them over to the orphanage and commit them to its protection. The great river that flows through the city is called the Moscow, therefore, they say, they called the city Moscow. On one side there is the mint and a printing house for Frankish books. They work there night and day.

In matters concerning their own country's workers and artisans, and in the presence of fine varieties and abundance of goods, the Russians cast aspersions on the fame of the flourishing bazaars of other Christian countries. When extolling the good qualities of their own country, and the varieties of men and nationalities, they call one a thousand, a worthless stone a gleaming gem, and bankrupt, penniless people men of wealth and riches. They display great energy in praising each other and their wares. The rich and small, in alliance, heap honors on themselves.

Production of most varieties of fruits is impossible because of the harshness and coldness of the weather in their country. In order to gain notoriety by the possession of any kind of stuff from other countries, the wealthy people construct well-cared-for and enclosed greenhouses. In the harshness of winter they heat them with stoves at great cost. They grow a quantity of jasmine, sweet lemon, and other things from among the fruits peculiar to warm weather countries.

They[73] have fruits and vegetables such as artichokes, cauliflower, sweet lemons, and pomegranates brought from remote regions in order to show them to guests who arrive in their

[73] The manuscript picks up again (f. 43b), corresponding to the bottom of page 66 in the printed text.

country. When their nobles give a party they prepare a good table. Sometimes exotic fruits appear in small shops in their markets and bazaars. But, when a customer appears, they ask the price of a yellow ruby for each grape of the bunch, and for each seed of the pomegranate they ask the price of a grain of a red ruby. You can figure from this what expensive things must cost.

Their minted coins of the *dinar* type are restricted to three kinds, a gold coin which they call the imperial and which circulates with a value of two thousand *akçe*, and coins of one-half and one-quarter [the value] of that one. In silver there are seven varieties, a ruble at two hundred *akçe*, a half ruble, a third ruble, a quarter ruble, a fifth ruble, a tenth ruble, and a twentieth ruble. In addition, there are copper coins of one, two, four, and ten *akçe* each. Only the copper coins are seen in the market and bazaar. Moreover, if a silver coin which they call a ruble is given for the price of any article of commerce, the owner of the article accepts the ruble with satisfaction, giving a premium of four or five *akçe* each because of its perfect value. Owing to the great value of their gold coins, the nobles give them to children as remembrances on important occasions. The poor can see a few gold coins when the nobles play cards. Or they may see them in their dreams. They make paper money in their factory. They print banknotes on an eighth of a sheet of paper, with a watermark on both sides, like the *altmışlık* we know.[74] There are four denominations of printed ruble in circulation—twenty-five, fifty, seventy-five, and one hundred. On the bottom of each there are the signatures in Russian characters of three or four officials. They are given for the payment of bills just as *akçe* would be given. They are given and received in daily business, and are absolutely never refused.

After that, because of the harshness of the winter, we departed from the road we had taken in coming to Moscow. This would increase the number of our stations and shorten the daily distance. We arrived at Tula on 1 *Muharrem* 1190, which

[74] The *altmışlık* was a 60 *para* piece minted by Sultan Mustafa III.

fell on a Wednesday [21 February]. The *kapıcılar kethüdası* whom
the ambassador had sent to the capital earlier with letters
arrived. He gave the ambassador a written command from the
grand vezir concerning the independence of the Tatars and the
article on the prisoners. It was further communicated that
should the courier meet the ambassador on the road, the
ambassador should send a full summary of the letter to the
prime minister through the general, our official escort.

He immediately had a summary prepared. After he had sent
it to the prime minister with the cognizance of the general,
sealed together with a friendly letter, we arrived at the town of
Orël on Tuesday, 14 *Muharrem* [5 March], traveling by way of
the stations. The ice had broken up on the great river that flows
through that town, and its bridge had been demolished. It was
necessary to stay over in Orël. On Sunday we crossed the river
by means of rafts. On Friday, the beginning of *Nisan* [22
March], when we crossed the Dnepr River located before the
fortress of the city of Kiev, a thirty-one-gun salute was fired
from the fortress. We crossed over to the suburb of the old
fortress called Podol, and stayed there for one week. On
Friday, 8 *Nisan* [29 March], we set out. At that point there
arrived the answer to the full summary of the grand vezir's
order that had been sent from Tula earlier to the prime minister.
After forwarding the reply to Istanbul, we arrived at Polonnoye within Poland on 18 *Rebiyülevvel* [7 May]. We expected
word of the time of the arrival of the Russian ambassador, who
would be returning from Istanbul, when we met and joined the
first and second caravans that had been sent on ahead at the
time of our departure from Moscow. A letter came to our
official escort in which it was written that the Russian ambassador would arrive in the region of Hotin at the end of June.
Our official escort came to the ambassador on the matter of our
having to stay in Polonnoye until that time. When he was
asked why he and his officers were wearing black, which is a
sign of their mourning, he explained that news had come of the

death of the wife of the empress's son.[75] The prayer, "May God
keep them in black always," was uttered.

After that, the Russian ambassador wrote to the general that
he would arrive at Hotin on 12 *Cemaziyelevvel* [28 June]. Wishing to arrive at the bank of the Dnestr simultaneously, we set
out from Polonnoye on 3 *Cemaziyelevvel* [20 June]. On Friday,
12 *Cemaziyelevvel* [28 June], the Russian ambassador arrived at
the outskirts of Hotin early in the morning, and in the afternoon the ambassador arrived before Zhvanets.

Description of the Mubadele at the Time of the Return

The *mubadele* ceremony was carried out in the same manner and
place as at the time of the departure of the ambassadors. At the
time of the return, however, it was requested that the *mubadele*
be carried out with the participation of the official escorts. It
was decided to have the *mubadele* on 14 *Cemaziyelevvel* [30 June].
Husayn Pasha was informed that on that day the Russian
ambassador's *mihmandar*, who was from among the *mir-i mirân*,
would ride side by side with the Russian ambassador to the
place of the exchange with the veziral complement of that great
intellect, the governor of Hotin, Mehmet Pasha.[76] No matter
how Husayn Pasha exerted himself to arrange things in this
way, he was unsuccessful. The Russian ambassador would in
no way acquiesce in riding side by side with his *mihmandar*. He
was obstinate and insistent, saying, "In the earlier exchange the
[Ottoman] ambassador's official escort was a major general who
was given the rank of lieutenant general after the exchange. My
official escort must ride in front of me in a reciprocal fashion."
Husayn Pasha learned that in truth the ambassador's official
escort had ridden in front of him. In the grand vezir's letter
that had arrived, the grant of a veziral complement was
contingent on the official escort's riding side by side with the
ambassador. It was not proper for the official escort to march

---

[75] She died in April 1776, K. Waliszewski, *Paul the First of Russia*, p. 15.
[76] Husayn Pasha is unidentified.

in front of the veziral complement. Therefore, the pasha would be furnished with a *mir-i mirân*'s complement. They set out in that manner. When our ambassador had returned from Moscow, a thirty-gun-salute was fired from the Kiev fortress. The Russian ambassador requested that the same number of cannon be fired in his honor from Hotin fortress. The requested number of guns were fired, and they got to the place of the exchange on the bank, marching in procession. They alighted at the tent that Husayn Pasha's *kethuda* had set up for the customary ceremonies. After that, the ambassador rested for a time in that tent after completing the *mubadele* and crossing over to this side. Then, in procession with his *kethuda*, *divan katibi*, *mihmandar*, and the officers of Hotin, he departed for his tent that had been set up on the plain of Hotin, and he settled in. We stayed in Hotin for eight days. On Friday, 20 *Cemazi-yelevvel* [5 July], we set out. According to the grand vezir's order that arrived, we left by the route indicated by the voivode of Moldavia. We crossed the river at Tutora and stayed there for one day. On Monday, 6 *Cemaziyelâhır* [22 July], we went to Măcin by way of the river. Thanks and praise be to God, in our passage through the villages of Moldavia this time, and especially the town of Galați, we found that they were ten times more flourishing than at our earlier passage. The peasantry's seeming tranquility and good condition is definitely evidence of the auspicious favor of His Excellency the *şahinşah* whose hallmark is beneficence, and of the blessing of the bountiful favor of the padishah who is marked by justice. We prayed that God would lengthen the days of his life and good fortune that gladden mankind and make this world resemble paradise.

After that, we stayed in Măcin for one night, and the next day we set out by way of the Dubrucaova. We spent a night each in Hacıoğlu Pazarı, and Kırk Klise. On Thursday, the last day of *Cemaziyelâhır* [15 August], we arrived at Silivri and set out the next day. On Saturday, 2 *Recep* [17 August] we passed through the gates of the auspicious walls of the abode of the

sublime sultanate. Straightaway we arrived at our usual dwellings. Prayers that are the requirement of our sacred duty and
devotion to God were offered for the augmentation of the
lustre and majesty of His Excellency, the asylum of the
caliphate.

Some Conditions and Information Seen and Heard

The cossack hetman Pugachev, who was mentioned in
passing, above, after making his appearance on the scene, daily
increased his supporters and partisans. He defeated the large
body of troops the empress had repeatedly organized to repel
and oppose him and that she had sent against him. After
scattering them, every time he was attacked, he added to his
side a great many of the troops whom he had defeated, for they
were of the same sort. His troops exceeded eighty thousand
men. He attacked in many directions and invaded and subdued
many forts and towns. From time to time he sent antagonistic
messages that would frighten the empress. The spread of his
terrible fame aroused complete terror. There was no hope of
getting rid of him. After the peace, however, one of his aides,
who had covetously relied on the empress's insincere promises,
deceiving the hetman, suddenly seized him and surrendered
him to the empress. In this way she was successful in killing
and destroying him. Although it was said that the empress's
coming to Moscow apparently was for the purpose of honor-
ing the ambassador who would arrive from the Sublime State,
in truth, she could not stay in Saint Petersburg for fear of her
cossack adversaries. We learned this, upon reaching Moscow,
from the Muslim prisoners who know their language and conditions through long residence among them. Now one of the
relatives of that adversary has come forward. With the desire
of taking blood revenge from the empress, he has set about to
increase his followers and augment his army. It is said that he
possesses a good-sized army, and that he recently wished to
attack impetuously. But, the realization of this wish was not
possible. May God make it so.

Prussia and Austria, from among the three states who shared
mutually in the partition of the Kingdom of *Leh* that is called
Poland, put forward difficult demands and proposals. Russia at
the time did not support those demands, and therefore, the
Poles are ostensibly more inclined to the Russians than they are
to the others. The Austrians, being dissatisfied with their portion of the partition of Poland, attacked some Polish territory
close to their share. The Poles were very upset. They again
began to prepare troops out of the necessity for defense. They
sent a general named Bruce, from among their generals, to the
empress to ask for help.[77] In order not to damage the ties of
friendship, she looked favorably on their request. The Polish
boyars with whom we dealt on our return said, "The empress
will help and assist us with sixty thousand troops. The troops
we have raised amount to thirty thousand, altogether that is
ninety thousand. Shortly, we shall finish their training and
preparation. With the delivery of the troops and material, our
alliance will take form. We shall proceed to repel the menace of
Austrian aggression. The ambassador explained that he had
seen with his own eyes that in the Russian gun factory at Tula
the empress had ordered the manufacture of thirteen thousand
stands of weapons, and the Poles had appointed a major to
inspect and receive them.[78]

When the ambassador inquired of some people well-versed
in Russian affairs, they confirmed that the Poles had asked for
help, and that the empress had promised to assist them. When
it was asked, "Will she really help?" they explained, "The
empress's intention is to help the Poles in this matter. But,
independence for the Crimea, which is a principle of the treaty
concluded this time with the Sublime State, has not yet been
accepted and settled in an agreeable fashion. It is definite that

[77] The Polish national biography records one Bruce, William Bruce, who was
born in Scotland, taught in Würzburg in the 1690s, and settled in Poland where
he distinguished himself as a teacher, diplomat, and soldier. It does not record
whether he left any heirs to the name. See *Polski Słownik Biograficzny*, 3:3–4.
[78] On 28 August 1775 Ambassador Gunning reported that a General Branicki
had ordered 30,000 arms for the Poles, PRO S.P. 99/2 no. 55.

so long as this matter is unsettled and Russia is not entirely at
ease, she will not engage in any action that might provoke war
with Austria or with any other state." Moreover, when we
arrived in Poland, the general who was our official escort said
during a conversation with the ambassador, "Although you
did not show me the letter that arrived from the Sublime State
at Tula after your departure from Moscow, and which concerned the independence of the Crimea, and of which you sent
a summary to the prime minister, I have information that the
communication concerned some suggestions on the form of
the article dealing with independence. My government too is
taking precautionary measures."

All of the troops introduced into Poland by Russia before
the start of the imperial campaign are still in Poland. After the
peace Russia did not cease sending troops, ammunition, and
supplies into Poland. On our return from Moscow they even
sent several thousand troops and a good deal of cannon supplies
with our official escort. When asked the reason for this, the
general said, "In order to meet [our] ambassador, and because
the Austrians are presuming to engage in various types of
aggressive actions, we are bringing them as a precaution with
a view to protecting the frontier regions from aggression." At
present there are in every town and city within Poland up to
eight or ten hours from Muslim borders anywhere from a
thousand to five thousand troops with their supplies and
ammunition. In the places in which they are located they said,
"We are guests. This area is not under our jurisdiction."
Nevertheless, such sovereign matters as the arrest and confinement of criminals, the assignment of police to patrols in
various areas and regions, and defense and protection, were in
the hands of the Russians.

It is obvious from appearances and from the fact that they
use printed paper in place of hard cash in their buying and
selling, as explained above, that their financial situation at
present is difficult and disquieting. Moreover, the owners of
some goods that General Potemkin, who looks after the

empress's private affairs, bought for the empress crowd into
the general's office almost every day, demanding hard cash.
While we were in Moscow they assembled brokers and pur-
chasers, and sold many varieties of furs that had been collected
and registered in a special place in Moscow for a long time. It
was understood that their sale at this time was for the purpose
of obtaining funds to meet the additional unforeseen expenses
of the ambassadors who had arrived recently. From this situation and other conditions, their financial need is self-evident.
But, it was reported and observed that they were one and all
most concerned to protect from any diminution the specific
revenues that had been assigned and earmarked in the time of
Peter the Great for the pay and other expenses of the soldiery
and the stockpile of munitions. No matter what other financial
worries they may have, these are never allowed to spread to
and affect the military organization and the good ordering of
military affairs. Their regular and standing troops were always
ready and prepared. Since it was not possible to have much
discussion and conversation on matters considered sensitive by
the Russians outside of what was known and customary,
nothing else could be learned.

> It is the time that is customary for the slave of the benefactor
> to present his service in hope of forgiveness and grace.
> Yet, I should never have dared offer these incoherent words
> to the majesty of the state, had I not been so commanded.

Reception of Repnin by the Ottoman
sultan. (Brückner, *Katharina*, p. 333.)

II

The Russian Embassy to
Constantinople in 1776

A description of the reciprocal exchange of ambassadors extraordinary and plenipotentiary: Russian, General in Chief, Lieutenant Colonel of the Izmailovskii Regiment and Cavalier of various orders, Prince Nikolai Vasil'evich Repnin; Turkish, Pasha of Three Horsetails,[1] Abdülkerim, Rumeli beylerbeyi, *located at Hotin on the Dnestr River, 13 July 1775, on a vessel specially designed for the preliminaries between these ambassadors and commissars authorized for the purpose by both sides; from the Russian side, General in Chief and Cavalier Fedor Matveevich Voeikov, and from the Turkish side, Pasha of Three Horsetails, Mehmet of Hotin; of the ceremony on that occasion; and following that, the mentioned journey of the local ambassador from Hotin to Constantinople, Moldavia, Walachia, Bulgaria, and Rumeli; with detailed descriptions of meetings and honors that were extended to the ambassador in noted cities and towns lying along his route, and the manner in which the ambassador entered those cities and above-mentioned Turkish capital, and following this the visit with the grand vezir and the audience with the sultan.*

July

12th. In accordance with the stipulated ceremony, a reciprocal crossing was arranged over the Dnestr River at Hotin for the embassy carriages and entourages, and a large part of these already spent the night in the suburbs of Hotin.

13th. On this day, for which the exchange of ambassadors was set at ten o'clock in the morning, the whole entourage of the embassy here, clad in rich dress, gathered before the tent of the ambassador, where each was assigned the place that he was to occupy during this ceremony. At noon, when all had been arranged, a signal was given by the cannon of the ambassador's camp, which was answered at that very moment from the

---

[1] The horsetail, or *tuğ*, consisting of horsetails affixed to a pole surmounted by a ball, was an ancient symbol of authority among the Turks. Rank determined the number of horsetails. Here the rank of *Rumeli beylerbeyi* entitled Abdülkerim to three horsetails, and in the Russian text he is "trekhbunchuzhnyi Pasha," a pasha of three horsetails. He was, therefore, superior in rank to the hospodars of Moldavia and Walachia, who had only two horsetails (N. Iorga, *A History of Roumania*, trans. Joseph McCabe, p. 191).

Turkish camp, as a sign that all was ready there too; whereupon all, having taken their places, marched out in the
following order:

Detachment detailed for the exchange	Interpreter Palladoklis and Secretary Marklovskoi along-side[3]
Entourage of Major General and Cavalier Baron Igel'strom	Carriage with the marshal of the embassy, with him a priest[4]
Entourage of General in Chief and Cavalier Voeikov	One haiduk at each door
Ambassadorial entourage	Interpreter Kruta at the carriage[5]
Major Markov, as chief quartermaster[2]	Master of the Horse Prince Kherkheulizev
Two fourriers with standards	Twelve draft horses
Hussar noncommissioned officer	Maître d'hôtel
Six hussars, two abreast	Eighteen lackeys, two abreast
Hussar trumpeters	Two jägers
Hussar kettledrummer	Four runners
Twenty-four hussars by platoons	Thirteen waiters
Musicians	Twelve noblemen of the embassy
Infantry in their formation	The carriages in which were the
Runner of the marshal	ambassador and General
His four lackeys, two abreast	Voeikov
	On the right side of the

[2] It is not clear whether this Major Markov, the chief quartermaster, is the same Major Arkadii Ivanovich Markov who was listed as the counsellor of the embassy and the one who carried out the discussions with the *reis efendi* quoted in the introduction, pp. 47–49. Counsellor Markov is mentioned in *SRIO*, 15:648. At another point, Rumiantsev wrote to Repnin that he was complying with all requests for promotions of members of the embassy, except Markov, whom he considered too young for promotion (*SRIO*, 5:196).

[3] Anton Pallodoklis, from the island of Mitelina. He asked to be released from the service at the conclusion of the embassy mission in order to return to the island (*SRIO*, 15:519).

[4] The marshal of the embassy was Iakov Ivanovich Bulgakov, 1743–1809. He is discussed in the introduction as the author of the text. He was also active in the Russian theater (*Istoriia Moskvy*, 2:596).

[5] Joseph Kruta elected to remain in Constantinople at the conclusion of the mission. Peterson recommended him as weak in written matters, but valuable for personal contacts with Turkish officials, many of whom he knew personally (*SRIO*, 15:518). See also, Jan Reychman, "Une famille de drogmans orientaux en Pologne au XVIIIe siècle," in *Rocznik Orientalistyczny*, 25 (1961): 83–99, esp. p. 97.

carriage, Secretary of Oriental Languages Panaiodoros[6]

Adjutant General Rontsov

On the left side of the carriage, one staff officer each for the adjutant general, and General in Chief Voeikov

Four pages at the reins

Two haiduks at the carriage doors

Six Izmailovskii grenadiers alongside; aides-de-camp behind the carriage, Igel'strom and Saltykov, and two junior officers as aides-de-camp of General in Chief Voeikov

Two chamber pages

Embassy Secretary Markov's runner

Two of his lackeys

Interpreters Valts and Shchepot'ev, Severin and Vilkens

Carriage, in it both secretaries of the embassy

One haiduk at each door

Interpreter Hangerli at the carriage[7]

Cuirassier trumpets and kettledrums

Cuirassier detachment

Arriving at one o'clock at the bank of the river where the ferryboats were lying, the ambassador went to the tent of General in Chief Voeikov. At that time the transport of exchange entourages from each side was begun. Then the ambassador, conjointly with the mentioned general in chief, two official escorts, and the remainder of the entourage that was with them went to Major General and Cavalier Shirkov's tent, which was set up nearby and beneath which a table had been prepared for him. After this he returned to the former tent and awaited the transport of the entire cortege, which lasted a little more than three hours. About four o'clock the signal was given from the Turkish camp that the ambassador there was ready for the crossing. A reply was quickly given from one of the cannons here, and the ambassador ceremoniously boarded his

[6] Collegial Assessor Panaiodoros. Peterson reported in a special memorandum that this particular interpreter had shown himself to be such an ardent supporter of the Russians that he could no longer conduct business with the Turks on a personal basis, and in fact that he must leave Constantinople with his family because of the danger he was in (*SRIO*, 15:520–21). Panin replied on 5 January 1776 that Moscow was in need of persons as knowledgeable in Turkish as Panaiodoros and instructed him to return with Repnin (*SRIO*, 15:588).

[7] Dmitrii Hangerli. Peterson recommended that he be assigned perhaps to an interpreter's position in one of the colleges of the Russian administration after the embassy departed, since he had aroused so much ill-will among the Turks that he could not remain in Constantinople (*SRIO*, 15:519).

ferry, as did the Turkish ambassador. Arriving simultaneously at the raft on which the exchange was to be held, both ambassadors with their entourages boarded the vessel at the same time and took their seats in armchairs and chairs that had been placed there for them and for the commissars and escorts who were with them.

After the customary mutual greetings, General in Chief and Cavalier Voeikov took the [Russian] ambassador by the right hand and presented him to the governor of Hotin, Mehmet Pasha. The latter did likewise, presenting to [Voeikov] the Turkish ambassador. On completion of this exchange, a signal was given with a flag placed on the ship for that purpose, whereupon twenty cannon were fired from both sides, while the infantry stationed in parade formation on either side fired three rounds from their small arms.

After this, the pasha of Hotin gave his right hand to the ambassador and led him, ahead of his entourage and both *mihmandar*s, to the transport raft, where he seated him on his right side in his own ambassadorial armchair that had been brought especially for this.

After both ambassadors reached the bank, shots were fired from ten cannon on each side upon a given signal. Then the ambassador was led by the Hotin pasha himself to his headquarters, where he was treated with every possible consideration and honor. Upon leaving the tent, the Hotin pasha gave the ambassador a richly outfitted horse as a mark of good will, asking him to ride it to the quarters intended for him, which the pasha would take as a token of his friendship and indulgence. The ambassador agreed to this, returning on the occasion a courteous compliment. In this manner the ambassador departed for his quarters, preceded and followed by his entourage, and then by the Turkish entourage. The carriages followed after the entire cortege. As soon as the ambassador had mounted, all the troops drawn up in parade formation fired three rounds from their rifles, and as he rode past, twenty-five shots were fired from the cannon of the Hotin fortress.

About six o'clock in the evening the ambassador arrived in his quarters and was accompanied by two *mihmandar*s to his tent. They were detained there for some time and were served coffee, confections, and cold drinks. After this the two *mihmandar*s retired to their dwellings, wishing the ambassador rest and quiet after his labors.

In the evening the Hotin pasha sent supper for fifty persons to the ambassador who was his guest and who had had no time to order the preparation of food.

The second *mihmandar*, the *kapıcıbaşı*, sent gifts of Turkish materials. Articles and money were presented in reciprocation to him and to those who were sent by him.

14th. In the morning the marshal of the embassy was sent to the Hotin pasha with gifts. During the exchange ceremony he had distributed two hundred gold pieces to the pasha's entourage, and one hundred gold pieces to the entourage of the two *mihmandar*s.

The *kâhya bey* and the *divan efendi* came to the ambassador from the pasha.[8] Gifts were sent by the *divan efendi*.

15th. After dinner the son of the Hotin pasha paid a visit to the ambassador.[9] Toward evening a supper like that of the first day was sent by the Hotin pasha.

16th. For his part, the ambassador sent a supper on rich service to the Hotin pasha. The maître d'hôtel and the embassy people who bore it were dressed in parade livery.

17th. Supper was again sent to the Hotin pasha toward evening, and it was again borne in ceremonial fashion. On this day an announcement came from the ambassador to his two *mihmandar*s that it was his intention to depart from Hotin the day after next. As a consequence, on the next day

18th. The *kâhya bey* and the *divan efendi* were sent by the Hotin

---

[8] *Kâhya* is another pronounciation of the word *kethuda*.

[9] This was one act of courtesy which Repnin felt he could not reciprocate. On 18 July 1775 Repnin wrote to Panin of the courtesies extended to him by Melek Mehmet Pasha of Hotin, "once he sent to me his son, who has the rank of *kapıcıbaşı* and master of the sultan's horse. To this instance of etiquette I was unable to respond, not wanting to send my daughters to His Excellency" (*SRIO*, 6:310).

pasha to wish him a pleasant journey. In conformity with this the marshal of the embassy was dispatched by the ambassador with farewell compliments. In the evening the order was given for the whole entourage to prepare for a ceremonial departure from Hotin on the following day.

19th. In accordance with the instructions of the previous day, the ambassador's entourage, as well as the entourages of both his *mihmandar*s gathered at his headquarters at the appointed hour.

Before the departure of the ambassador, the *divan efendi* came to him once again to take leave and to wish him a happy journey in the name of the Hotin pasha and on his own behalf. Following this the ambassador mounted at noon and set out with his and the Turkish entourages, which traveled in the following order:

*Çavuş*es and the Turkish convoy	The ambassador, around him four runners
Cuirassier trumpeters	
Cuirassier kettledrums	Behind him both secretaries of the embassy
Major Tutol'min with half of the cuirassier detachment	Adjutants
Master of the Horse Prince Kherkheulizev	Pages
	The other half of the cuirassiers with the cornet
Cavaliers of the embassy, mounted two abreast	*Kâhya*s of the *mihmandar*s, with their music
Marshal of the embassy	
Two Turkish *mihmandar*s without entourages	Ambassadorial carriages

Twenty-five cannon shots were fired during the departure from the city. During the entire time of his sojourn in Hotin the ambassador was visited daily by the two *mihmandar*s assigned to him, as well as by other distinguished people of the pasha's entourage.

After traveling five hours distance from Hotin, they arrived in the village called Larga where they spent the night.

20th. Spent the night at the town of Gordineshty, having traveled for five hours.

21st. At two o'clock in the afternoon the ambassador arrived at Kosteshty where he was met by a chorus of Moldavian musicians sent by Hospodar Ghika. Traveled four hours this day.

22d. Rest day. In the morning three boyars arrived at the camp, sent by Hospodar Ghika to meet and accompany the ambassador to Jassy. On behalf of their prince they brought him various fruits which were left at the dinner table.

23d. At six in the morning the ambassador, accompanied by his entourage and the mentioned Moldavian boyars, rode out of the town of Kosteshty, and after traveling two hours made camp at the town of Stefănesti, where he was met by the district *ispravnik* [district administrative officer]. After dinner the third *vestiar maray* [treasurer] arrived at the camp, sent by Princess Ghika, with four horses for the ambassador and the princesses. Having spent the night, on the next day,

24th. The ambassador rode from the town of Stefănesti in the morning and after a five-hour ride arrived at Tabăra where he was met by the *ispravnik* of Jassy with a few *Arnauts* [Albanian troops].

25th. Rest day.

26th. Left Tabăra and after riding three hours made camp near Trifeşti, where they spent the night.

27th. After riding three hours halted near Sculeni. Immediately upon the arrival of the ambassador at that town the brother and the brother-in-law of the hospodar arrived. They were sent by the latter with congratulations on the ambassador's nearing Jassy satisfactorily, and with a profession of the mentioned hospodar's pleasure at his forthcoming meeting with the ambassador. On this occasion he gave him a letter of the same contents and presented various fruits.

In accordance with this missive, the secretary of Oriental Languages, Panaiodoros, was sent to the hospodar with respectful compliments and with a letter of reply.

After luncheon a relative of the hospodar, Prince Mavrocordato, arrived with his wife. Toward evening the Moldavian hetman arrived with some 150 troops who were appointed to accompany the ambassador to Jassy.

They, Prince Mavrocordato and his wife, and the Moldavian hetman were invited by the ambassador to take supper with him.

28th. At 8:30 the ambassador left the camp with his entourage along with the mentioned hetman and his troops. Five versts from Jassy the ambassador found Moldavian troops drawn up in two files alongside two tents erected opposite each other, on the right side for the ambassador, and on the left for his wife. Before he dismounted, a few courtiers of the hospodar approached them. Two of them held water pipes in their hands. They walked alongside his horse and at the door of the carriage in which were seated the ambassadress and the princesses. Approaching the tent, the ambassador was met by the hospodar himself, with his children, who led him inside. Two tables were set up there with liqueurs and cold food, one in the middle for the ambassador, and the other toward the edge for his two *mihmandars*. Shortly after entering the tent the ambassador sat at the table that was prepared for him, along with the hospodar and then part of his entourage. His *mihmandars* took their places at their table and spent some time resting. When the ambassador rose to ride on, the hospodar presented him with a horse and all the trappings, which the ambassador accepted. He promised, out of courtesy, to ride into the city. After this, the hospodar requested that he be allowed to ride on ahead to Jassy in order to make arrangements for his reception in the house assigned to him, to which the ambassador agreed. The hospodar mounted and departed, leaving with the ambassador his two sons and a number of boyars.

The ambassadress in turn was received and shown hospitality in the special tent of the Moldavian hospodar's wife and the most distinguished ladies of her court. When she took her place in the carriage, the wife of the hospodar went on ahead for the same reason.

The ambassador's entrance into Jassy was arranged in the following order:

The Moldavian hetman with all his entourage and banners	Two *mihmandar*s
	The ambassador
Entourages of the two *mihmandar*s	The two secretaries of the embassy
Cuirassiers, trumpeters, kettledrums	Secretary of Oriental Languages Panaidoros and the interpreter
Major Tutol'min with half of the cuirassiers	Hangerli
	Adjutants
Moldavian boyars	Hussars with draft horses
Master of the Horse Prince Kherkheulizev	Carriages
Noblemen of the embassy	The second half of the cuirassier detachment under Cornet Litkhen
Marshal of the embassy, at his sides the two sons of the Moldavian hospodar	Turkish musicians with the *kâhya*s of the *mihmandar*s

They rode into the city of Jassy in this order with the bells of all the churches ringing. Moldavian troops were drawn up on each side along the street on which the embassy quarters were located, and they presented a salute with their arms and banners. When the ambassador entered the courtyard and began to dismount, the troops fired three rounds from the small arms and as many as possible from the cannon. The hospodar himself was standing on the porch with members of his court and led the ambassador to his quarters. His wife was met in the same manner by the wife of the hospodar and her boyar ladies. On entering his quarters the ambassador, the ambassadress, and their children were served refreshments of cold drinks. After this, they went to the table prepared by the hospodar. Present were he, his princess, his two sons, a few leading boyars and their wives. Other persons of the court stood behind the chairs of the ambassador and the ambassadress. Moldavian music was played during the dinner. When it was over, there were Moldavian dances, while the hospodar and his whole entourage took leave of the ambassador and returned to their own places.

The ambassador arrived at his quarters in Jassy at one o'clock in the afternoon, having ridden three hours, or fifteen versts.

29th. In the morning one of the secretaries of the embassy was sent with gifts to the Moldavian hospodar and his wife. On his return the ambassador himself went to visit him and the ambassadress was likewise with the wife of the hospodar.

30th. There was a luncheon of ninety places at the ambassador's, to which were invited the hospodar, his wife, their sons, and the most prominent citizens of both sexes from Jassy. During the dinner the ambassador's music was played. Afterwards, there was Moldavian dancing while the ambassador and the hospodar played cards.

31st. Toward evening the first *mihmandar*, Kara Ahmet Pasha, visited the ambassador.

August

1st. The ambassador rode to hunt at the invitation of the hospodar some ten versts from Jassy, where he stayed until six o'clock in the evening. Luncheon was served there.

2d. In the morning the second *mihmandar*, the *kapıcıbaşı*, came to visit the ambassador.

Toward evening the hospodar's marshal was sent to ask the ambassador to luncheon on the following day, to which was also invited the entire ambassadorial entourage. The ambassadress and the princesses were asked by the wife of the hospodar herself, who came to visit her that day with her daughters.

3d. The ambassador and the ambassadress with their daughters and part of the entourage were served lunch with the hospodar who attended with his family and a few ladies of his court.

4th. Nothing worthy of note occurred.

5th. The ambassador and his two *mihmandar*s rode out after lunch to hunt with the hospodar.

6th. After luncheon, at five o'clock, the ambassador and his family and part of the entourage went at the request of the hospodar up a mountain called Galata, two versts from the city. His tent had been set up to receive them. Immediately after arriving there, various games of horsemanship in the Turkish and Moldavian style were begun on the mountain. During this time coffee, confections, and various cold drinks were served. At dusk the table at which those present had been served at one place was closed. After dining, the children of the Moldavian hospodar and his courtiers entertained with national dances. At the conclusion of everything a small display of fireworks was set off near the mountain. After this the ambassador mounted and rode to his own quarters, to which he was accompanied by the hospodar himself.

7th. In the morning the ambassador was visited by the first *mihmandar*, Kara Ahmet Pasha. After this, distinguished clerical as well as secular officials visited the ambassador.

8th. The metropolitan of Jassy came to the ambassador. Toward evening the order was given to the whole entourage to prepare for departure from Jassy on the following day, and instructions were given to those responsible for the departure. The ambassador, his family and all the entourage went to the hospodar, who on the previous day had asked them to take supper with him.

9th. At seven o'clock in the morning the hospodar came to the ambassador and after staying with him a while departed, telling him that he did not yet wish to take leave of him. He still hoped to be his host at breakfast a short distance from the city. After his departure, Princess Ghika and the Moldavian ladies arrived and stayed with the ambassadress until she entered her carriage in order to be on her way. Because she was with child and therefore not very hale, the princess excused herself for not being able to accompany the ambassadress from the city.

When all carriages were ready, the cortege departed from Jassy in the following order:

The Moldavian entourage under the leadership of the hetman	The carriage in which the ambassador was sitting, the two sons of the hospodar at his side, and the Secretary of Oriental Language Panaiodoros and the Adjutant General Rontsov on horseback
The entourages of the two *mihmandar*s	
Cuirassier trumpeters and kettledrummers	
Major Tutol'min with half of the cuirassiers, swords drawn	The carriage in which the secretaries of the embassy were sitting
Cornet Brink[10]	
Draft horses of the embassy	The carriage with the princess and princesses, along with the interpreter Kruta on horseback
Moldavian boyars	
Master of the Horse Prince Kherkheulizev	Various other carriages of the embassy
Noblemen of the embassy, mounted	The other half of the cuirassiers with drawn swords
Both *mihmandar*s, mounted, and between them the marshal of the embassy along with the interpreter Hangerli	*Kâhya*s of the *mihmandar*s with their music

After riding about three versts, they stopped at a tent which had been set up at the command of Prince Ghika and at which the Moldavian troops were positioned. There he received the ambassador and the ambassadress in the manner of their arrival in Jassy and escorted them inside where they seated themselves at a prepared breakfast. After he had been there for a short while, the ambassador took leave of the hospodar, thanking him for all his courtesies during the stay in Jassy. He went on his way accompanied by the Moldavian hetman with his entourage and two boyars, all three of whom had been commanded to accompany him to Focşani.

After traveling five hours from Jassy, they made camp near a postal station called Scînteia. There the ambassador was met by the district *ispravnik*.

[10] Karl Brink. Repnin made a special request to Rumiantsev to have the "Polish Cornet Karl Brink" assigned to the embassy (*SRIO*, 5:163).

10th. Leaving at six o'clock in the morning, the ambassador continued his way to the postal station called Uncești, lying four hours from the previous one, and there he made camp and spent the night.

Toward evening two Moldavian boyars who lived in the vicinity of this place came to the ambassador to pay their respects.

11th. Leaving at five o'clock in the morning, they arrived at the town of Vaslui, where they took quarters. The journey that day was four hours long.

12th. Rest day.

13th. Left Vaslui at five o'clock in the morning. Traveled for four hours and halted in camp at Dekolin.[11] The night was spent there.

14th. Left at five o'clock in the morning. Arrived at the city of Bîrlad, where they took quarters in homes of the inhabitants.

15th. Rest day.

16th. Left Bîrlad at five o'clock in the morning and after spending five hours on the road arrived at Guru-Paraskevului,[12] where camp was made.

17th. Left at five o'clock in the morning and arrived at the town of Tecuci, where quarters were taken in the homes of the inhabitants.

18th. Rest day.

After lunch the local archbishop came especially from Brăila to visit the ambassador.

In the evening three Walachian boyars arrived at the town to pay their respects to the ambassador, but since it was already late, their introduction was postponed until the following day.

19th. In the morning before his departure, the ambassador met with the mentioned Walachian boyars, and after their greetings he set out on the road that lay before him. Traveling four hours, he arrived at Pomistraveskului,[13] where a camp was pre-

[11] Unidentified, possibly Crasna.
[12] Unidentified.
[13] Unidentified, perhaps close to present-day Petreşti.

pared for him. Waiting under a tent for him there were the *spatar*, that is, the captain of the Walachian troops, and the archimandrite Varlaam of the Focşani Monastery, who had ridden out to meet him.

20th. Set out on the march at five o'clock in the morning and after traveling four hours they arrived at the Milcov River which separates Moldavia from Walachia. The Moldavian hetman formed his troops on the Moldavian bank. The ambassador released the latter there, along with the entire Moldavian cortege which had accompanied him, charging him to thank Hospodar Ghika for the courtesies and for all the services which he had rendered during their crossing of Moldavian territory. Likewise, he expressed his gratitude to the hetman for his correctness and diligence in carrying out those matters entrusted to him.

After crossing over to the Walachian side, the ambassador was met by the Walachian *spatar* and the hospodar's secretary, Gospodin Rakoviţa, both of whom congratulated him in the name of the prince on his safe arrival. The troops of the former, which amounted to some one hundred men, were drawn up in two ranks, and when the ambassador rode between them they rendered a salute with their banners and played the trumpets and other instruments. When they had ridden to their tent and dismounted, the mentioned *spatar* and secretary Rakoviţa repeated their congratulations on his safe arrival. The latter remained for luncheon, while the former excused himself because he was required to execute certain arrangements for entertaining the embassy.

21st, 22d, and 23d. They remained at this place for three days in order to take care of certain necessities.

24th. At five o'clock in the morning they left the village of Vîrteşcoiu and after riding for six hours arrived at the village of Slobozia, on the Rîmna River, and there they occupied quarters in the homes of the inhabitants and spent the night.

25th. Left at five o'clock in the morning and after traveling for three hours arrived at the village of Topliceni near the town of Rîmnicu Sărat, where the ambassador was met by the seignior himself and a few Walachian boyars who were his neighbors. They conducted him to the lord's home in which quarters were designated for him. After luncheon the wives of the mentioned boyars came to pay their respects to the ambassadress.

26th. Rest day.

27th. In the morning at five o'clock they left the village of Topliceni and after traveling for seven hours, stopped at the town of Buzău where they spent the night.

28th. Arrived at the village of Margineanu, five hours' distance from the previous one, and made camp there.

29th. Rest day.

30th. Set out at five o'clock in the morning and after traveling seven hours, arrived at Podikuram,[14] where camp was made on the bank of the Ialomiţa River. The Actual State Councillor in the service of Her Imperial Majesty, Prince Cantacuzene, rode out to meet the ambassador at this place.[15]

31st. Departed at six o'clock in the morning and after traveling for four hours, made camp at the village of Creaţa. On arriving there the leading official of the embassy, the chief quartermaster, was quickly sent to Bucureşti to accept the quarters assigned for the ambassador and his entourage.

At four o'clock in the afternoon the archbishop of Rîmnicu and three leading Walachian boyars arrived at the camp. The first addressed a congratulatory speech to the ambassador in the name of the prince on the occasion of his safely approaching their capital, while the others offered him a letter from the hospodar that contained similar congratulations on his coming arrival in Bucureşti. After the departure of the archbishop and the boyars from the headquarters, in which they had been served coffee, cold drinks, and confections, various fruits and

[14] Unidentified.
[15] Cantacuzene had visited Repnin in Kiev to discuss unspecified business (*SRIO*, 5:190). On 9 June 1775 Repnin wrote to Peterson that Cantacuzene had left for Bucureşti with letters for the hospodar from both Repnin and Panin (*SRIO*, 5:195).

other items for the table were brought to the ambassador in the name of the hospodar. In consonance with this presentation, Panaiodoros, the secretary of Oriental Languages, rode to Bucureşti with the compliments of the ambassador for the hospodar.

September

1st. In the morning at seven o'clock they set out and, before coming within five versts of Bucureşti, the ambassador and the ambassadress were met by the hospodar and his wife in the same manner as at Jassy. They were conducted to special tents where they were served various drinks and fruits. When the ambassador rose, after sufficient rest, the hospodar requested his permission to go ahead and brought him a horse with rich trappings, which he promised out of courtesy to ride into the city. After giving the hospodar time to go on ahead, he mounted the mentioned horse. The ambassadress, who had likewise allowed the wife of the hospodar to go on ahead, entered her carriage and they rode into the city in the same manner as they had entered Jassy. Two sons of the hospodar rode ahead in the ambassador's entourage, at the sides of the marshal, then his first *mihmandar*, but the second was not there because of illness. After the ambassador rode the two secretaries of the embassy, between whom was the mentioned Actual State Councillor Prince Cantacuzene. Again, upon their entrance into Bucureşti there was ringing of bells, cannon and rifle fire, a reception and refreshments at their quarters, and all other honors identical to those which were shown the ambassador and the ambassadress on their arrival in Jassy.

The ambassador arrived in Bucureşti at two o'clock in the afternoon, after traveling three hours from where they had spent the night.

2d. The marshal of the court arrived in the morning from the hospodar and his wife to inquire about the health of the ambassador and the ambassadress. The general's adjutant,

Rontsov, of the embassy staff, delivered presents to the hospodar and his wife. At eleven o'clock the ambassador and all his entourage paid a visit to the hospodar. After luncheon the ambassadress visited the wife of the hospodar. After this, the hospodar went to the ambassador and sat with him the entire evening and stayed for supper.

3d. In the morning the marshal of the hospodar again came to the ambassador and the ambassadress with compliments. After luncheon the wife of the hospodar arrived with her daughter and with the most distinguished ladies of her court and stayed until eight o'clock in the evening. On the same day the general's adjutant, Rontsov, asked the hospodar and his family to luncheon on the following day, to which the most prominent Walachian boyars had also been invited.

4th. There was a dinner for seventy persons at the ambassador's where the following persons were present: the hospodar with his entire family, the Russian Actual State Councillor Cantacuzene, and the most distinguished citizens of both sexes of Bucureşti. After luncheon the guests were regaled with national dances, while the ambassador and the hospodar played cards. Before leaving, the hospodar requested the ambassador and the ambassadress and their family to have luncheon with him on the following day. His entourage was also invited.

5th. The ambassador and the ambassadress and the princesses and the entourage had luncheon at the hospodar's.

6th. The name day of her imperial highness, the grand sovereign princess. The ambassador and his entire entourage heard the divine liturgy in the Monastery of the Forty Martyrs after which a service was held for the health of her highness.[16] After leaving the church, the ambassador visited the archi-

[16] The word service used here is a translation of *sobornoi moleben*, indicating a service said by several priests, probably from various churches. This suggests that the ambassador's visit was an important event for all the clergy in the area. For the liturgy itself see Isabel Florence Hapgood, *Service Book of the Holy Orthodox-Catholic Apostolic [Greco-Russian] Church, Compiled, Translated, and Arranged from the Old Church-Slavonic Service Books of the Russian Church, and Collated with the Service Books of the Greek Church.*

mandrite of the monastery, who had invited him to call. When he returned home, the metropolitan of Bucureşti and two other Walachian bishops arrived. They were seated at the luncheon table to which the hospodar, his family, and his entire court had been invited on the previous day. There were seventy places set. Vocal and instrumental music continued during this time. Trumpets and kettledrums played during the toast to the health of her highness. There was a ball after the luncheon.

7th At five o'clock in the morning the ambassador and his first *mihmandar* went hunting at the hospodar's invitation, some five versts from the city, where a table had been prepared under a tent for him and his entourage, and which was attended as well by the wife of the hospodar and the most distinguished ladies of her court. Afterward, a Turkish comedy was presented and in the evening there was a small display of fireworks. All this was concluded at ten o'clock in the evening and the ambassador returned to the city.

8th. This date had been set for leaving Bucureşti, but it was postponed to the eleventh of the month on the urgent request of the Walachian hospodar. The excuse was that not everything had been prepared for the departure.

9th. In the evening the hospodar and his wife, along with a few persons of both sexes from the court, came to the ambassador and the ambassadress and stayed with them until nine o'clock in the evening. Then, Actual State Councillor Prince Cantacuzene of the Russian service invited the ambassador and the ambassadress to lunch with him on the following day. He also invited part of the entourage.

10th. The Cavalier Feast Day of Saint Alexander Nevsky.[17] The ambassador in the company of his entourage heard the divine liturgy in the Monastery of the Forty Martyrs, after which prayers were offered. Returning from there, the ambassador and his family, and the entourage, visited the above-

[17] The feast day was celebrated in honor of Saint Alexander Nevsky, and also in honor of the holders of the Order of Saint Alexander Nevsky. Repnin had been awarded this medal by the empress for his service in Poland.

mentioned Actual State Councillor Cantacuzene and lunched with him. The hospodar, his family, and entire court were also present. In the evening the whole entourage was informed that the departure from Bucureşti would be the following day.[18]

11th. At seven o'clock in the morning the entire train was sent on ahead, except for the carriages and the saddle and draft horses. At nine o'clock the hospodar and his wife arrived at the ambassador and ambassadress's and after staying with them for a short time, they rode out of the city to where breakfast had been prepared, following the example of the procedure employed on their departure from Jassy.

At ten o'clock the ambassador left Bucureşti at the head of the Walachian, Turkish, and his own entourages. The ambassador himself rode in a carriage, with the above-mentioned Actual State Councillor Prince Cantacuzene, the two sons of the hospodar rode on horseback at either side of the carriage. In other respects the entire order of march was arranged as it had been for the departure from Jassy. After traveling about four versts, they stopped near the monastery called Vakareshti, near which tents had been erected with tables set up in one for the ambassador and in the other for the ambassadress. When they had stopped for a while at his place, the ambassador rose and after expressing his gratitude to the hospodar for all the courtesies that had been rendered by him, set out on his way. The ambassadress expressed the same things on her own behalf. After traveling an hour and a half, they arrived at the bank of the Sabar River, where they made camp and spent the night.

12th. Departed at six o'clock in the morning and after riding four hours arrived at Călugăreni and made camp there.

13th. Left at six o'clock in the morning and arrived at the village of Daia after traveling four hours and made camp there.

---

[18] Repnin's notes indicate that on 10 September he received a petition from the boyars of Walachia. It was written in practically illiterate Russian. In general, the boyars were asking for greater security in their positions, a firm regulation of the amounts of tribute to be collected and paid to the Porte, and representation at the Porte through the Russian ambassador (SRIO, 6:346–47).

14th. Set out at six o'clock and before coming within four versts of the city of Giurgiu the ambassador found a reception group sent there to meet him, consisting of:

Turnacı Ağası Çadırcıoğlu
Mehmet
Abdullah Aga, *turnacı* of
Giurgiu
Voivode Musa Aga
Turnacı Ağası Abdullah Baki,
sent from Tsar'Grad [Istanbul]
to aid the two *mihmandar*s in
travel arrangements
Two *çorbacı*s
Twenty *serdengeçti* agas
A few janissaries

The leaders at this meeting, who were also the main persons under the commandant of the city of Giurgiu, addressed salutory compliments to the ambassador on his arrival.

As the ambassador rode past the city of Giurgiu, some seventy cannon shots were fired from the fortress and from the ships lying opposite it. Three versts after the city the ambassador stopped on the bank of a stream, the Romadan, which flows from the Danube, and camp was made there. When he entered his headquarters he was followed by the captains of the above-mentioned group, who were served coffee.

At two in the afternoon galleys for transporting the ambassador and his entourage across the Danube arrived at the camp, and cannon were fired. At four o'clock the ambassador went to inspect the place where the crossing was to take place, and on this occasion he was saluted by cannon shots from the ships.

15th. In the morning the chief quartermaster was sent across the Danube to select a campsite. On his return, the transport of the carriages was begun, a number at a time, and this lasted throughout the day.

After luncheon, the above-mentioned chiefs of Giurgiu

arrived to pay their compliments to the ambassador and were served coffee and confections.

16th. Early in the morning the rest of the train was taken across and at eleven o'clock the ambassador and his family, accompanied by his whole entourage, rode to the bank of the Danube, and when they arrived there the carriages and saddle horses were taken across. The Walachian convoy was released, except for the *spatar* himself, who wanted to accompany [the ambassador] farther. He and part of his entourage boarded galleys which had been prepared especially for him. The ambassadress and the princesses boarded another, and still two more were filled by the two Turkish *mihmandar*s and their entourages and three officials sent from Giurgiu to accompany the ambassador, namely: *Çadırcıoğlu* [Mehmet], *turnacı* [*ağası*], the *turnacı* of Giurgiu [Abdullah Aga], and the voivode [Musa Aga] of that city, who had been at the meeting two days before. As soon as they cast off from the shore, shots were fired from two cannon on the mentioned galleys. At the same time cannonade was audible from the fortress in Giurgiu. When they reached the middle of the river, the signal was given from two cannon in Ruse (Ruščuk), from Giurgiu several shots were immediately fired in answer, the full number of which could not be determined because of the distance of the two fortresses, one of which was three and the other eight versts from the crossing.

When they had tied up at this bank of the Danube, shots were again fired from the ships and the ambassador disembarked from the galley. He was received by his two *mihmandar*s. When he alighted on the bank, the second *mihmandar* congratulated him on his safe arrival and introduced him to those who had been sent from Ruse to meet him: the *zagarcıbaşı* Akvalı Mehmet Aga, Mustafa Efendi of the *hacegân* of the divan, Ismail Aga of the *haseki* agas, and Hacı Ahmet Aga, who were the first officials of the commander in chief there. After this he was introduced to the *baş çuhadar* who was the envoy of Osman Pasha of Silistra. He had a letter of greeting and a horse outfitted in the Turkish style, which the second *mihmandar*, the *kapıcıbaşı* [Kara Hisarî Ahmet Bey], requested the ambassador to ride to his headquarters in the name of Osman Pasha, and he did this.

Turkish troops were drawn up in two ranks along the bank, eighty cavalry of the *serdengeçti* agas in one, and one hundred janissaries in the other. The ambassador was accompanied to his headquarters in this manner, where in addition to his two *mihmandars*, all the mentioned Turkish officials who had been sent to meet him were seated and given refreshments in accordance with their custom. After some conversation, they withdrew, and the ambassador replied to the letter of the pasha of Silistra, after which presents were sent to him with his envoy the *baş çuhadar*.

17th, 18th, and 19th. Remained at this place for a lack of transport carts.[19]

20th. After receiving the carts and sending the baggage train on, the ambassador and his family, accompanied by his entourage, set out amid the sound of cannonade from the fortresses of Giurgiu and Ruse. The commander in chief of the latter place accompanied him for half of the march with a small number of Turkish cavalry. Having traveled two and a quarter hours, they came to the camp at the town of Chervena Voda and spent the night here.

21st. Although it had been planned to continue on the way this day, an extremely heavy rain poured down during the night and lasted until noon, which caused a large part of the Turks with carts to become separated, and so it was necessary to stop for the entire day.

22d. At seven o'clock in the morning, after sending on the baggage train, the ambassador broke camp and arrived at the village of Senovo at four in the afternoon. They made camp

[19] The difficulties encountered here were more severe than the text indicates. Carts were in short supply, the horses were usually not broken to harness, and the rains were making the Balkan passage especially difficult. Nevertheless, he managed to arrive in Constantinople earlier than he had anticipated (*SRIO*, 6:356–57, 367).

after riding for five and one-half hours. The carts arrived in the
night because the road, naturally slippery and full of ruts from
the rain, had become very difficult.

23d. The order to get the carts underway came at daybreak,
but because of the shortage of carts, many of which had lost
the way, they started late. The ambassador himself, after eating
breakfast, left with his family and part of the entourage at
eleven o'clock in the morning. When he had traveled half the
way to the next town, called Razgrad, he found the chief
commander of the *turnacı*s of that town, who had ridden out to
meet him. With him were a few other officials, among them
some one hundred men of the Turkish foot and mounted
troops. The *turnacı* commander, having extended the appropriate greetings, accompanied the ambassador with the entire
entourage mentioned above to the camp that had been made at
the outskirts of the town. In order to avoid separating the
people, it was decided not to take quarters in the city.

The ambassador arrived at this camp at four o'clock in the
afternoon after traveling for three hours. The baggage train,
because of the bad road, arrived in part during the night, and
the rest during the following day.

24th Rest day.

25th. After sending out the baggage train and carriages,
which were to skirt the town, the ambassador and the rest of
his entourage, accompanied by his two *mihmandar*s and the
above-mentioned *turnacı*, rode through Razgrad. There the
turnacı took his leave of the ambassador and on returning home,
left fifty men from his troops to convoy him to Shumen.

After traveling five and one-half hours along a most difficult
road on which many carts broke down and were left behind,
they arrived at a camp lying near the village of Uzunlar
[Dlŭzhko] and spent the night there. Hasan, the *turnacı ağası* of
Shumen, that is, the commander of the troops in that city, and
Ahmet Bey, the leading citizen, with his entourage, came to the
camp for a meeting with the ambassador.

26th. When the ambassador had gone about a verst from the

place where he had spent the night, he was met by the above-mentioned *turnacı* and Ahmet Bey, and they accompanied him. Before coming within three versts of the camp assigned near Shumen, he was met by the *müftü* and kadi and all the *serdengeçti*s of Shumen, and the aga and the *bayraktar* janissaries who had with them about one thousand foot and horse troops, who stood in two files right up to the camp.

27th. Rest day.

28th. They were scheduled to set out extremely early. Horse-drawn carts had been released here, however, and they were supposed to collect more from the Shumen district, but because of the slowness with which they could be assembled, they could not move from the spot before eleven o'clock in the morning, and even then they had to leave a considerable part of the train behind. Some one hundred and fifty cavalry troops were sent from Shumen to accompany the ambassador across the entire district. They were under the leadership of the above-mentioned *turnacı* and Ahmet Bey, who had accompanied the ambassador all the way to the town of Karnabat. After traveling five hours they arrived at the village of Smyadovo and made camp there.

29th. Everything was ready at the appointed hour, and first the train and then the ambassador set out at seven o'clock in the morning. The difficult crossing of the Balkans began here, and although it was no more than a three-hour trip, all the carriages and carts did not arrive until evening at the village called Chalik Kavak, near which they made camp.

30th. Left camp as early as on the previous day and continued the crossing of the Balkans, coming to the village of Dobrol after four hours, near which camp was made. Less than half an hour from this place the commander in chief in Karnabat, *Kapıcıbaşı* Abdurrahman, rode out to meet the ambassador, and after the appropriate greetings, accompanied him to the headquarters. The baggage train assembled during the night. This was the end of the Balkans, where the road levels out again.

October

1st. Started at nine o'clock in the morning, later than on previous days because some of the carts were changed here. Before the ambassador came within half an hour of Karnabat, the kadi and all the officials of Karnabat, spiritual and civil, came out to meet him, and with them were some two hundred foot and mounted troops. The kadi rode up to the ambassador. Congratulating him on his safe arrival, he rode ahead of him along with the first *mihmandar*, the pasha of two horsetails; the second *mihmandar* was not there because of illness. Having ridden about two hundred paces, they found lined in a row the citizens of Karnabat, spiritual as well as temporal, whom the kadi said he had sent out to meet the ambassador as a greater proof of respect and welcome. Then *Kapıcıbaşı* Abdurrahman, who had been at the meeting the previous day with the ambassador in Dobrol, met the ambassador after overtaking him by another road. He spent the night in that village and after getting the whole baggage train on the road in the morning he managed to get ahead of the ambassador in order to meet him as he approached Karnabat. Doing this with appropriate greetings, he rode between the pasha and the kadi and accompanied the ambassador right to his headquarters, which he entered after him and where he was seated, as were the two escorts from Shumen, that is *Turnacı Ağası* Hasan and Ahmet Bey. Coffee was brought to them, and after sitting awhile they retired, wishing the ambassador rest and quiet.

The ambassador entered the camp near Karnabat at three in the afternoon. The remaining part of his entourage and carriages assembled toward night. The journey was five hours long.

2d. Rest day. The Shumen escorts *Turnacı* Hasan Aga and Ahmet Bey paid their respects to the ambassador. At this time through the marshal of the embassy they presented appropriate gifts as a mark of their pleasure in accompanying the ambassador all the way across their district.

The quartermaster general of the sultan, Ali Pasha of Chirmen, a pasha of two horsetails, who goes out only to meet the sultan and the vezir when they have with them the sacred banner of the Prophet, arrived. This pasha made camp near the ambassador and sent forthwith notice of his arrival, requesting permission to visit the ambassador. Receiving the answer that the ambassador awaited him, he came to him with all his entourage. During the usual greetings he said that he had been commissioned by the Porte to meet the ambassador beyond the Balkans and accompany him in a few marches to Edirne. He added on his own behalf his most respectful compliments, to which answer was given in appropriate fashion. During their conversations they were served coffee, confections, and sherbet. After staying awhile, he returned to his quarters and at that time sent the ambassador as a gift a horse without accoutrements.

3d. The ambassador set out early in the morning, accompanied by his two *mihmandar*s who had been with him the previous day, Ali Pasha of Chirmen, the *kapıcıbaşı* of Karnabat, the kadi, and other city officials. The latter took leave of the ambassador and returned to Karnabat after riding with him about an hour, but the *kapıcıbaşı* accompanied him further. After five hours of travel they arrived at the village of Kaftan, near which they made camp.

4th. The leading part of the train was sent on at four o'clock in the morning and the ambassador himself left camp at daybreak. After traveling seven hours he arrived at the village of Popovo, beyond which camp was made at five o'clock in the afternoon. As they rode through the village, the inhabitants scattered wheat and salt before them along the road.[20]

Abdurrahman, the *kapıcıbaşı* of Karnabat, returned after accompanying the ambassador beyond the border of his district. Before doing so he went to the ambassador to take his

[20] The offering of bread and salt (wheat and salt in the text) is a traditional sign of welcome well-known among the Russians, but also common in Eastern Europe. There may be other things to consider in the present instance, for example, a feeling of relief over the end of devastation caused by the war.

leave. The ambassador expressed his gratitude for all the courtesies shown him and sent him several furs as a present.

5th. Left as early as on the previous day and after traveling eight hours stopped in camp near the village of Hanlıyenice, where they arrived at five o'clock in the afternoon. In all populated places that the ambassador passed through, the inhabitants strewed the road with wheat and salt.

6th. Left at seven o'clock and having traveled three hours, made camp at Giol'bab,[21] one and one-half hours' distance from Edirne. As soon as the ambassador's arrival became known in that city, the *bostancıbaşı* sent his *çuhadar* with his compliments and with fruits, fish, and items for the table.

In order to hasten his arrival in Constantinople, the ambassador determined to merely ride through Edirne without taking quarters there, so as not to make his departure more difficult by scattering his entourage throughout the sprawling city for just one night. For this reason he sent word to the official who was the chief quartermaster for that day, ordering him to designate a campsite for the next day one-half hour beyond Edirne. The whole entourage was given the order to be prepared the following day for a ceremonial entry into the city.

7th. In the morning the ambassador and all the entourage rode in the following order:

The entourages of both *mihmandar*s, Ali Pasha of Chirmen, and various other Turkish officials	Second Master of the Horse, Cornet Brink
	Draft horses
Chief Quartermaster Major Markov	Master of the Horse, Prince Kherkheulizev
Two cuirassier noncommissioned officers as fourriers	Noblemen of the embassy, two abreast
Hussar detachment with trumpets and kettledrums	The two Turkish *mihmandar*s, and between them the marshal of the embassy
Grenadier detachment with the banner and music	The ambassador in a carriage in

[21] Unidentified.

which both secretaries of the embassy sat in front of him Alongside the carriage rode the Secretary of Oriental Languages and Collegial Assessor	Panaiodoros, the adjutant general of the embassy staff, the aide-de-camp, and a haiduk at each door The whole cuirassier detachment

Before coming within half an hour of Edirne, the *bostancıbaşı* and the janissary aga rode out from there. First the mentioned aga rode to the carriage and congratulated the ambassador on his safe arrival. Following him, the *bostancıbaşı* immediately did the same. After this they both took their places in front of the *mihmandar*s and the marshal of the embassy, while their entourages rode on ahead with the various Turks. After them rode the *naip*, or deputy of the mulla of Edirne, in whose name he greeted the ambassador, adding his apology that the latter was unable to ride out because of his age and even more because of decrepitude. Approaching the city, the *bostancıbaşı* rode up to the ambassadorial carriage a second time. He expressed his regret that he would not be staying with them in the city, and requested that [the ambassador] at least do him the honor of staying in the house prepared for him and allow him to be his host for whatever brief period of time he would allow. The ambassador agreed to this. One verst from the city *bostancı*s were drawn up on the right side and janissaries on the left, in all some two thousand men, without rifles or pikes. After riding through all the more important streets, along which troops had been stationed and where there was a multitude of onlookers, they arrived at the house that had been designated to accommodate them. The ambassador alighted from his carriage there and was received at the gate by the *bostancı* and other officials. He was conducted to the room prepared for him and furnished with sofas and carpets. As soon as the ambassador was seated they began to bring him, in accordance with the Turkish custom, confections, coffee, sherbet, perfumes, and rose water. During these refreshments the *bostancıbaşı* introduced the most distinguished leaders and inhabitants of Edirne. About half an hour later the ambassador

rose and departed, accompanied in the same manner as when he
was met, that is, the *bostancıbaşı* and all the leaders of the city,
as well as the *naip* or deputy of the mulla of Edirne. They
accompanied him to the camp located near Kaçılar kiosk, a
half hour's distance from the house in the city where the
ambassador had been entertained. *Bostancı* and janissary troops
were stationed in two rows right up to the camp. On arriving
at the camp the ambassador invited the *bostancıbaşı* and various
other Turkish officials to his headquarters. They as well as his
*mihmandar*s accompanied him, and he served them at his place
according to their custom. He then dismissed them, expressing
his pleasure at all the honors which had been shown him.[22]

After lunch the *bostancıbaşı* sent the ambassador and the
ambassadress, as well as the secretary and marshal of the
embassy, various fruits and confections.

The first deputy of the French nation and all the distinguished
French merchants located in that city came to the camp to pay
their respects to the ambassador. They brought him various
French wines and liqueurs, declaring that they had been ordered
to do so by the ambassador to the Porte, the Marquis de
Saint Priest.[23]

8th. After waiting on the baggage train for some time, the
ambassador sent the lead wagons on ahead and departed at
nine o'clock in the morning. He was accompanied by his first
mihmandar, but he had not had time to travel two versts when
the *bostancıbaşı* with the janissary aga and other officials over-
took him in great haste. The *bostancıbaşı* went to the ambassador
and excused himself for not being able to reach him at his
quarters because of official matters that had arisen for him. The
above-mentioned *naip* also rode out to this place. He returned
after accompanying him about a verst, after expressing appro-

[22] Repnin wrote that his reception in Edirne had been carried out with greater
honors than those shown Count Rumiantsev in 1740 (*SRIO*, 15:430).
[23] Although the French were notably anti-Russian during the war, Saint Priest
received two Russian medals in April 1779, the Orders of Saint Andrew and
Saint Nevsky. The award was made for his assistance in bringing about the
Convention of Aynalı Kavak, Mikhail I. Pyliaev, *Staraia Moskva*, p. 59.

priate compliments to the ambassador. Continuing on his way, the ambassador arrived at the village of Kuleli, and made camp there after traveling seven hours.

9th. Left at daybreak and after traveling eight hours arrived at a camp near the town of Lüle Burgaz, from where the kadi and various principal leaders and inhabitants came out to meet the ambassador and accompany him to his headquarters.

10th. Departed at daybreak and after traveling eight and one-half hours made camp this side of the town of Çorlu. Here Ali Pasha of Chirmen, having announced beforehand that he had an order from the Porte to accompany him to this place, came to take leave. He was seated and served coffee and confections. After he had returned to his own place gifts were brought from him via the interpreter Hangerli.

11th. Left also at daybreak and after traveling eight hours arrived at the city of Silivri, from whence a welcoming party composed of all the leaders of the city rode out. They accompanied the ambassador to his camp laid out this side of the city. On arriving at this camp they found there Gospodin Actual State Councillor Peterson and with him the interpreter Tamara, who had come from Constantinople to meet the ambassador.

12th. At seven o'clock in the morning they set out on the march and after traveling six hours they arrived at the town of Büyükçekmece. From there a welcoming party, composed of leading people, came to them and accompanied the ambassador to his camp, occupied near the town.

13th. Set out on the march and after traveling three hours arrived at Küçükçekmece, where a tent was set up for the ambassador's breakfast. There the dragoman [the Porte's translator], Kostaki Muruza, who had been sent by the vezir to meet him, was waiting with congratulations for the ambassador on his satisfactory arrival, which the above-mentioned dragoman accomplished in appropriate phrases as soon as the ambassador had dismounted. After this, he was conducted into the tent where the ambassador seated himself in the armchair

set for him. Actual State Councillor Peterson was seated on his
right side, while on his left was the mentioned dragoman.
When coffee had been brought to him, he was invited to breakfast and seated next to the ambassador. When they had finished,
they mounted and rode to a camp near San Stefano [Yeşilköy].
The Porte's interpreter rode in the ambassador's entourage,
and after arriving there he stayed for a time, during which they
made arrangements concerning the day of arrival; and he then
took leave of the ambassador, who sent with him his respects
to the grand vezir.

From Küçükçekmece to San Stefano is a distance of one and
a half hours. From Ruse to the last stop, not only in the camps,
but also in the towns passed through where there were kadis
and other official persons, they met and accompanied the
ambassador everywhere with all honors and courtesy.

14th. In accordance with the agreement arrived at on the
previous day with the Porte's interpreter, the marshal of the
embassy rode to the Porte with an announcement of the
ambassador's arrival in San Stefano. With him were an
interpreter for the Turkish language, two officers of the
embassy, two runners, and six hussars in embassy livery.

In the morning the Prussian envoy, Gospodin Zegelin, came
to meet the ambassador, with whom he had lunch.[24]

During the first hour after noon the marshal of the embassy
returned from the Porte. Half an hour after his return the
teşrifatçı, or chief master of ceremonies, sent by the grand vezir,
arrived at the camp. With him was the first dragoman, Kostaki

[24] Zinkeisen, *Geschichte*, 6:128–29, records that Zegelin was well-regarded by the
Russians and useful to them. Zegelin wrote Repnin on 19 October 1775 that
King Frederick had ordered him to postpone his departure until after Repnin's
arrival (*SRIO*, 15:423–24). Repnin was pleased to have the opportunity to
obtain Zegelin's views on the situation in Constantinople (*SRIO*, 15:440). The
Porte was not too pleased with Zegelin, and he did not receive a robe of honor
during his last audience with the grand vezir (*SRIO*, 15:544). When Zegelin
left his post he offered the Russians his mother-in-law's house in Izmir for
18,000 rubles. She was a Pizani, perhaps related to one of the Russian interpreters
of the same name (*SRIO*, 15:521–22).

Muruza, whom the ambassador received while sitting in an armchair. After hearing their compliments, which consisted of the vezir's congratulations on his safe arrival, he asked them to be seated on chairs, the *teşrifatçı* on his right and the dragoman on his left. Then they brought him coffee, confections, and sherbet. During these refreshments the *teşrifatçı* apologized in the name of the vezir in case there were any deficiencies in provisions or treatment, asking him to ascribe this to nothing other than their lack of understanding. He then expressed the wish of the vezir to see the ambassador soon, and asked when it would be convenient to make his entry. [The *teşrifatçı*] was answered with return compliments that, wishing to meet His Excellency the Vezir, [the ambassador] was prepared to enter the day after next, that is, 16 October, if from its side the Porte would make the necessary arrangements for an appropriate reception. To this the *teşrifatçı* replied that all was ready to receive him as the most esteemed and honored guest of the Porte. Whereupon they agreed that the entry would be on the designated day mentioned above. After this the *teşrifatçı* and the dragoman rose and, bidding farewell to the ambassador, brought him the usual gift of fruit and flowers from the vezir. They then departed from the headquarters, escorted by a few junior officers of the embassy.

15th. Orders were given to the entire entourage to be prepared for the entry on the following day. Rich livery was distributed and the order of march was drawn up.

At four o'clock, after luncheon, the ambassador learned through his dragomans, who had been at the Porte, and also through the second Turkish master of ceremonies, who was serving in the camp for certain internal assistance, that the present *çavuşbaşı* had had a severe attack of pleurisy which would prevent him from fulfilling the previously suggested rites, and that this incident had caused the Porte the greatest anxiety lest this prevent the entry of the ambassador and cause suspicion that it was contrived to diminish the honor due the ambassador. In order to avoid such suspicion, the Porte suggested, through these dragomans, that he send his own doctor to examine the patient. The ambassador answered that he was not in the least suspicious of the good faith of the Turkish ministry. In no way, however, could he agree to carry out the entry without the presence of the *çavuşbaşı* at the ceremony, according to the prescribed order. The ambassador wished personally either to postpone it until [the *çavuşbaşı's*] recovery, or to have another person appointed in his place immediately, and he dispatched dragoman Pizani with this answer. As soon as this was announced to His Majesty the Sultan, the latter at once appointed Said Efendi as *çavuşbaşı*. He had previously served twice in this rank and now had seniority over the present one and was his superior in all respects. At one in the morning the first dragoman of the Porte, Kostaki Muruza, arrived at the camp with this information. After reporting to the ambassador about the arrangements made by the sultan, he went on to Davut Pasha where the reception ceremony for the ambassador was to begin during the night of the fifteenth to sixteenth.

16th. The entire infantry detachment and all the people who were to march on foot were conducted to Davut Pasha and waited for the ambassador at the same tents under which tables had been prepared for him and his entourage.

At daybreak, that is, about seven o'clock, the ambassador set out in the parade carriages, but on approaching Davut Pasha he mounted his horse. Upon arriving at a small stream at eight-thirty o'clock he was met on this side by the Porte's interpreter. Having crossed the stream, a few paces beyond which there was a fountain, he met the *çavuşbaşı*. After the usual greetings and questions about health, the *çavuşbaşı* rode twenty paces ahead of the ambassador, accompanying him to the tents set up at Davut Pasha for serving lunch. Not far from there stood two janissary *ortas* in parade attire, while the Russian infantry was located right around the tents. When the ambassador rode up to them, he was saluted by dipping of the banner, playing of music, and beating of drums.[25]

Dismounting, he went into the tent, accompanied by the *çavuşbaşı* and his entourage, and seated himself on a sofa. Opposite him was the *çavuşbaşı*, while alongside at a little distance were the marshal and the secretaries of the embassy, and also as many cavaliers of the embassy as could be seated. At this time they began to bring coffee, confections, sherbets, and perfumes. When this ceremony had been performed, the interpreter of the Porte summoned first the marshal of the embassy and the secretaries of the embassy, and then the cavaliers, and escorted them to the tent in which tables had been prepared for them. The ambassador remained alone with the *çavuşbaşı*, having with him the Secretary of Oriental Languages Panaiodoros for translating the conversation between them. At half-past ten luncheon was served, at which the ambassador and the *çavuşbaşı* both sat on taborets. *Yemeklik* agas, the *masraf efendisi*, and other servants of the vezir waited on them. The table was covered with gold brocade and before the ambassador was a gold service.

The secretaries and the marshal of the embassy dined with the Porte's interpreter. Cavaliers of the embassy, various officers and other ranks, including the domestic servants, dined in separate tents. After luncheon they again brought coffee and perfumes.

Meanwhile, horses sent from the Porte and numbering 120 were accepted and inspected. In addition to this there were two horses brought from the sultan's stables for the ambassador, and both of them with fine, rich trappings. [The ambassador] rode one of them and the other was led by the reins. At 11:30, when the whole entourage had arranged itself in formation, the ambassador mounted his horse, and the march into the city began in the following order:

[25] This ceremony had been prearranged and was based on the precedent of 1740. Repnin wrote to Peterson on 17 September from Shumen, enclosing a copy of the 1740 ceremony. He instructed Peterson to insist that the earlier format should not be altered, and all details should be observed. These matters were fulfilled according to Repnin's wishes. See *SRIO*, 6:358–64 for a description of Rumiantsev's entry into the city in 1740, and Repnin's comments on it.

1. *Alay çavuşu*
2. Fifty *divan çavuşları*
3. *Asesbaşı*, with the people belonging to him
4. Four janissary kamor [humbaracı?] agas
5. The janissary *kapu kethudası* and the *subaşı* of Constantinople, with their people

Persons of the Embassy

9. Major Markov, as chief quartermaster
10. Two noncommissioned officers as fourriers
11. Hussar trumpeters
12. Hussar kettledrummer
13. Lieutenant Verderovskoi
14. Hussar detachment
15. Infantry music
16. Infantry detachment
17. Interpreter Bodisko
18. Two noncommissioned officers
19. Carriage with the second priest Leontii with four lackeys alongside, two on each side
20. Carriage with the first priest Dorofei with four lackeys alongside, two on each side
21. Cornet Brink, second master of the horse
22. Two noncommissioned officers

6. Two janissary *çorbacı*s with two janissary *orta*s that went on either side of the ambassadorial entourage. One of these was designated to maintain guard in his house, whereas the other was simply for the entry ceremony
7. The *turnacı* with his entourage
8. The *çavuşlar katibi* and the *çavuşlar emini* alongside

23. Four draft horses of the embassy in Turkish harness, each led by two *çuhadar*s
24. Sergeants of the Izmailovskii Guard Regiment, Princes Ukhtomskoi and Levashev
25. An empty carriage of the embassy, with pages at the reins, and six haiduks at the sides
26. The maître d'hôtel, mounted
27. Sixteen *çuhadar*s, two abreast
28. Two footmen
29. Thirty-six lackeys
30. Four jägers
31. Twelve singers
32. Thirteen waiters, mounted two abreast
33. Master of the Horse, Prince Kherkheulizev
34. Twelve draft horses in local harness
35. The student Dandrii[26] and the clerk Marklovskoi

[26] Dandrii was one of the four students who remained in Constantinople after the departure of the embassy, in order to continue the study of Turkish. The others were Vasili Ozerov, Ivan Ravich, and Anton Marinii (*SRIO* 15:519).

Interpreters

36. Hangerli and Shchepot'ev
37. Vilkens and Severin
38. Palladoklis and Loshkarev
39. Mel'nikov and Pizani
40. Kruta and Dandrii
41. Thirteen Greek officers in Russian uniform
42. Cornet Besh
43. Ensigns Berg and Lutaev
44. Second Lieutenants Rozendal and Kleman
45. Secretary of the embassy military staff Trashchinskii, and Captain Mansurov
46. Captain Marklovskoi and chief legal officer Alekseev
47. Captains Masalov and Shreder
48. Captains L'vov and Elchaninov
49. Director of the consular officer in Smyrna [Izmir], Ferrieri
50. Cornet Olsuf'ev and Second Lieutenant Novosil'tsov
51. Aide-de-camp Berg and Second Major Goven
52. Captain Lieutenant Count Razumovskoi and Premier Major Neledinskii-Meletskii
53. Premier Majors Sikstel' and Polikarpov
54. Lieutenant Captain of the Fleet Pleshcheev and Lieutenant Colonel Bok

55. The marshal of the embassy with his people
56. *Ahor kâhyası* with twenty *müteferrika* agas and about ten *sipahi* officers
57. The *silâhdar katibi* and the *silâhdar emini*
58. The *sipahiler katibi* and the *sipahiler emini*, with four agas of the *Bölükât-ı erbâa*
59. The dragoman of the Porte, with his *çuhadar*s
60. The *teşrifatçı efendi*, or the first master of ceremonies, with his people
61. The *kapıcıbaşı mihmandar*, with his people
62. The *Sipahiler Ağası* İsmail Bey and the *Silâhdar Ağası* Tahir, with their people
63. *Çavuşbaşı* Said Efendi in his parade turban, his people with him, rode in the middle of the road, twenty paces ahead of the ambassador
64. The ambassador. Next to him were six grenadiers of the Izmailovskii Guard Regiment, six haiduks, and eight runners
65. The two secretaries of the embassy
66. Secretary of Oriental Languages Panaiodoros and Adjutant General Rontsov

67. Aides-de-camp Igel'strom[27]
    and Soltykov
68. Medical officer Gokhfel'd
69. Six pages
70. Cuirassier trumpeters

71. Cuirassier kettledrums
72. Major Tutol'min, and
    following him, completing
    the march
73. A cuirassier detachment

In this order, with banners unfurled, music playing, drums beating, infantry with rifles at shoulder arms, the cavalry with carbines on the knee,[28] infantry officers with fixed bayonets, the cavalry with rifles instead of swords but without bayonets, turbans and divan attire on all the above-mentioned Turks, they entered Constantinople through the Edirne gate, came out in the Fener district, and after passing the suburb called Eyyub, arrived at *Ağa Çeşmesi* fountain at the end of the settlement. There the *çavuşbaşı* suggested to the ambassador that he rest, to which he agreed. He commanded his entire cortege to halt. He dismounted and was served coffee and sherbet. When he rose to mount his horse in order to continue on the way, the *çavuşbaşı* asked his permission to remove the large turban and ride through the open country in his ordinary one. The ambassador agreed to this with the understanding that when they began to approach Pera he would again put it on, which he in fact did, for the entry into Pera was carried out in the same order and formation as into Constantinople, but because it took place at seven o'clock in the evening they had to light torches. When they arrived at the house prepared for the ambassador, only he rode into the courtyard. The Turks, beginning with the *çavuşbaşı* himself, dismounted at the gate, crossed the courtyard on foot, and entered the quarters where

[27] Aide-de-camp Igel'strom was probably a son or younger relative of General Igel'strom, Abdülkerim's official escort. An aide-de-camp could not have a position higher than class nine, i.e., the rank of captain. Most aides were in class thirteen, according to the table of ranks of 1722 (*PSZ*, 6:486–93).

[28] Further description of Russian military ceremonies at the time are contained in the following documents: "II. 11.782 A. Marta 31 [11 April 1763]. Ustav voinskii o konnoi ekzertsitsii," *PSZ*, 16, supplement: 46–105, especially p. 51, par. 29, describing one of the salutes mentioned here, *karabin na koleno*; "I. 11.773. Marta 12 [23 March 1763]. Pekhotnyi stroevyi Ustav," *PSZ*, 16, supplement: 1–46, especially chap. 14, pp. 31–32, "O soliutatsii Ofitserskoi ruzh'em na meste i na pokhode," and chap. 15, pp. 32–33, "O znamennykh priemakh."

the ambassador, seated in an armchair, received them. Chairs were placed on both sides and the *çavuşbaşı* and various other Turkish officials were seated according to rank and were served coffee, confections, and various cold drinks. All retired after this, with decorous compliments from both sides.[29]

17th. After luncheon the interpreter of the Porte came to the ambassador with the sultan's fruit-server, the *yemişçibaşı*, and after first conveying appropriate compliments from the vezir and inquiring after the ambassador's health, he brought fruits and confections that had been sent him. Staying awhile, he presented [the ambassador] with a gift from the vezir consisting of articles of diamonds and a few pieces of rich brocade. In addition, he announced that he was also commissioned to congratulate the ambassadress, whereupon he was admitted to her presence and, after extending appropriate compliments in the name of the vezir, he presented both to her and to the princesses gifts from the same vezir, consisting of articles of diamonds and brocade materials.[30] On both of these visits the mentioned dragoman of the Porte was served coffee.

18th. Secretary of the embassy Vild was sent to the Porte in the morning, instructed to thank the vezir, his *kâhya*, and the *reis efendi* for the extraordinary courtesies shown the ambassador on the day of his arrival.

That morning, the ambassador's arrival was announced by the cavaliers of the embassy to the ambassadors residing in Constantinople, and by officers to ministers of second rank, namely: ambassadors, the French Marquis de Saint Priest, the Venetian Cavalier Gradenigo, Gospodin Weiler of Holland,

[29] Accommodations for Repnin in Constantinople had been arranged by Peterson. He secured the house of the former Danish envoy, in Pera. The Porte built additions for the ambassador and his family, and furnished two of the rooms, as was the custom for ambassadors extraordinary. Peterson also procured the sedan chair used by the ambassador. Wine for the household was purchased through local importers (*SRIO*, 5:165–66). A special dessert service was ordered from Viennese manufacturers through the Russian ambassador there, at a cost of 2,000 rubles (*SRIO*, 5:169–70).

[30] Repnin was not pleased with the gifts he and his family received and complained of the workmanship being European rather than Turkish. He also was critical of the quantity (*SRIO*, 15:435).

the Roman imperial internuncio, Gospodin Thugut; envoys, the Prussian Gospodin Zegelin, and Celsing of Sweden. With each of these cavaliers of the embassy and officers were two lackeys in rich embassy livery and one student of Oriental Languages. They responded to this message by each sending his secretary of the embassy or one of the cavaliers attached to it with just such a cortege and with salutatory compliments. Soon after this they came one after the other to pay a visit with their entire entourages and were received in ceremonial apartments.[31]

After luncheon all the aforesaid ambassadors and envoys, as well as the wives of the French and Venetian ambassadors and the Prussian envoy, visited the ambassadress, leading their entourages. They spent the evening playing cards.

19th. Before noon the ambassador, accompanied by his entourage, paid visits to the three ambassadors, and after luncheon to the envoys and wives of the ambassadors, and to the Prussian envoy Zegelin. The ambassadress did the same on her own behalf.

According to the preliminary agreement with the Porte regarding the ceremonial reception and entertainment of the ambassador, during both the visit to the vezir as well as the audience with the sultan, the former was set for 9 December.[32] As a result of this, at ten o'clock in the morning of the appointed day the ambassador left his house, carried on a sedan

[31] The representatives included the following:

France	François Emmanuel Guignart, Compte de Saint Priest
Venice	Bartolommeo Gradenigo
Netherlands	Weiker (or Weiler)
Austria	Johann Amadeus Franz de Paula, Freiherr v. Thugut
Prussia	Herr v. Zegelin
Sweden	Ulric Celsing (succeeded his brother Gustav in 1770)

The English ambassadors, not mentioned in the text, were John Murray until 25 May 1775, who was relieved because of illness. He died shortly after leaving his post. Anthony Hayes was his temporary replacement from May to October 1776. The new ambassador, Sir Robert Ainslee, was appointed in September 1775 and arrived at his post on 2 October 1776.

[32] This description of Repnin's visit to the grand vezir and the sultan is one of the few parts of the journal published by the Russian Imperial Historical Society. It was reproduced (in *SRIO*, 15:531–38), with minor alterations in language. The text is essentially that of Repnin's reports to Catherine from Pera, dated 15 December 1775. On this seven-week gap in the narrative see p. 35.

chair at the head of his entourage. The *kapıcıbaşı mihmandar* rode on horseback ahead of the sedan chair, with the *çorbacıbaşı* of the guard and his janissary *orta*, all in ceremonial turbans. Arriving at Tophane pier, he boarded a fourteen-oared caique sent by the Porte's *çavuşbaşı*. His entourage was accommodated in seventy six-oared caiques, also sent from the Porte. Arriving at the Constantinople side, the ambassador was met, as he alighted from the caique, by the *çavuşbaşı*, who led him to a specially prepared and appointed room not far away. There, while the entourage was going over the horses and getting into formation, they were refreshed with confections, coffee, rose water lavations, and smoking. When the whole entourage had mounted and arranged itself in formation, the ambassador left the room ahead of the *çavuşbaşı* and other Turkish officials who were there, and near the entrance mounted a richly outfitted horse also sent from the Porte. In all there were 120 of these horses besides the ambassador's. Then they set out in the following order:

1. The *alay çavuşu*
2. The *asesbaşı* with the janissary *orta*
3. The *subaşı*
4. Forty *çavuş*es
5. Major Markov as chief quartermaster
6. Four noncommissioned cavalry officers as fourriers
7. Four staff clerks
8. Captain L'vov as master of ceremonies
9. Sergeants Smirnov and Semenov
10. Cornet Brink, the second master of the horse
11. Noncommissioned officers Bukhanovskoi and Shchorba
12. Four draft horses in Turkish harness, each led by two *çuhadar*s
13. Twelve draft horses in European harness, levy hussars in rich livery
14. Hussar sergeant major
15. Maître d'hôtel
16. Sixteen *çuhadar*s, two abreast
17. Two unmounted footmen
18. Twenty-four lackeys
19. Thirteen waiters
20. Twelve Greek officers, two abreast
21. Fourteen students and interpreters, two abreast
22. Eighteen junior officers, two abreast

23. Four staff officers, two abreast
24. Ferrieri, the former agent of the fleet in Smyrna
25. The first master of the horse
26. Ten noblemen of the embassy, two abreast
27. Marshal of the embassy
28. Four *divan çavuşları*, assigned to the ambassador's person
29. The *çorbacı* guard
30. The *çavuşlar emini* and the *çavuşlar katibi*
31. The *kapıcıbaşı*
32. The pasha's *çavuş*, twenty paces ahead of the ambassador
33. The ambassador, around him six grenadiers of the

Izmailovskii Guard Regiment, six haiduks, four runners, two jägers
34. Following him, Gospodin Actual State Councillor Peterson, after him the Duc de Braganza, who wished to see the ceremony out of curiosity
35. Both secretaries of the embassy
36. The adjutant general and the first dragoman Pizani
37. Two aides-de-camp
38. The doctor and the medical officer
39. Two chamber pages
40. Four pages
41. Five noncommissioned officers
42. Several Turks in addition

Having ridden to the Porte via another courtyard, the whole entourage dismounted before coming to the entrance. The ambassador rode right up to the entrance and was received there by the Porte's interpreter, who along with the *çavuşlar emini* and the *çavuşlar katibi* went before him. They accompanied him into the reception chamber. The *teşrifatçı*, or first master of ceremonies, came to meet them on the stairs and likewise went before the ambassador. Entering the chamber, the ambassador stopped briefly at the door, not seeing the entrance of the vezir who entered at that very moment. When they came up to each other they bowed and after this went to their appointed places. Before seating himself, the ambassador handed the vezir the rescript from Her Imperial Majesty, which he received standing and placed on the cushion next to him. At the same time, a note from His Excellency Count

Nikita Ivanovich Panin was handed the vezir's *mektupçu*
[secretary] through one of the secretaries of the embassy, which
the *mektupçu* gave to the *reis efendi*, who likewise laid it on the
cushion next to the vezir.[33] After this, the vezir and the
ambassador sat down at the same time, one on a sofa and the
other on an armchair placed opposite. The chargé d'affaires
Gospodin Peterson sat on a taboret not far from the ambassador's armchair.

After a declamation of the usual Turkish greetings, the vezir
extended a proper welcome to the ambassador, inquiring after
the state of his health. Having completed the appropriate
courtesies on both sides, the ambassador apprised the vezir of
his commission in the following speech:

> Her Imperial Majesty, my sovereign most august, and most
> gracious, bestowing on me the character of her ambassador
> extraordinary and plenipotentiary in execution of the treaty
> of peace concluded, and confirmed by imperial ratification,
> between Her Imperial Majesty and His Majesty the Sultan,
> and their empires, has deigned to command me to bear
> witness most firmly to His Majesty the Sultan concerning
> the imperial intention of Her Imperial Majesty to preserve
> firmly and inviolably that sacred peace and the restored
> neighborly amity in the full measure of fidelty to all
> provisions of the treaty, which is the firm foundation
> thereto. Her Imperial Majesty hopes that His Majesty the
> Sultan also will always conform to it completely. Your
> Excellency knows that my most gracious and most august
> sovereign in her praiseworthy and peace loving sentiments
> has deigned to command me to make assurances of her
> imperial goodwill and has deigned to bestow this through
> this most gracious rescript, hoping that you will not refrain
> from assisting in every way and will lend every effort for
> the best maintenance of this treaty of peace inviolably ordained
> between both empires. I have here the honour of submitting
> to your excellency that imperial rescript, as well as the note
> of His Excellency Count Panin, who did not wish to fail to
> inform Your Excellency of all these matters, hoping that as
> a result you would lend every effort toward obtaining for
> me as soon as possible a gracious audience with His Majesty
> the Sultan. I commend myself otherwise to your benevolence,
> which I will consider an honor to merit, and to observe

---

[33] The text of Panin's note is found in *SRIO*, 135:375–76.

with assiduity everything which may increase the good
harmony between both empires on the basis of the
inviolably concluded provisions of the peace treaty.

When the dragoman of the Porte had translated this speech
to the vezir, [the vezir] then answered it personally. The dragoman of the Porte translated [the answer] for the ambassador;
it had the following content:

His Imperial Majesty, my most gracious and most august
sovereign, the refuge of the world, wishes to consolidate
and preserve that sacred peace concluded between both
empires. You may have no doubts that from our side the
utmost care and effort have been applied toward this very
thing, just as we have perceived with genuine satisfaction
that for this embassy was selected the person of Your
Excellency, in whom dwells the capacity and the industry to
further the common interests of both parties.

After this, they began to bring the vezir and the ambassador
confections, coffee, sherbet, rose water, and smoking articles.
They then served in the same manner the chargé d'affaires and
other officials of the ambassador's entourage, except for lavations and smoking materials, which they did not bring them.
At the conclusion of this ceremony they brought the ambassador a sable garment covered with brocade, which he put on
without rising from the armchair. They then clothed the
chargé d'affaires, the marshal, and the two secretaries of the
embassy in coats of sable [with the paws left on], covered with
cloth and trimmed with strips of the same sable fur. Ten
cavaliers of the embassy were clothed in ermine covered with
camlet. For the rest, one hundred caftans were distributed to
the ambassadorial entourage. As soon as this distribution was
completed, the entourage got into formation and the ambassador was informed of this. He then took leave of the vezir,
accompanied by those Turkish officials, except the *çavuşbaşı*,
who had conducted him to the visit and met him on his arrival
and escorted him now in the same order right to the landing
where all the Turks remained. Accompanied by the *çorbacı* and

his entourage who were the escort, he crossed over to Pera in the same boats on which they had crossed over to Tsar' Grad.[34]

In all, his stay at the vezir's was about an hour.

10th. At eleven o'clock in the morning the marshal and the secretaries of the embassy went to the Porte with presents from the ambassador. The first [the marshal] went to the vezir and the other two to his *kâhya* and to the *reis efendi*. They were received with every possible courtesy and served coffee and other things according to local custom. The secretaries of the embassy, however, who were with the *kâhya* and the *reis efendi*, were seated. They were each presented a gold watch with diamonds, and in addition to this, the marshal of the embassy was clothed in an ermine coat. The dragoman accompanying them was given three hundred *levok*s, and the people who carried the gifts were given four hundred and seventy *levok*s.

11th. About noon, that is, the day before the appointed audience with the sultan, gifts were brought to the saray [palace]. The junior officers Captain L'vov and Secretary Trashchinskii, and the interpreter Bodisko, as well as the gold-inlay craftsman Martini were sent with them, from whom the first and the last were left at the saray, one to guard the things which had been sent, and the other to arrange them in proper order.

At six o'clock in the morning on 12 December the ambassador was carried from the courtyard in a sedan chair to the Tophane landing with his entourage and the *kapıcıbaşı mihmandar*, who rode on horseback ahead of the sedan chair, and the *çorbacı* guard, in the same order as on the visit to the vezir. From there they crossed over in the caique of the *çavuşbaşı*, while the entourage was on the seventy caiques sent from the Porte.

[34] In regard to this meeting with the grand vezir, Repnin wrote to Catherine that it was the same as the one carried out by Count Rumiantsev in 1740, with the following changes, recorded in *SRIO*, 15:530: (1) the *çavuşbaşı* waited for Repnin at Tophane landing, and not vice-versa, (2) his entourage received more fur garments, but twenty fewer caftans, (3) Repnin handed Catherine's rescript to the grand vezir while he was standing, (4) Panin's note was refused by the grand vezir, and was then given to him by his first secretary, the *mektupçu*.

On arriving at the other side, the ambassador went straight
to the same chamber in which he had stopped on the day of the
visit to the vezir. At the entrance he was met and conducted
upstairs by the *çavuşbaşı*, who was waiting for him there. The
ambassador remained there about an hour so as not to wait on
the street. He had mounted messengers to notify him when the
gate of the saray opened and the vezir was ready to go there.
In the meantime, the entourage was mounting and arranging
itself in the order of march, while the *çavuşbaşı* was serving the
ambassador coffee, confections, and other things.

When the *çavuşbaşı* received news that it was time to go, he
informed the ambassador. They mounted and set out, departing in the very same order as when they had gone to the vezir
—the *çavuşbaşı* twenty paces ahead of the ambassador, and after
him both secretaries of the embassy with the imperial rescript
of Her Imperial Majesty.

When they had come opposite the Porte, between it and the
sultan's pavilion, the ambassador and his entourage stood in
one line along the wall of the saray, giving room to pass to the
vezir, who in a few minutes rode by with his entire entourage.[35]
After his passage, the embassy entourage formed itself into the
previous order and marched without stopping to the saray
itself. There, going to the second gate, the ambassador dismounted at the vestibule on the right and was met there by the
Porte's interpreter.[36] Instead of waiting on a bench in this gate
until they conducted him to the divan, as all ambassadors
usually do, he was taken to the room of the *kapıcıbaşı* guards,
which was specially furnished with sofas for this occasion.
There the *çavuşbaşı* and the interpreters of the Porte entertained
the ambassador and stayed with him without leaving until it

[35] The text printed here was sent to Catherine in a later report. Repnin com-
mented on the meeting, saying that he had been received with coolness. The
grand vezir was late, and Repnin was forced to wait in the street as he rode by.
As he passed Repnin, he turned away so as not to have to recognize him. Repnin
responded by engaging those about him in conversation (*SRIO*, 15:539).
[36] For detailed descriptions and diagrams see Barnette Miller, *Beyond the Sublime
Porte*.

was announced that it was time to go to the divan. The *çavuşbaşı* preceded the ambassador, striking the pavement with a silver staff. The embassy entourage went ahead of him, while behind the ambassador were both secretaries of the embassy with the imperial rescript. Thirty paces from the gate on the right side of the way a thousand janissaries were standing. Once the ambassador passed by, they threw themselves at the food which had been set out for them. On the left side were standing several draft horses, among which were a few with diamond-studded harnesses.

Before they came to the chamber of the divan, the *kapıcılar kâhyası* came out to meet [the ambassador] and proceeded with the *çavuşbaşı* on the left side. He too had a silver staff in his hands with which he struck the pavement, alternating with the *çavuşbaşı*, and in this manner the ambassador entered the divan. At the same time the vezir entered through other doors and seated himself at the usual place,[37] while the ambassador seated himself on a taboret which had been placed for him opposite.[38] Then the vezir sent his interpreter to the ambassador to ask after his health. After an answer had been given thereto by the ambassador, along with the appropriate salutations from him, the ambassador sent him the Porte's interpreter. The vezir was delaying in inviting the ambassador to the *nişancı* bench, in accordance with the treaty. The ambassador instructed the interpreter to say that the ambassador would go there himself if this invitation from him were delayed. For this reason the Porte's interpreter came to him immediately to ask him in the name of the vezir to the *nişancı* bench. As a result of this, he crossed over from there and sat down in the middle on the right side of the *nişancı*. Then the court began and lasted not more than half an hour. At its conclusion the vezir sent the *reis efendi* to the sultan with a written report concerning the ambassador's admission. When the *reis efendi* returned with the

[37] Here again the diplomatic game is indulged in, with neither side wishing to enter the room first (*SRIO*, 15:539).

[38] The text omits the fact that the grand vezir did not bow in recognition of Repnin, who sat down without looking at the grand vezir (*SRIO*, 15:539).

sultan's firman, tables were set. The ambassador dined alone
with the vezir.[39] With the *kapudan paşa* were the marshal, the
two secretaries of the embassy and the Duc de Braganza, who
was present among the cavaliers of the embassy. They dined at
the tables of the *nişancı* and the *defterdar*. During the luncheon
the imperial rescript was held alternately by the noblemen of
the embassy. On conclusion of the luncheon the ambassador
returned to the *nişancı* bench and there various other Turkish
customs, such as washing and smoking, were observed.[40] After
this, the ambassador was led out and seated on a bench halfway
between the divan and the last gate of the saray. At this place
he was clothed in a sable coat covered with brocade, whereas
the marshal and the secretaries were clothed in ermine. One
hundred caftans were distributed to the entourage. During this,
several of the sultan's masters of the horse rode by in front of
the ambassador on rather richly outfitted horses.

After sitting on this bench about a quarter of an hour the
vezir went to the sultan, and a little while later the ambassador
himself was conducted there. At the last doors presents were
held by the *bostancıs*. There two *kapıcıbaşıs* took the ambassador
by the arms, along with his entourage of sixteen men, each of
whom was led by two *kapıcıbaşıs*, with only the Porte's interpreter ahead of the ambassador.

On entering the chamber where the sultan sat on the throne,
and after bowing three times, the ambassador delivered the
following speech:

> On the occasion of the felicitiously concluded, sacred peace
> between Her Imperial Majesty, my most august and most
> gracious sovereign, and Your Majesty the Sultan, and both
> exalted empires, the All-Russian and the Ottoman, fortified
> by mutual sovereign imperial ratifications, and in accordance

[39] Before the luncheon the Russian was allowed to wash only after the grand
vezir. Repnin let this pass without comment. After lunch, however, the grand
vezir received a white towel and Repnin one of a dark color. He did not over-
look this. He dropped the dark cloth on the floor and took out a white one from
his pocket. The vezir noticed this. Conversation at the table was indifferent and
of few words (*SRIO*, 15:540).
[40] Repnin received his rose water and smoking items almost last. He refused,
therefore, to accept either (*SRIO*, 15:540).

with and fulfillment thereof, Her Imperial Majesty, bestowing
on me the character of her ambassador extraordinary and
plenipotentiary, has deigned to command me to bear
witness most firmly to Your Majesty the Sultan concerning
the genuine intention of Her Imperial Majesty to preserve
firmly and inviolably that sacred peace and restored
neighborly amity in the full measure of fidelity to all
provisions of that treaty of peace inviolably concluded and
solemnly strengthened by imperial ratifications, serving as
the foundation to the present good accord of the two
exalted empires. Her Imperial Majesty hopes that Your
Majesty the Sultan is pleased to be possessed of such
benevolent and peace-loving sentiments, with a genuine
intention for the inviolable maintenance of this sacred peace
in all its provisions, as is attested to in the imperial rescript
of Her Imperial Majesty to Your Majesty the Sultan. I
personally consider it a signal honor that I have the good
fortune to present myself before Your Majesty the Sultan,
and I will consider myself even more fortunate if I will have
been found worthy during the time of my sojourn here to
bear the favor of Your Majesty the Sultan, which I will
endeavor to merit with all possible diligence toward
increasing the good harmony between both exalted
empires, on the basis of the treaty of eternal and sacred
peace concluded between them.

The rescript was received by the *kapudan paşa*, who handed
it to the vezir. He placed it next to the sultan.

After the translation of the ambassador's speech by the
Porte's interpreter, the sultan said a few words in a loud voice
to the vezir, who replied:

His Imperial Majesty, my most gracious and most august
sovereign, the emperor, the refuge of the world, has
commanded me to inform you that it is his imperial will
that the treaty of peace concluded between his empire and
the All-Russian empire should be preserved and fulfilled
forever.

When the Porte's interpreter had translated this, the ambassador, after bowing to the sultan, departed from the audience
chamber, and after him the whole entourage.

The *kapıcıbaşı* and various others who were with him at the
audience led the ambassador to the place where they took them
by the arm. The ambassador, preceded by his *mihmandar*, the

kapıcıbaşı, the *çavuşlar emini*, the *çavuşlar katibi* and the *çorbacı*
guard, was escorted to the chamber of the *kapıcıbaşı* guards
and waited there, not on his horse as is the custom with other
ambassadors, until all the lesser ranks such as the aga of the
janissaries, the *kapıcıbaşı*s and various others in the saray rode
away. When he was apprised that the vezir was already leaving,
then he left the room and mounted his horse so as to leave
immediately thereafter for the return trip. He did this in the
same formation in which he arrived, except that the *çavuşbaşı*
did not accompany him.[41]

The ambassador and his entourage rode in the fur garments
and caftans that had been given them up to the turn in the
saray wall where they removed them and returned home,
accompanied in the same manner as from the visit to the
vezir.[42]

---

[41] Once again, as Repnin was leaving, the grand vezir passed by without recog-
nizing him, and Repnin ignored his host. Repnin did make a point of bowing to
the *reis efendi*, who was the only one who showed him any courtesy during the
audience (*SRIO*, 15:540–41).

[42] Repnin reported that the audience with the sultan was carried out in the same
manner as that of Count Rumiantsev in 1740, with some of the same type of
minor differences recorded in note 34; see *SRIO*, 15:531.

*A description of the ceremonial entertainments which took place at
the Ottoman Porte, given by the Grand Vezir and sundry Turkish
Ministers to Her Imperial Majesty's ambassador extraordinary and
plenipotentiary, General in Chief, Lieutenant Colonel of the
Izmailovskii Guard Regiment and Cavalier of various orders,
Prince Nikolai Vasil'evich Repnin; likewise of the farewell audience
with His Majesty the Sultan, the farewell visit with the Grand Vezir
and, in conclusion, of the departure of the Ambassador from
Constantinople on the twenty-fourth day of April in this year 1776.*

The first luncheon was at the vezir's on the eighth day of
February in rooms at the Porte where the sultan holds receptions when he arrives there.

It had been proposed that this luncheon would take place in
tents in one of the residences of the sultan beyond the city
called Saadabad, but in consideration of the winter and the cold,
the likes of which were almost beyond recollection in Constantinople, he was entertained at the Porte in accordance with
a preliminary agreement of the ambassador thereto in the
following manner.

On the day before, that is, 7 February, his *mihmandar,*
Kapıcıbaşı Ahmet Bey, and the dragoman of the Porte, Kostaki
Muruza, came to the ambassador to invite him to the vezir's
for luncheon on the following day. As a consequence of this
the ambassador, on the appointed day, was carried from the
courtyard on a sedan chair at 8:30 in the morning to the
Tophane pier, preceded by his *mihmandar,* the *kapıcıbaşı,* and
the *çorbacı* of the guard with his janissary *orta,* and accompanied by his own entourage. There he boarded a fourteen-
oared caique of the *çavuşbaşı,* while his entourage was distributed among forty other caiques sent from the Porte. On these
they went over to the batardella galley of the *kapudan paşa,*
standing opposite the pier, at the ladder of which he was met
and received by the pasha commanding it. He was conducted to
the main stateroom where he was seated on a rich sofa that had
been prepared for him, and was served coffee, sherbet, and

smoking articles. A large part of his entourage was also present during this time and was entertained in various ways. As soon as he boarded the galley the anchor was weighed and a large flag hoisted, while the entire galley was decked out with penants. There were no volleys in this instance because of the occurrence of a holiday for the birth of a daughter to the sultan, and the minor holiday following immediately thereon, and because the prohibition against firing from cannon in the port of Constantinople and the channel had been renewed because of the pregnancy of still another sultana.

After sailing on this galley about half an hour, the ambassador informed the commander of his wish to return again to the caique so as to cross over more quickly. As a result of this the anchor was dropped and the ambassador and all his entourage boarded the caique, and the commander of the galley himself also made the transfer so as to accompany him to the Porte. Such a courtesy had not been shown before. On reaching the Constantinople side, they found sixty horses ready there, in addition to the richly outfitted one for the ambassador sent from the vezir. They mounted and rode to the Porte, the ambassador preceded by the pasha of the galley, and the *kapıcıbaşı* who was his *mihmandar* who rode at the pasha's left. Before they came within thirty paces of the Porte, janissaries and persons of various rank at the Porte were drawn up in two files. Riding to the same place as on the day of the visit at the vezir's, the ambassador dismounted and was received there by the Porte's interpreter. After he ascended a few steps of the interior entrance, the *teşrifatçı efendi* met him and led him to the pavilion of the sultan designated for the reception. As soon as he entered, the vezir came in at the same time from the other side, preceding the *reis efendi*, the *çavuşbaşı*, and all the distinguished ranks of the Porte except the vezir's *kâhya*, who was absent because of illness. The vezir, standing, bowed to the ambassador and asked him to be seated next to him on the sofa.

Although an armchair was prepared for [the ambassador], [the vezir] gave him a choice of places to sit, saying that he wished to have [the ambassador] closer to himself. The ambassador answered that he preferred the sofa for the reason that he wished to be closer to the vezir. Thereupon, both seated themselves next to each other at the same time. A little farther away on the other side of the vezir sat the *reis efendi*, the *çavuşbaşı*, and the two *tezkireci efendi*s. Right after this they brought the vezir and the ambassador pipes, then coffee. At the same time the ambassador's entourage was invited to go to other rooms, set off for them according to rank, and in which they were served in the same courteous manner according to the Turkish custom.

The vezir, extending a welcome to the ambassador by asking him to be the master in his home and to order whatever he wished, inquired whether he wished the games and amusements that he had prepared for [the ambassador's] entertainment to begin. The ambassador answered with a courteous compliment, whereupon the vezir ordered the games to begin. These were performed in the courtyard beneath the windows of the pavilion where the vezir and the ambassador were sitting. They consisted of dancing in the Asiatic tradition and that of various Greek islands. As they continued, the vezir and the ambassador conversed in a mutually courteous and amicable manner.

About eleven o'clock in the morning the vezir asked the ambassador to tell him the time at which he usually lunched so that he could order the table to be prepared at that hour, because being determined to entertain that day with a table which would be pleasant for his guest, he did not wish to burden him with any change in his daily habits. The ambassador, thanking the vezir in a decorous manner for his courtesy, answered that, since he was experiencing the utmost pleasure in being entertained by such an esteemed and benevolent host, he would forgo all his own customs and asked the vezir not to feel constrained in any way. Therefore, he himself should determine the time for the luncheon. A short while after these declarations, articles for washing their hands were brought to

the ambassador and the vezir, and about half an hour after noon
a table was brought to the sofa. In addition to the two, the
reis efendi also sat at [the table] and they ate lunch. A service was
placed before the ambassador, that is, a spoon, knife, and fork
of gold set with diamonds; and the plates that he was given
were all gold. During the luncheon the vezir continued to
show every courtesy to the ambassador and make every effort
to entertain him. At this time, separate tables were set in other
rooms for the secretaries and the marshal of the embassy, for
the noblemen of the embassy, for staff and junior officers, for
chancellery ranks, and, finally, for the waiters and liverymen
too. Everyone was served according to his rank and calling
and entertained lavishly and with every kind of courtesy.

At the completion of the vezir's and the ambassador's
luncheon, they were brought at one time articles to wash their
hands, and then coffee, rose water, and smoking articles. Then
the *reis efendi* retired, and the vezir, after sitting a little while,
asked the ambassador's permission to absent himself for the
purpose of attending to his prayers. Receiving a decorous
answer to this, he ordered that they begin to enact the comedy
in the courtyard at this time for the amusement of the ambassador. When this was begun, [the vezir] rose and went to his
room, leaving behind the *teşrifatçı efendi*, the Porte's interpreter,
and various officials. When some ten minutes had elapsed, the
vezir returned, again begging forgiveness of the ambassador
that he was compelled to leave him. He commanded the
acrobats to begin their acts, which lasted more than half an
hour. Then the vezir asked the ambassador whether he would
not find it an amusing change to see the magicians, who were
conducted into the very pavilion where the ambassador and the
vezir were sitting. This also lasted about half an hour. After
this, two boys who sang Arabian songs were brought in.

As the time for the prayer called *ikindi* drew near, the ambassador ordered that the vezir be told that [the ambassador]
wished not to detain him from the fulfilment of his duty, and
also that he feared hisurb presence would dist [the vezir],

especially since he was aware that the vezir was not very well at that time and had not yet fully recovered from the attack of podagra which had befallen him; [the ambassador] therefore asked to be excused for not staying longer. He thanked the vezir for all the honors and courtesies that had been accorded him. The vezir replied that the presence of the ambassador could not be a burden to him and that on the contrary it cured his podagra altogether. At the same time, however, since the ambassador might already be uneasy, he did not wish to detain him. Following this, sherbet and smoking articles were brought to the vezir and the ambassador. Simultaneously he was clothed in a sable coat covered with cloth, in the pocket of which three kerchiefs had been placed and in which was wound a gold watch set with diamonds. The marshal and the secretaries of the embassy received ermine coats and two kerchiefs each. The cavaliers of the embassy, the master of the horse, and three dragomans were clothed in camlet caftans called *kerrâke* and each was likewise given two kerchiefs. The pasha of the galley, the *kapıcıbaşı*, and the Porte's dragoman received caftans. After this, the vezir and the ambassador, expressing to each other their polite regards, rose at one time and each went his own way, the vezir to his rooms, accompanied by the *reis efendi*, the *çavuşbaşı*, and various other persons of rank at the Porte who had gathered there at this time, while the ambassador prepared for his departure.

The ambassador was accompanied from the Porte in the same manner as he had been received, by the *teşrifatçı efendi*, the interpreter of the Porte, and then various other officials thereof, and rode to the pier, preceded by the pasha of the galley, and by his *mihmandar* the *kapıcıbaşı*. When he arrived at the pier, the vezir's master of the horse announced to him that the horse which he was riding, with all its accoutrements, was being presented to him by the vezir, for which the ambassador ordered him to extend his thanks and went to the caique. On this he crossed over to the galley. There its commander, the above-mentioned pasha, notified in advance of his arrival, met

him and seated him at the same place as when he went to the
Porte and served the ambassador coffee, rose water, and smoking articles, as before. Then when the anchor was dropped as
they neared the pier, the pasha accompanied the ambassador to
the ladder, and he returned about six o'clock in the evening to
Tophane in the caiques used previously. He was accompanied
by the *kapıcıbaşı*, and the *çorbacı* guard with his janissary *orta*,
and the entire embassy entourage.

An ermine coat which had been made for Gospodin Actual
State Councillor Peterson was sent to him at his house by the
vezir. He was not present at the festivities because of illness.

The second luncheon was the *kapudan paşa*'s on 15 February,
in the sultan's palace called Aynalı Kavak.

Because of several repairs at the arsenal and, further, lack of
sufficient space there for the games and entertainments prepared
for this luncheon, the *kapudan paşa* sent the admiralty interpreter Mavroyiani and his own *kapıcılar kâhyası* on 13 February
to invite the ambassador and all his entourage to luncheon on
the fifteenth of that month, at the above-mentioned palace of
the sultan. Thus, on the appointed day toward the end of the
tenth hour in the morning, the ambassador, in his decorations,
left the courtyard, preceding his *mihmandar* the *kapıcıbaşı*, and
the *çorbacı* guard with his janissary *orta*. He was accompanied
by Gospodin Actual State Councillor Peterson and the whole
entourage to the Tophane pier where he boarded the fourteen-
oared caique of the *kapudan paşa*, having with him the mentioned actual state councillor. The remainder of the entourage
was situated in other caiques, the number of which was sixty.
As they sailed past the admiralty, trumpeters had been brought
on board the disarmed warships standing there, and they played
their trumpets for the ambassador's passage. This was repeated
also on his return.

On arriving at Aynalı Kavak, the interpreters of the Porte
and the admiralty, the *kapıcılar kâhyası* of the *kapudan paşa*, a
host of admiralty officers, the vezir of the agas, and other main
persons in the house of the *kapudan paşa* arranged themselves

with the junior officials alongside and the senior officials in front of the ambassador. They led him to the room designated for the reception. Along the passage several hundred persons of various naval ranks were in formation on either side. He was met by the *teşrifatçı efendi* on the interior stairway. Just as the ambassador entered the room, the *kapudan paşa* appeared at another door at the very same moment, surrounded by his entourage, which consisted of the most distinguished persons of naval rank. Approaching one another with an even step, they bowed and greeted each other with mutual courtesy. After which the *kapudan paşa* asked the ambassador to be seated in an armchair upholstered in velvet and covered with gold braid. Gospodin Peterson was invited to take a chair placed a short way from the ambassador's armchair. The *kapudan paşa* himself, however, sat on a sofa in accordance with the custom, and next to him, a short distance away, was the *tersane emini*, that is, the ranking officer of the admiralty. Then pipes and coffee were brought simultaneously to the ambassador, the *kapudan paşa*, and Gospodin Peterson. After this, the marshal, secretaries, cavaliers of the embassy, as well as others, were requested to go to the special rooms that had been designated for them.

After some conversation between the ambassador and the *kapudan paşa*, Turkish comedies with dances were begun. In order [for the ambassador] to see them the *kapudan paşa* invited the ambassador to a pavilion located near the room where they were sitting. On repairing there the ambassador seated himself on a sofa next to the *kapudan paşa*, but at his right hand, while Gospodin Peterson sat on a chair. When it came time for the midday prayer, the *kapudan paşa* requested of the ambassador permission to absent himself for the fulfillment of his duty, suggesting to him in the meantime to view the palace and garden if he wished. Whereupon they rose together. The ambassador, accompanied by the *teşrifatçı efendi*, the interpreters of the Porte and the admiralty, and a few officials of the *kapudan paşa*, as well as his own entourage, went to view the palace while the *kapudan paşa* departed to the interior rooms.

Half an hour later they met again in that room where a table had been set and where the ambassador found the *kapudan paşa* standing, awaiting him. The ambassador, the *kapudan paşa*, Actual State Councillor Peterson, and the *tersane emini* ate at this table. The ambassador sat at the right hand of the *kapudan paşa*, Gospodin Peterson next to the ambassador, and the *tersane emini* next to the *kapudan paşa*. A gold service studded with diamonds had been set before the ambassador, whereas silver was placed before Gospodin Peterson. The ambassador had gold plate before him and the actual state councillor had silver. At table the *kapudan paşa* treated the ambassador with all possible courtesy and politeness. The marshal and the secretaries of the embassy, the noblemen of the embassy, persons of chancellery rank, and sundry officers lunched in other rooms at various tables. The Porte's interpreter and the *kapıcılar kâhyası* of the *kapudan paşa* lunched with the former in order to serve them, while officials of the *kapudan paşa* were placed at other tables, scrupulously ensuring that [the Russians] were courteously and abundantly served.

At the conclusion of the luncheon, during which Turkish chamber music was played, the ambassador and the *kapudan paşa* were brought smoking articles and coffee, as well as rose water to wash their hands; the same was done for the other two present with them. After this, they went back to the former pavilion, from which they watched the continuing games and where as before the ambassador sat on the sofa at the right hand of the *kapudan paşa*.

Every kind of refreshment in the Turkish custom, such as serving coffee, sherbet, washing with rose water, and smoking was also observed with the marshal, the secretaries, noblemen, and persons of other rank in the embassy. About four o'clock in the afternoon, when all observances had been fulfilled by the *kapudan paşa* with all possible complaisance, courtesy, and kindness, the ambassador ordered that it be suggested, along with appropriate compliments, that it was time for him to be returning home. Whereupon the *kapıcıbaşı*, returning his compliments, with regrets that the ambassador was leaving so soon, ordered sherbet, rose water, and smoking articles to be brought. On completing this ceremony, the *teşrifatçı efendi*, approaching the ambassador, announced that the *kapudan paşa* was presenting him a horse with all trappings. In addition they brought him two Algerian blankets as well as two from the island of Chios, and two kerchiefs. The actual state councillor was presented with a brace of pistols and two kerchiefs. Two kerchiefs each were given to the marshal, the secretaries and cavaliers of the embassy, and one each to the other ranks. The ambassador expressed his gratitude for this as well as for the other courtesies shown him, and rose. The *kapudan paşa* rose at the same moment, and they left the pavilion side by side. Following this, the ambassador, having taken leave in a proper manner, left for the pier, while the *kapudan paşa* retired to the inner rooms. The ambassador was accompanied to the caique in the same manner and to the same places as when he was met.

Returning to Tophane on the caique on which he had come, the ambassador found there the horse that had been presented to him by the *kapudan paşa*. He returned home at 4:30 in the afternoon.

The third luncheon was at the vezir's *kâhya*, on the bank of Tsar' Grad port in the sultan's palace called Valide Saray, on 22 February.

Two days in advance, that is, on 20 February, the *kâhya* of the vezir's *kâhya* came to the ambassador to invite him to luncheon on the twenty-second of that month. Whereupon, on the appointed day the ambassador, with all his entourage, accompanied by his *mihmandar*, the *kapıcıbaşı*, and the *çorbacı* of the guard with his janissary *orta*, went to Tophane pier where he boarded the fourteen-oared caique that belonged to the vezir's *kâhya* and that was sent by him, while his entourage was in fifty caiques also sent by him, and made the trip in the same way as they did going to the two previous luncheons. Arriving at the pier of Valide Sarayı about 10:30, he was met by the Porte's interpreter and the *kâhya* of the vezir's *kâhya* with other

officials of his house, and on the interior stairway [he was met]
by the *teşrifatçı efendi* and was conducted to the room designated for his reception. In it near the door were standing
persons of distinguished ranks of the Porte, namely: the two
tezkirecis, the *beylikçi*, and the *mektupçu*, while before him was
the vezir's *kâhya* himself. He bowed courteously to the ambassador and in a decorous manner invited him to sit on the sofa
at the first place on his right side. When the ambassador sat
down, the vezir's *kâhya* did the same. Next to the ambassador,
a little way away, the marshal and the two secretaries of the
embassy were seated at taborets. The two *tezkirecis*, the
beylikçi, and the *mektupçu*, however, were seated on a special
sofa a little way from the *kâhya* bey. Immediately after this,
coffee and pipes were brought, and when they had been sitting
a little while, musicians were brought into the same room, and
during the playing of the music various local dances were
begun. As the time of the midday prayer drew near, the vezir's
kâhya requested permission of the ambassador to absent himself for it, suggesting to him that if he wished he could view
the palace during this time. The ambassador assented, rising
from his place, which the *kâhya* also did at the same time, and
both went their ways simultaneously, the ambassador accompanied by the *teşrifatçı efendi*, the *kapıcıbaşı*, the Porte's interpreter, and sundry other Turkish officials. After a quarter of an
hour they said that the vezir's *kâhya* had finished his prayers
and was awaiting him in the previous room, where he returned
and found a set table behind which the vezir, standing, asked
him to be seated at the first place at his right hand. The service
placed before the ambassador was gold plated, as were the
plates, and the two lunched at their table, while at another
table in a separate room the secretaries of the embassy lunched
with the *kâhya* of the vezir's *kâhya* and the dragoman of the
Porte. The cavaliers and persons of other rank of the embassy
were also entertained at various tables, and all of them lavishly
and cordially.

After the luncheon the usual ceremony was carried out, that

is, they washed their hands and received rose water and smoking articles. After that, the vezir's *kâhya* asked the ambassador to go to another room in order to see from there them dance in the courtyard and walk on tightropes; the ambassador went and was again seated at the first place on the sofa. At the same time and in that very room other games were begun, which lasted until three o'clock in the afternoon. Then, the ambassador ordered that an appropriate compliment be made to the vezir's *kâhya*, thanking him for his courteousness and adding that he did not wish to disturb him further. Where-upon the vezir's *kâhya*, offering a polite answer, called for sherbet, rose water, and smoking articles. On completion of this, the *teşrifatçı efendi* brought the ambassador three kerchiefs from the vezir's *kâhya* announcing that in addition the vezir's *kâhya* was presenting him a horse with accoutrements, which they were exercising in the courtyard. The marshal, secretaries, and noblemen of the embassy were each given two kerchiefs, while the others of the ambassadorial entourage were each given one. The *kapıcıbaşı*, the *teşrifatçı efendi*, and the dragoman of the Porte were clothed in *ferace*s [fur-lined robes]. After this, the ambassador rose, and the vezir's *kâhya* did also and ac-companied the ambassador to the door during his leave taking. The persons of other ranks were accompanied to the place where they had been met.

The ambassador returned to his house in Pera in the same manner in which he came from there and found at his house the horse presented to him by the vezir's *kâhya*.

The fourth luncheon was at the Janissary Aga's in the sultan's palace called Bahâriye, on 29 February.

The ceremony of this luncheon was carried out on the basis of the one given before it by the vezir's *kâhya*. For which reason, two days before, that is, on the twenty-seventh, the *baş ezancı efendi* of the janissary corps came to the ambassador to invite him to it on the twenty-ninth. On the aforesaid day the ambassador, following the previous order and having with him the *kapıcıbaşı* and the *çorbacı* with his *orta* of janissaries,

crossed in the fourteen-oared caique sent by the Janissary Aga.
Arriving at the pier of the above-mentioned palace, he was met
there by the Porte's interpreter, the *kâhya* of the Janissary Aga,
and the *baş ezancı efendi*, who led him through the officials of
the janissary corps, standing some four hundred strong along
either side up to the room designated for the reception. There
the Janissary Aga himself, along with the main persons of rank
among the janissaries, met him. After the usual greetings, he
asked him to be seated on the sofa at his right hand and at the
first place. The marshal and the secretaries of the embassy were
seated on taborets. Following this was the serving of coffee and
proffering of pipes. During the midday prayer the ambassador
went as before to view the palace. After this, he lunched alone
with the Janissary Aga; the marshal and the secretaries of the
embassy lunched with the Porte's interpreter and with the
kâhya of the Janissary Aga. The games and entertainments
were the same as during the luncheon at the vezir's *kâhya*. On
conclusion of all ceremonies, the *teşrifatçı efendi* announced to
the ambassador that the Janissary Aga had presented him a
horse with all its trappings, which was being exercised at the
windows in front of them, and brought him in addition three
kerchiefs. The marshal, the secretaries, and the noblemen of the
embassy were each given two kerchiefs. Persons of other ranks
each received one. After this, the ambassador took leave of the
Janissary Aga and rode away in the same order as from the
vezir's *kâhya*, accompanied by the same people and to the same
places as was done on his arrival. He returned to his house in
the previous caiques about four o'clock in the afternoon.

The fifth luncheon was at the *defterdar*'s, in the sultan's
palace called Kâğıthane, on 7 March.

On the fifth the *cizye baş bakı kulu*, that is, one of the pursers
subordinate to the *defterdar*, was sent by the *defterdar* to invite
the ambassador to this luncheon on the seventh. On the
appointed day the ambassador, accompanied by the *kapıcıbaşı*,
and the *çorbacı* of the guard with his janissary *orta*, arrived at the
Tophane pier and departed from there on the fourteen-oared

caique sent by the *defterdar*. His entourage was on another fifty caiques sent by him also. They arrived at the place of the entertainment where he was met at the pier by the Porte's interpreter, the *baş bakı kulu*, the *kâhya*, and other officials of the department and house of the *defterdar*. The *teşrifatçı efendi* came to meet him at the interior entrance and, joining the persons of rank indicated previously, escorted the ambassador to a room designated for his regalement, where the *defterdar* himself, standing, awaited and received him. After they had executed mutual bows and greetings, the ambassador was seated on a sofa at the first place. The marshal and the secretaries of the embassy were also seated on taborets. Before the luncheon the ambassador, accompanied by the *teşrifatçı efendi*, the *kapıcıbaşı*, and the interpreter of the Porte, went to view the palace while the *defterdar* attended the midday prayer. Following this, the ambassador lunched with the *defterdar*, the marshal and secretaries of the embassy with the *defterdar*'s *kâhya* and the Porte's interpreter. The cavaliers of the embassy and the remainder of the embassy entourage also lunched at separate tables. Games and entertainments in the local manner went on without interruption. Before the departure the ambassador was presented a horse with trappings, and in addition to this three kerchiefs. The marshal, the secretaries, and the cavaliers were each presented two kerchiefs, while the other ranks received one each. During the return the ambassador was accompanied by the same people and to the same places where they met him, in exactly the same manner as at the previous ceremonial luncheons.

The sixth luncheon was the *reis efendi*'s, on the Asiatic bank, in the sultan's palace called Küçük Göksu, on 14 March.

Two days beforehand the *kesedar efendi* had come from the *reis efendi* to invite the ambassador to this luncheon, to which Her Imperial Majesty's extraordinary envoy and minister plenipotentiary currently in residence at the Porte, Gospodin Stakhiev, had also been invited. On the fourteenth the ambassador, along with the mentioned envoy and the *kapıcıbaşı*, as

well as the *mihmandar* of the envoy Stakhiev, a *gedikli zaim*, and
both the ambassador's and the envoy's *çorbacı*s of the guard
with their janissary *orta*s, left Tophane pier. With him in the
fourteen-oared caique sent by the *reis efendi* was the envoy,
while the entourage was in fifty other caiques also sent by him.
On his arrival at the aforesaid palace, the ambassador was met
at the pier by the *kesedar efendi*, the Porte's interpreter, and
other officials of the house of the *reis efendi*. The *teşrifatçı efendi*
met him at the interior entrance, and in the room intended for
his entertainment the *reis efendi* himself received him while
standing, having with him both *tezkireci*s, the *beylikçi*, and the
mektupçu. The ambassador was seated on the sofa at the first
place, and next to him on taborets were the envoy, the marshal,
and the secretaries of the embassy. In other regards all ceremonies relating to the reception and entertainment were
observed precisely according to the example of the last three
luncheons. The *reis efendi* and the envoy lunched with the
ambassador at his table. The *kesedar efendi* and the dragoman of
the Porte lunched with the marshal and the secretaries of the
embassy. During the entire time of the ambassador's stay with
the *reis efendi*, various games and entertainments were presented
continuously. Before his departure he was presented with a
horse and trappings and three kerchiefs, the envoy with three
kerchiefs, the marshal, the secretaries, and the cavaliers with
two, and the rest with one. The ambassador was accompanied
by the same people and to the same places where each met him,
and he returned to his house in the same manner as was
previously carried out in such instances.

   At this luncheon the vezir was present, incognito, in a tent
erected for him, from where he viewed all the games and
entertainments presented on this occasion. He sent the ambassador his compliments, explaining his regrets that the ceremony
would prevent him from seeing and amicably conversing with
the ambassador on this occasion. He sent the ambassador and
the envoy each a tobacco-pipe as a present. It was ordered by
the ambassador to send him a courteous reply on his behalf,
with thanks for the friendly gift.

On the following day a horse with trappings was also sent from the *reis efendi* to Gospodin Envoy Stakhiev.

In accordance with the preliminary agreement with the Porte concerning the farewell audience with the sultan and likewise concerning the farewell visit with the vezir, the audience was scheduled for the ninth and the visit for the eleventh of April.

On both of these occasions, in regard to the receptions and honors shown the ambassador, the same ceremony was observed during the first audience with the sultan and the visit at the vezir's, with only one difference, that everything was carried out with greater precision and courtesy. The *çavuşbaşı* both times notified the ambassador in advance concerning this arrival at the place where he was to meet him, and rode a few paces ahead of him. During the trip from the pier to the saray the ambassador did not wait for the vezir at all, but on arriving at the saray he was conducted as before to the chamber of the *kapıcıbaşı* of the guard rather than through the gate. Then when he had entered the divan he sat on the *nişancı* bench. He lunched with the vezir as usual. He was introduced, with his entourage of fifteen people, to the sultan and made a speech of the following content:

> Her Imperial Majesty, my most gracious and most august sovereign, on the strength of the twenty-seventh article of the treaty of peace concluded between both empires, has deigned to bestow on me the character of her ambassador extraordinary and plenipotentiary, for attestation to your majesty of her peace-loving and amicable sentiments, which I have fulfilled. Returning now to present myself at the foot of her imperial throne, I consider it my special good fortune that I achieved on this occasion the distinguished honor of seeing Your Majesty, which I will never cease to preserve preciously in my memory as the most felicitous occasion of my life, to which I shall forever ascribe my special fame.

In response to this speech the ambassador was given an answer through the vezir, at the sultan's command. It consisted of amicable compliments from the sultan to her imperial majesty. The sultan gave the vezir a rescript for her imperial majesty which the *kapudan paşa* handed to the ambassador. As he was leaving the audience chamber, the *büyük imrahor*, or the sultan's master of the horse, informed him that his majesty was presenting the ambassador a horse with trappings of the divan. Then he was again conducted to the chamber of the *kapıcıbaşı* of the guard, where he waited for the vezir's exit from the saray. After this, he himself returned to the pier and then to his house, accompanied this time as from the first audience.

During the visit at the vezir's, which was carried out on the basis of the previous one, the ambassador delivered no speech, but he did pay [the vezir] appropriate respects, consisting of his thanks for all the courtesies and acts of goodwill that had been accorded him. He added that the ambassador would always consider it his pleasure to remain in his benevolent regard and to give evidence thereof, to which the vezir replied with reciprocal assurances. Following this, confections, coffee, sherbet, rose water, and smoking articles were brought to the ambassador. Then the vezir himself handed him the rescript of the vezir to her imperial majesty. The *mektupçu* gave the note for his excellency Count Nikita Ivanovich Panin to one of the ambassador's secretaries of the embassy. After this, the ambassador took leave of the vezir and departed from him. At the entrance a horse was brought to the ambassador, the one that the *teşrifatçı efendi* had announced was being presented to him with all accoutrements by the vezir. The ambassador returned from the Porte in the same order as he went, except that the *çavuşbaşı* did not accompany him.

On both these occasions the ambassador was clothed in a sable coat covered with brocade. The marshal and secretaries of the embassy were clothed in ermine coats, while persons of other rank in the embassy were given caftans.

On the day after the ambassador's visit at the vezir's, the Porte sent him two horses, a gift in the style of the previous ones, for his excellency Count Nikita Ivanovich Panin. In addition, [the Porte] commanded it to be announced to the ambassador that preparations for his departure would be completed by 21 April. Whereupon, the ambassador with all his entourage left Constantinople for his return journey on the twenty-fourth day of the month, with everything in a satisfactory condition.

*A description of the return journey from Constantinople to Hotin of
Her Imperial Majesty's ambassador extraordinary and plenipotentiary
at the Ottoman Porte, General in Chief, Lieutenant Colonel of the
Izmailovskii Guard Regiment and cavalier of various Orders, Prince
Nikolai Vasil'evich Repnin, and the ceremonial exchange between
himself and the Turkish ambassador effected on the Dnestr on the
nineteenth of June of this year 1776.*

April

24th. At eight o'clock in the morning the new *mihmandar*,
pasha of two horsetails, Husayn Pasha, arrived at the house of
the ambassador, and shortly after him the former assistant also
arrived, *Kapıcıbaşı* Ahmet Bey, who prior to this had been
awarded the rank of *kapıcılar kâhyası*, that is, the sultan's
adjutant general. When everything had been prepared and
arranged for the departure, they set out at ten o'clock on the
march. It began with the Turkish entourage with the banner
and the pasha's horsetails, then the *çorbacı* of the guard with his
orta of janissaries. Behind them followed a part of the mounted
detachment of cuirassiers and hussars with trumpets and
kettledrums, carbines on the knee, the cavaliers and the marshal
of the embassy, the new *mihmandar* Husayn Pasha, and the
kapıcılar kâhyası Ahmet Bey preceding the ambassador. After
the ambassador came the secretaries of the embassy, and his
adjutants, then the remaining part of the cuirassiers and
hussars in the same formation as the lead part, and finally the
pasha's music. After departing from Pera, the marshal of the
embassy was sent with the dragoman Pizani to the Porte with
expressions of gratitude to the vezir, the *kâhya*, and the *reis
efendi* for all the extraordinary honors and courtesies that had
been accorded them during their sojourn in Tsar' Grad. Two
aides-de-camp were also sent with farewell compliments to the
ambassadors and ministers residing at the Porte. The above-
mentioned Ahmet Bey escorted the ambassador about four
versts from Pera and took leave of him with wishes for a

pleasant journey, while the ambassador, continuing his journey with the pasha of two horsetails, various other Turks, and his own entourage, arrived at Küçükçekmece at one o'clock in the afternoon, two and one-half hours' distance from Tsar' Grad, and camp was made there.

25th. Halted the whole day so as to put the carriages and baggage train into condition for continuing the extended journey.

In the morning noblemen from all the ambassadors and ministers residing in Pera, as well as several of the most prominent residents of Pera came to wish the ambassador a pleasant journey; some of them remained for luncheon and spent the night in the camp.

The çorbacı of the guard, having accompanied him from Tsar' Grad with his orta of janissaries, was released by the ambassador and on this occasion he presented appropriate gifts.

26th. Set out at eight o'clock in the morning and after traveling three and a half hours made camp at the town of Büyük-çekmece, from where the kadi and other Turkish leaders rode out to meet the ambassador, about a verst from their dwellings.

27th. Left at six o'clock, made camp within sight of but without reaching the town of Silivri, from where a welcoming party also rode out, composed of the kadi and the chief leaders of the city.

28th. Rest day. The mihmandar visited the ambassador.

29th. Arrived at the village of Kınıklı and made camp there.

30th. Having traveled three hours, made camp near the town of Çorlu, from where the leading inhabitants of that place rode out to meet the ambassador. In this town a courier came from Gospodin Lieutenant General and Cavalier Igel'strom with a message concerning his departure from Kiev with the Turkish ambassador.

May

1st. Arrived in camp near the town of Karıştıran, six hours'

distance from Çorlu and were met by the Turkish leaders of
this place.

2d. Rest day.

3d. Having traveled four hours, made camp near the town
of [Lüle] Burgaz, from where the kadi and other leaders came
out to meet the ambassador and, having escorted him to his
headquarters, returned to the city.

4th. Departed at six-thirty, stopped in camp near the village
of Asılbeyli, one and one-half hours' distance from the city of
Kırklareli, from where the *müsellim* aga, that is, the chief
commander of the city, and the *turnacı* were sent out to meet
the ambassador, and with them was an entourage of several
persons. On the morrow

5th. when they arrived at the outskirts of Kırklareli itself,
in addition to the above-mentioned two, the kadi and the
voivode, with all the other officials rode out to the meeting,
and in addition to this there were about one hundred janissaries
in formation.

6th. Rest day.

7th. Left camp early and after a march of four hours stopped
near the village of Erikler.

8th. Having traveled four hours, made camp near the village
of Kanara.

9th. Arrived in the village of Fakiya and made camp nearby
after traveling four hours.

10th. Rest day and change of carts.

11th. Traveled four hours and stopped in camp near the
village of Karabunar [Grudovo].

12th. Having traveled three hours, arrived in camp near the
village of Rusokastro.

13th. After traveling five hours arrived in camp on the outskirts of the city of Aytos, from where the kadi, various other
city leaders, and about one hundred cavalry personnel from
among their subordinates rode out for the meeting. All
together they escorted the ambassador to his headquarters.

14th. Rest day.

15th. After traveling two and one-half hours, arrived at the village of Nadur and set up camp there.

16th. After traveling three and a half hours, made camp between the mountains and a place called Subaşı.[43]

17th. Arrived at the village of K'opryu-k'oy and made camp nearby, having traveled five hours.

18th. After traveling six hours, arrived at the town of Provadiya, from where the kadi and various other city officials rode out for a meeting, and after riding through the city ahead of the ambassador, escorted him to the camp situated near it.

19th. Rest day, and all carts, oxen, and horses were changed on this day.

20th. Likewise a rest day, at the request of the *mihmandar* so as to give him time to improve the preparation of provisions in advance.

21st. At dawn the quartermaster was as usual sent on with the lead wagons to the village of Kozluduza, but the ambassador left at seven o'clock in the morning and arrived at Kozluduza (a distance of four hours from Provadiya) at noon, where he was met by the local voivode.

22d. At six o'clock the ambassador left the camp and, after traveling six hours, was met by the local commanders, the kadi, the *kapıcıbaşı*, and the *serdar* on the road as he entered his camp on the outskirts of Bazargıc.

23d. At noon the ambassador set out on the road with his entourage, and when he had traveled six hours, arrived in a camp set up near the ruined village of Musubei at seven o'clock in the evening, where he was met by the kadi of Kovarna, who came there with the provisions of that town.

24th. Rest day.

25th. After leaving at seven o'clock in the morning and traveling six hours, the ambassador arrived in camp near the village of Bektir Kioi [Furca] during the noon hour.

26th. The ambassador left camp at seven o'clock, and when

43 Unidentified.

he had been on the road for four hours, arrived in camp set up near the village Mamut-Kuius at ten o'clock.

27th. After traveling four hours, the ambassador arrived in camp near the village of Celebichioi.

28th. Rest day for the change of carts.

29th. After traveling five hours, the ambassador arrived at noon in camp near the village of Satişchioi.

30th. Leaving there early in the morning and marching for four hours, the ambassador halted in camp near the village of Casimcea.

Captain L'vov was sent from here to Măcin in order to inspect the boats and to prepare everything necessary to cross the Danube.

31st. After traveling seven hours, the ambassador made camp near the village of Cerna.

June

1st. After traveling four hours, arrived at the camp set up directly on the bank of the Danube near the town of Măcin. Four agas and *odabaşıs* of Brăila, with one hundred janissaries, rode out from there to meet and accompany him to his headquarters. On the same day the *kapıcıbaşı*, or commander in chief in Brăila, came to the camp with compliments for the ambassador and to help him with the crossing.

2d and 3d. The transport of the carts continued.

4th. When the last carts had been dispatched, the ambassador himself left after them, without delay, at noon, on two covered boats, accompanied by the pasha, and amidst cannonade and the playing of Russian and Turkish music. When the ambassador was in view of Brăila there was a salute of several cannon shots from the fortress and from those standing beneath the fortress and from various ships sailing on the Danube.

When he alighted on the shore two versts from Galaţi, the ambassador was met by a senior Turkish *ispravnik* and by three boyars sent from Jassy for the meeting. All of them, preceded by some one hundred men of the Moldavian mounted troops with banners, rode ahead of him to the camp set up at the outskirts of the city itself, where the ambassador arrived at five o'clock in the afternoon.

5th. Rest day, for assembling and repairing of the baggage train, and for receiving new horses and carts.

6th. At seven in the morning the ambassador left the camp, and after traveling four and a half hours, arrived in camp near the village of Penevul.[44]

7th. Traveled four and a half hours and made camp in a place called Dcherul.[45]

8th. Traveled four hours and stopped near the village of Puțeni.

9th. Having traveled four hours, made camp in the valley called Recea.

10th. Traveled four hours and made camp on the outskirts of the city of Bîrlad.

11th. After traveling four hours, halted near the village of Dekolin.

12th. Arrived at the town of Vaslui, four hours from Dekolin.

13th. Arrived at the location Uncești, having traveled four hours.

14th. Traveled four hours and made camp in the location called Scînteia.

The hetman, with a considerable number of mounted troops, and the third *spatar* Debasta with a letter, arrived here to meet the ambassador. They were sent by the Moldavian hospodar, to whom the ambassador dispatched an answer with Major Markov, who was sent to secure quarters in Jassy. The hetman and the *spatar* remained in the camp and were invited to dine.

After luncheon the lead train was sent to Jassy.

15th. At five o'clock in the morning the remainder of the

---

[44] Unidentified, probably near present-day Pechea.
[45] Unidentified.

baggage train was sent off and at seven the ambassador and all his entourage set out.

Before coming within an hour of Jassy, the chamberlain, or the first boyar, was sent by the hospodar with compliments. Half an hour from the city the hospodar himself, with all his boyars, was awaiting the ambassador in a tent. Receiving and entertaining the ambassador at a table prepared with cold food and liqueurs, he requested permission to go on ahead to Jassy for the meeting in the ambassador's house. After this, the ambassador mounted and rode into Jassy in the precise order and with the same honors, without the slightest diminution, as were used on his way to Tsar' Grad. He rode to the firing of cannons and rifles by the military personnel standing along the streets, and to the ringing of bells. The hospodar himself met the ambassador at the lower stairway of the house allocated for him, but the wife of the hospodar, who was sick in the village, the sister of the hospodar's wife, and many Moldavian ladies gathered in the mentioned house to meet the ambassadress.

Having dined at a table prepared by the hospodar, all departed toward evening.

16th. The Metropolitan of Jassy, with all the boyars of the divan, were at the ambassador's on a visit, and after this, the ambassador went to the hospodar on a return visit, having been invited on the previous day. He stayed for luncheon.

17th and 18th. Rest days, and on these days the ambassador and all his entourage took supper with the hospodar.

19th. At daybreak the lead wagons were sent off.

At nine o'clock the hospodar came to the ambassador at his house where, after remaining a short time, he asked the ambassador to be allowed to ride on ahead to the tent prepared for him a half hour from the city. The ambassador soon followed him, in the same order and with the same honors as were observed during his entrance into Jassy.

After they arrived at the above-mentioned tents, in front of and outside of which Moldavian troops stood in formation, the hospodar received the ambassador before the tent and asked him to be seated at the table set for breakfast. After sitting there about half an hour, the ambassador rose, took leave of the hospodar, and set out on his way. He was accompanied by the Moldavian hetman and a considerable number of troops and three boyars. After traveling two hours, [he] arrived at his camp on the location Sculeni.

20th. Traveled three hours and halted near the village of Trifeşti.

21st. Traveled three hours and stopped near the village of Tabăra.

22d. Arrived in camp near the town of Stefănesti, six hours' distance from Tabăra.

23d. After crossing the Pruth River and traveling two hours, made camp near the village of Kosteshty.

From here, since this was the border of the Moldavian principality, the forces accompanying the ambassador from Jassy turned back.

The *vekilharç* aga came from Hotin to meet the ambassador with a letter of welcome sent by Melek Mehmet Pasha of that place. Surrendering it, he said he had been commanded to accompany the ambassador to Hotin and to make an examination to insure that nothing at all should be lacking on the way.

24th. Traveled five hours and halted near the village of Gordineshty.

The Secretary of Oriental Languages Panaiodoros was sent ahead to inspect the crossing on the Dnestr and all the preparations made for it. In addition he was ordered to stop at Melek Mehmet Pasha's and convey appropriate compliments from the ambassador, and if he could find an occasion, to arrange in advance the order for the ceremony of the exchange on the return trip.

25th. Traveled six hours and made camp near the village of Larga.

26th. After traveling three and a half hours, arrived in camp near Uchevlar.[46]

46 Unidentified. The place name means "three houses."

Two hours later, the *kâhya* of the pasha of Hotin came to the camp with a letter of greeting and compliments for the ambassador. Among other things, he brought the pasha's regrets that because of illness he could not entertain him personally in his tent that would be pitched on the bank of the Dnestr. One hundred cavalry personnel arrived with the *kâhya* to convoy the ambassador. A written greeting was given in reply to the pasha's letter.

Gospodin Lieutenant General Igel'strom arrived for a meeting with the ambassador and for a clarification of the ceremonial exchange, and spent the night in the camp.

27th. Rest day, and part of the baggage train was dispatched to Hotin.

Gospodin General Lieutenant Igel'strom rode back to the Turkish ambassador so as to arrive on the following day at the Dnestr and at the same time that the ambassador would arrive in Hotin.

28th. At ten o'clock in the morning the remainder of the train was sent on, whereas the ambassador himself left the camp with all his entourage during the first hour after noon, accompanied by his *mihmandar* and the Turkish convoy sent from Hotin. Awaiting him one-half hour from that city were about one thousand janissaries in formation, and all the persons of leading rank from the city, and the pasha's entourage. This was under the leadership of the pasha's *kâhya* who rendered the ambassador a proper greeting and rode several paces ahead of him on the left side of the *mihmandar*. On the arrival at Hotin, the fortress of that city saluted the ambassador with thirty-one shots from the cannon. After arriving at his quarters, the pasha's *kâhya*, the kadi to the city, and the janissary aga were conducted into the tent to the ambassador, who seated them and ordered refreshments of confections, coffee, and cold drinks for them. He dismissed them after some conversation with an expression of his pleasure at their courtesy. The marshal of the embassy and the Secretary of Oriental Languages Panaiodoros were sent immediately after the arrival to the pasha to announce the event, and the doctor of the embassy went with them to offer his services to the pasha on account of the illness that had seized him.

Somewhat later the Turkish ambassador arrived at the Dnestr and made camp near the village of Braga opposite Hotin. In accordance with the preliminary conditions, both ambassadors sent to each other at the same time notification of their arrival, with appropriate compliments. The Russian sent Vild, the secretary of the embassy, and the Turk sent his *kâhya*.

Toward evening supper for fifty places on gold-plated service was brought from the Hotin pasha.

Two *çorbacı*s with their janissary *orta*s were sent to the ambassador in order to guard his residence.

29th. The crossing of the baggage train continued from morning until night.

After lunch the ambassador sent Vild, the secretary of the embassy, to the pasha to ascertain the state of his health and further to inquire whether everything was ready for the next day's exchange. The pasha sent his *silâhdar* simply with compliments for the ambassador.

The order was given in the evening to the whole entourage to be in readiness for the ceremony on the following day.

30th. Early in the morning the entire embassy entourage gathered at their quarters in rich dress.

At eleven o'clock the *kâhya* with the chief leaders of the city, and the pasha's entourage and music came to the ambassador. The *kâhya*, the kadi, the janissary aga, and pasha's *silâhdar* were seated and served confections and coffee. Shortly thereafter the *mihmandar* arrived with all the emblems of rank of the pasha of Hotin, a pasha of three horsetails, except the horsetails. These included the number of *şatır*s and draft horses with emblems belonging to that rank, all of which the pasha of Hotin gave to him that day in the ambassador's honor. As everyone had already assembled at the ambassador's quarters, they left at twelve o'clock for the exchange, which took place in the following order.

1. In the middle of the Dnestr, at the same place as the preceding year, a raft expressly intended for the exchange had been secured, and on it armchairs had been placed on both sides, whereas chairs were arranged a little behind the ambassadors' chairs for their *mihmandar*s, who were present at the ceremony only as witnesses.

2. On either side five hundred infantry were drawn up on the banks of the river in parade formation.

3. At noon a shot was fired from a cannon on the Russian side to inform the Turkish ambassador that all was ready at the Russian ambassador's. As soon as this was answered, likewise by a cannon shot, the ambassador left his quarters. The *kâhya* of the Hotin pasha, at the head of the five-hundred-man mounted Turkish convoy, began the march, so that he could arrive earlier and receive the ambassador at the tent of the Hotin pasha set up on the bank, and so that no disorder or error could in any way occur. After them followed the entourage of the *mihmandar*, with his horsetails. Following this came the draft horses of the Hotin pasha, with the emblems, and then the ambassador's entourage and the ambassador in the same order as the year before; they were preceded by the *mihmandar* who was a pasha of two horsetails, surrounded by his *çuhadar*s and the *şatır*s of the Hotin pasha. At the end of the whole cortege was the Hotin pasha's music under the leadership of his *silâhdar* and *kapıcılar kâhyası*. The infantry marched with unfurled banners, with music and beating of drums, while the cavalry came with drawn swords, trumpets, kettledrums, and flying standards.

4. After the departure of both ambassadors from their quarters, ten cannon shots were fired from each side.

5. When the ambassador came opposite the Hotin fortress in his march, it fired a thirty-one-gun salute from the cannon.

6. When he came to the tent and dismounted, he was received by the Hotin pasha's *kâhya* and the *mihmandar*, who conducted him, walking ahead of him, into the tent, and there the ambassador seated himself alone on the sofa. The *mihmandar*

and the *kâhya* of the Hotin pasha, who was a rank higher than the *mihmandar*, a pasha of two horsetails, sat on chairs at the side, as did the marshal and the secretaries of the embassy. All the rest stood.

7. Since the Turkish ambassador rode up to the bank at the same time, the crossing of both entourages began. During this, coffee, sherbet, rose water, and smoking articles were brought to the Russian ambassador. Meanwhile, both ambassadors sent persons to each other with notice of their arrival at the bank, along with appropriate compliments. The Russian sent Lieutenant Colonel Bok, the Turkish, his *kâhya*.

8. After the crossing of the entourages and after the firing of signals from the cannon on both sides that all was ready for the crossing of the ambassadors themselves, the Russian arose and left the tent, preceding the *mihmandar* and accompanied by the *kâhya* and all the Turkish entourage. On coming to the ferry raft, he dismissed the *kâhya*, expressing to him proper regards and bidding him extend his compliments to the Hotin pasha. Having boarded the ferry raft with his *mihmandar*, and with the persons of chief rank from his own entourage, he arrived at the exchange raft and boarded it at the same time the Turkish ambassador tied up and boarded it with his assistant and part of his entourage.

9. Once on the raft, both ambassadors seated themselves on armchairs, opposite each other, while their *mihmandar*s were on chairs a little way back. After some conversation and mutual greetings, the ambassadors rose together and changed with each other, each going to the place of the other, and after mutually wishing each other a pleasant journey and good health, each went his own way.

10. As soon as the exchange of ambassadors had been accomplished in this fashion, at a given signal, twenty shots were fired from the cannon on each side and three rounds of rifle fire were given by the infantry standing on the banks.

11. When each ambassador had tied up to his own bank, ten rounds of cannon shot were again fired as they alighted, while

the infantry on both sides repeated the three rounds of rifle fire.

After the crossing of the ambassador, the pasha sent to him at his camp his *silâhdar* to inquire of his health and to offer apologies in case anything had been omitted during the exchange. The ambassador, through both the *silâhdar* who had been sent and Panaiodoros, the Secretary of Oriental Languages, whom he had dispatched out of reciprocity, ordered his thanks to be expressed for all the courtesies shown him.

July

1st. Rest day, for receipt of baggage carts and for dispositions regarding the further journey. Meanwhile, both ambassadors sent each other at the same time persons with presents and compliments; the Russian, his adjutant to General Rontsov, with the interpreter Kruta, the Turkish, his *kâhya* with the interpreter Karacı.

Travel Routes

Question marks indicate tentative identification. Where two names are given, the second is the present-day form of older place names.

Abdülkerim Pasha: Istanbul to Moscow

Istanbul
Küçükçekmece
Kınıklı
[Lüle] Burgaz
Edirne
Yambol
Chalik Kavak
Shumen/Kolarovgrad
Silistra
Călăraşi
Brăila
Galaţi
Izburuga [?]
Tutora
Chuchulya
Kotyudzhen'

Hotin
Dnestr River
Zhvanets
Dolzhok
Kamanice/Kamenets-Podolsky
Negin
Tynna [?]
Yarmolintsy
Shumovtsy
Masivtsy
Medzhibozh
Buzticnu [?]
Severiny
Polonnoye
Miropol'
Nastana Karşı

Chudnov
Pyatki
Berdichev
Belopol'ye
Utaşrahina [?]
Pavoloch'
Fastov
Motovilovka
Quarantine Station
Vasil'kov
Unnamed stop
Kiev
Dnepr River
Brovary
Semipolki
Kozelets
Nosovka
Nezhin
Komarovka
Borzna
Gorodische [?]
Baturin
Altynovka

Krolevets
Tuligolovo
Glukhov
Tolstodubovo
Sevŝk
Asmon'
Dmitrovsk-Orlovsky
Chuvardino
Kromy
Orël
Sergiyevskoye
Mtsensk
Nikol'skoye
Seriryovka [?]
Solova
Tula
Oka River
Vashana
Savino [?]
Serpukhov
Lupasnya
Bahary [?]
Moscow

General Repnin: Hotin to Constantinople

Hotin
Larga
Gordineshty
Kosteshty
Stefănesti/Stefanesti-Tîrg
Tabăra
Trifeşti
Sculeni
Jassy/Iaşi
Scînteia
Unceşti
Vaslui
Dekolin/Crasna
Guru-Paraskevului [?]
Bîrlad
Tecuci

Brăila
Pomistraveslkului/Petreşti
Focşani
Milcov River
Vîrteşcoiu
Slobozia
Rîmna River
Topliceni
Rîmnicu Sărat
Buzău
Margineanu
Podikuram [?]
Ialomiţa River
Creaţa
Bucureşti
Sabar River

Călugăreni	Karnabat/Polyanovgrad
Daia	Kaftan/Nedyalsko
Giurgiu	Popovo
Romadan River	Hanliyenice
Danube River	Giol'Bab [?]
Giurgiu Fortress	Edirne
Ruse/Ruščuk	Kuleli
Chervena Voda	Lüle Burgaz
Senevo	Çorlu
Razgrad	Silivri
Dlŭzhko	Büyükçekmece
Shumen/Kolarovgrad	Küçükçekmece
Smyadovo	San Stefano/Yeşilköy
Chalik Kavak	Constantinople/Istanbul
Dobrol	

Glossary and
Biographical Dictionary

The definitions and biographical information presented here
are not intended to be definitive. Rather, they are offered as aids
to a more immediate comprehension of what otherwise might
remain mere esoterica. Some of the entries, however, include
material not readily available elsewhere. For more extensive
information on Ottoman terms see the works by Gibb and
Bowen, Kepeci, Pakalın, and Uzunçarşılı cited in the bibliography.

Abdülhamit I. He was born in 1725, the son of Ahmet III. On
21 January 1774 he succeeded his brother Mustafa III and
became the twenty-seventh Ottoman sultan. The long war
with Russia was terminated early in his reign by the treaty
of Küçük Kaynarca. He died in 1789.

Aga of the janissaries. *See* **Janissary Aga.**

Ahmet III. Twenty-third Ottoman sultan, son of Mehmet IV. He
was born in 1673 and came to the throne in 1703. The last
half of his reign has become known as the "age of tulips,"
lâle devri. It was a period of opulence, and cultural and
intellectual activity, brought to a close by an uprising

participated in by the janissaries in 1730. Ahmet III was
forced to abdicate, and he died in 1736.

Ahmet Resmi Efendi. Ottoman statesman, historian, and man of
letters. He was born in 1700 in Crete. He came to Istanbul,
and by means of a successful marriage into the Ottoman
bureaucratic elite, he embarked on a distinguished career.
In 1757 he was sent as ambassador to Vienna, and in 1763 he
was sent in the same capacity to Berlin. He was involved in
the peace negotiations and wrote an important work on the
war period, 1768–74.

Alay çavuşu. The word *çavuş* means messenger, herald, or usher,
and *alay* means parade or procession. This was the official
who cleared the way for processions.

Aynalı Kavak. The palace here was also known as *Tersane Sarayı*,
Admiralty palace. It was located at Kasım Pasha on the
Golden Horn, and was one of Istanbul's largest buildings.

Bahâriye. A district on the Golden Horn between Eyyub and
Silahdarağa. Here leading personalities constructed summer
houses on the shore. The sultans maintained one such
establishment in this noted place of relaxation.

Baş defterdar. This official was the chief financial officer of the
Ottoman Empire. In this period the office was occupied by
Recâî Mehmet Emin Efendi.

Baş ezancı efendi. Second in command to the Chief of the Callers
to Prayer. He trained the candidates for positions as *ezancı*s.

Bayraktar. A junior officer in a janissary *orta* who was responsible
for the *orta*'s standard.

Beylikçi. As director of the central chancery office responsible for
the composition, issuance, and conservation of all regulations,
divan decisions, edicts, and orders, except those relating to
financial matters, he was the senior official under the *reis
efendi*. He was one of the *hacegân*.

Birun agas. Agas of the outside service: This term usually
designated those officials of the Ottoman sultan's imperial
household who were concerned with more than palace
affairs. These officials dealt with administrative, military,
and even religious matters. Great private households might
also have their own *birun* agas.

Bölükât-ı erbâa. The first four divisions, or *bölük*s, of the standing

cavalry. Two were known as *ulufeci* and two as *guruba*. On
the field of battle one *ulufeci* and one *guruba* division each
took up positions on the sultan's right and left flank.

Bostancıbaşı. This official was the senior officer of the *ocak* of
*bostancı*s. They originated in the group assigned to beautify
the grounds around Topkapı Sarayı when it was first
constructed, but gradually they came to assume other duties.
These included rowing the sultan's barge, guarding various
palaces and quays, and maintaining public security in the
capital and in Edirne. The *bostancıbaşı* in Istanbul was also
responsible for carrying out punishments decreed against
grand vezirs and other high-ranking officials. At the
beginning of the eighteenth century the *bostancı*s numbered
some 2400. The *bostancı*s of Edirne had their own
organization, composed of some 750 men at the beginning
of the eighteenth century. Here the *bostancıbaşı* was
responsible for law and order in the city and its suburbs.
He was, in fact, responsible for the government of the city.

Boyars. Baron de Tott described the boyars in the following
manner, "The boyards (an appelation given to the great
land-holders, a species of Nobility, whose only title is their
wealth; but wealth is everything, and the strictest order
scarcely can resist its influence) represent, with vast arrogance,
the Grandees of the country; tho' in reality, they are only
rich Proprietors and cruel tax-gatherers. Seldom do they live
in amity with their Prince, but generally are intriguing
against him, and Constantinople is the centre of their
factions. Hither doth each party carry his complaints and
his money, and the Sultan Erasker, of Bessarabia, affords a
ready refuge to those Boyards whom the Porte thinks proper
to sacrifice to its tranquility. The Tatar Prince gives safety
to the Boyard, and under his protection he is often
re-established; but for this protection he must pay.

"These various expenses, which the Boyards reimburse
to themselves by oppressing Individuals, added to the taxes
which the Prince imposes to pay his annual Tribute, and
other objects of expence which I have already mentioned,
overburden Moldavia so much, that, rich as is the soil, it is
scarcely sufficient" (De Tott, *Memoirs*, 1, pt. 2:37–38).

Bruce, Count Iakov Alexsandrovich. He was born in 1732. At
the time of this *mubadele* he was governor general of both

Moscow and Saint Petersburg. His appointment to the rank
of general in chief occurred in 1773. At the start of the
Ottoman war he had been a commander in the army of
General Golitsyn, and when the latter was replaced by
General Rumiantsev he stayed on as a division commander.
In 1770, however, he was replaced by the new field marshal
because of a military error. Piqued, he asked for release from
field duty.

This did not seem to harm his fortunes, for he was well
connected with the empress. Bil'basov suggests that he
participated in Catherine's accession to the throne (Vasilii A.
Bil'basov, *Istoriia Ekateriny Vtoroi*, 2:461). Bruce's wife was
Praskov'ia Aleksandrovna Rumiantsev, sister of his former
commander and very close confidante of Catherine until
1779. She is said to have "tested" Catherine's lovers before
they were installed as favorites (George P. Gooch, *Catherine
the Great, and Other Studies*, p. 38).

In later years Bruce was governor general of Saint
Petersburg. Of interest is the fact that he was a bitter
opponent of Novikov's ideas and publications. Repnin
lost favor with Catherine partly because of his association
with Novikov and his acceptance of the ideas of Freemasonry.

The history of the Bruce family in this particular case gives
another example of the small circle of relatives and intimates
who appear to make the history of the era. The family also
provides an example of the famous immigrant in Russia. The
founder of the Russian branch of the family, himself a
descendant of Scottish kings, arrived in Russia in flight
from Cromwell's England. Descent to the present count is
as follows: James (Iakov) Bruce and his son William arrived
in Russia, 1647. Villim Iakovlevich died in 1695, Roman
Willimovich lived from 1668 to 1720, Aleksandr Romanovich
from 1705 to 1752. Iakov Aleksandrovich who died in
1791, was the last male member of the line in Russia. A
history of another branch of the family that crossed paths
with the Russian branch in the time of Peter the Great is
found in Peter Henry Bruce, *Memoirs*. There is a biography
of Iakov Aleksandrovich in *RBS*, 3:414–16, and of other
members of the family on pages 413–19. A rather loose and
conversational account of the family is in Francis A. Stuart,
Scottish Influences in Russian History.

Cavalier. In this text the term refers to someone who has been

decorated with one of the imperial orders. For information
on the orders see *Istoricheskii ocherk rossiiskikh ordenov i
sbornik osnovnykh ordenskikh statutov*, compiled by I. I.
Vorontsov-Dashkov. A list of orders and the persons on
whom they were bestowed up to 1814 is in Dmitrii N.
Bantysh-Kamenskii, *Istoricheskoe sobranie spiskov Kavalerem
chetyrekh rossiiskikh imperatorskikh ordenov*. Several of the
Russian orders, with black-and-white drawings, are in
James Henry Lawrence-Archer, *The Orders of Chivalry*,
pp. 143–57.

Çavuşbaşı. Chief of the *çavuş* corps attached to the imperial divan.
He ushered petitioners into the meetings of the divan, and
was the grand vezir's deputy in that official's law court.

Çavuş katibi. This official was the secretary of the *çavuş* corps
attached to the imperial divan. He made a record of legal
cases sent to lower courts by the grand vezir and included in
that record the name of the *çavuş* who carried that instruction.

Çavuşlar emini. The *çavuş* corps under the *çavuşbaşı* consisted of
fifteen companies of forty-two men each. This official was
the commissioner of the whole corps, working as part of the
grand vezir's staff. The *çavuşbaşı*'s orders were transmitted
through the *çavuşlar emini*.

Çekke. *See* **Weights and measures**

Çerge. A small tent or two-poled open marquee.

Cizye baş bakı kulu. An inspector in the financial bureau
concerned with the *cizye* tax, the tax levied on non-Muslim
able-bodied men. It was a religiously sanctioned tax, for
which reason the Ottomans exempted children, women,
disabled and blind men, and the unemployed poor. The
revenues were usually assigned to military expenditures, in
keeping with the ghazi nature of the state.

Çorbacı. A janissary term applied to *orta* commanders.

Davut Pasha. A plain outside the walls of Istanbul. This was the
staging area for military campaigns.

Deste. A small booklet, usually containing some twenty-four
sheets of gold leaf.

Divanegân. Earlier this term designated volunteer light-cavalry
who joined campaigns for a share in the booty. Their later
positions perhaps resembled that of the *gönüllüyân*.

Divan katibi. In imitation of the central administration, provincial
  governors maintained a divan for the transaction of
  business. The secretary of this divan had the title of *divan
  katibi.*

Enderun agas. Agas of the inside service. This term usually
  designated those officials of the Ottoman sultan's imperial
  household detailed to the personal and private service of the
  sultan. In the palace they were under the direction of the
  head White Eunuch. Since the leading officials of the
  Ottoman government modeled their own households after
  that of the sultan, they would have servants in their employ
  (or slaves) who might be designated as agas of the inside
  service. Abdülkerim's retinue included a number of *enderun*
  agas. They may have been assigned to him from the imperial
  household for this embassy.

Eyyub. A district of the capital at the far end of the Golden Horn.
  The district takes its name from the disciple of the Prophet
  who fell in the siege of Constantinople led by Yazid in 669.
  It is a sacred place known for its mosques and cemeteries.

Fener. A quarter of Istanbul on the Golden Horn. In 1603 the
  Greek Patriarch located his establishment there at the
  Church of Saint George. Many prominent Greek families
  settled in that quarter, including those families that
  controlled the office of dragoman of the Porte. These
  prominent families were known collectively as the
  Phanariotes.

Gedikli agas. The term *gedik* had many meanings, mainly,
  privileged or enfiefed. Here we are dealing with servants of
  the outside or inside service who were perhaps senior and
  enjoyed special status.

Gedikli zaim. *See* **Müteferrika ağası**

Ghika, Gregory. The Ottomans were suspicious of this member
  of one of the leading Phanariote families. He had taken up
  with the Russians during the war and then had tried to
  make amends by betraying them. In 1777 he was executed
  by the Ottomans.

Gönüllüyân. In earlier usage the term designated volunteer
  cavalrymen who descended on the enemy in wild raids
  ahead of the regulars. Later, the term designated cavalrymen
  listed in the janissary registers, enjoying the rights and

privileges of janissaries, but without any pay. After serving
in battle they would be enrolled in the wage registers and
draw pay.

Grand vezir's kâhya. *See* **Kethuda/Kâhya**

Guard regiments. The information given by Abdülkerim needs
to be supplemented. Although the Preobrazhenskii and
Semenovskii Regiments were founded by Peter and did
play an important part in his wars with the Swedes, they
were not only a military force. For the nobility, service in
the guards as a common soldier was required before one
could be chosen for a permanent officer's assignment in the
army. In the eighteenth century they exercised an
extraordinary influence on politics. Kliuchevskii has
remarked that, "almost all the governments which
succeeded one another from the death of Peter I to the
accession of Catherine II were the work of the guards. In
thirty-seven years at the court, five or six revolts occurred
with their assistance. The Petersburg guard barracks were
the rival of the Senate and the Supreme Privy Council,"
Sochineniia, 4, lecture 70: 266. On the guards and Catherine's
accession see the same work, 4, lecture 74: 348–58. Further
discussion of the guards and other political elements in the
early years of Catherine's reign is found in Georg Sacke,
"Katerina II. im Kampf um Thron und Selbstherrschaft,"
Archiv für Kulturgeschichte, 23 no. 2 (1932): 191–216.
     The Semenovskii and Preobrazhenskii regiments were
founded in 1687, but were not called guard regiments until
1698. The Izmailovskii Guard Regiment was founded in
1730.

Habbe. *See* **Weights and measures.**

Hakan. One of the titles used by the Ottoman sultans, and other
Turkish rulers. It can be translated as ruler or lord.

Haseki aga. Second in command to the *bostancıbaşı*. Senior
*bostancı*s were also known as *haseki*s. Members of the
fourteenth, forty-ninth, sixty-sixth, and sixty-seventh *orta*s
of the janissaries were also called *haseki*s, the more respected
and venerable ones being called *haseki* aga. They formed a
special guard for the sultan and were distinguished by their
fine dress.

Hazinedar. A term composed of two elements, *hazine*, meaning

treasure, and *dar*, meaning possessing, or managing. In any establishment, royal, bureaucratic, military, etc., the *hazinedar* acted as treasurer.

Hetman. *See* **Spatar.**

Imrahor. The *büyük imrahor* and the *küçük imrahor*, the great and little master of the horse, were among the agas of the stirrup who were the principal officers of the sultan's outside service. The great master of the horse commanded all personnel attached to the imperial stables, and he had charge of the imperial pasturages. The little master of the horse was his assistant and was primarily responsible for carriages and pack horses.

Ispravnik. Walachia was divided into districts (seventeen in the early nineteenth century), each of which was governed by two *ispravnik*s or deputies. Their appointments were renewable each year. They were mainly concerned with the collection of tribute and other contributions.

Janissary Aga. This official was the commander of the janissary corps. He had his headquarters in Istanbul. Local janissary commanders were also known as the aga of the janissaries, but they were subordinate to their chief in the capital.

Kağıthane. A favorite place of relaxation at the end of the Golden Horn. The charming valley of the Ali Bey and Kağıthane streams, called by the Europeans the Sweet Waters of Europe, was a much-frequented picnic and outing spot. Here Sultan Ahmet III had a superb palace constructed, called Saadabad. In the revolt of 1730 that palace was considered a symbol of degeneracy by the rioters and was destroyed.

Kâhya bey. *See* **Kethuda/Kâhya.**

Kaimakam. When the grand vezir campaigned in the field with the imperial armies a deputy was designated to "stand in his station," that is, to be the *kaimakam*. He enjoyed almost all the authority of the grand vezir for that period. *Kaimakam*s were also designated to serve until a newly appointed grand vezir might arrive from some distant post. The *kaimakam* was usually the second vezir, and therefore, an important official in his own right.

Kantar. *See* **Weights and measures.**

Kapıcıs. The gatekeepers of the palace were divided into two
groups, one the *dergâh-ı âli*, the other *bâb-ı hümayun*. In the
first half of the eighteenth century their number stood at
about 600. Their ranks were usually filled by the sons of
leading governmental and military families. *Kapıcıbaşı* was
a term applied to the high officers and officials of the *kapıcı*
corps, and in this period they numbered about 150. Although
the gatekeepers of the imperial palace (the *dergâh-ı âlı*) did
keep watch at the gate to the second court of the palace
(*orta kapı*), they had more important roles as messengers,
chamberlains at palace functions, and as special agents on
important missions to the provinces. Here one of their
special functions at times was to act as official escort
(*mihmandar*) for a visiting ambassador.

Kapudan paşa. This official was the grand admiral of the Ottoman
navy. In the period covered by Repnin's stay in Istanbul the
grand admiral was Cezâyirli Pala-bıyık Gazi Hasan Pasha.

Karakullukçu. A janissary term used to designate under-officers
of an *orta*. They were used in police and security details.

Kese. An accounting term, in this period usually indicating 500
kuruş.

Kesedar efendi. An official in the *reis efendi*'s suite. He was
concerned with the filing of papers and the transaction of
business. He also reported to the *reis efendi* and other officials
on the conduct of business.

Kethuda/Kâhya. *Kethuda* (Persian), and its Turkish version, *kâhya*,
mean lord of the house, or major-domo. It is a ubiquitous
term since almost every official of note, and every important
Ottoman household had a steward. In the texts we find
such offices as *kapudan kâhyası*, *imrahor kâhyası*, *kapıcılar
kethudası*, and the grand vezir's *kâhya*, as well as the *kâhya*
of the grand vezir's *kâhya*. Each of these men performed a
myriad of functions for the men they served. For the
eighteenth century there is no doubt that the grand vezir's
kâhya was the *kâhya* par excellence. As the position of the
grand vezir grew in importance and status, that of his *kâhya*
did the same. The *kâhya* became in time the grand vezir's
deputy and managed most of his correspondence and daily
schedule, and in general acted as his confidant and personal
administrative secretary. In the eighteenth century,

therefore, it is not surprising to see instances of *kâhya*s
succeeding their lords in the grand vezirate.

Keyl. *See* **Weights and measures.**

Kile. *See* **Weights and measures.**

Kıyye. *See* **Weights and measures.**

Küçük Göksu. Known by the Europeans as the Sweet Waters of
Asia, this favorite outing ground is located on the Asian
side of the Bosphorus, between Anadoluhisarı and Kandili.

Masraf efendisi. This official was the secretary in charge of royal
expenditures. His major concern was provisioning the royal
palace.

Mehterhane. This is the Ottoman military music group. They
attended the sultan when he went into the field, and
serenaded him twice a day when he was in residence at the
imperial palace. Vezirs and pashas also had military music
units. For this *mubadele* Abdülkerim has been assigned a
group of musicians from the *mehterhane* to add luster and
pomp to his embassy.

Mektupçu. This official, who ranked among the *hacegân*, was the
grand vezir's general secretary. His bureau was concerned
with outgoing correspondence issued by the grand vezir or
that accompanied the sultan's firmans, and the vezir's
communications with the provinces.

Melek Mehmet Pasha. One of the leading Ottoman personalities
of the eighteenth century. Born the son of a *kapudan paşa* in
1720, he followed in his father's footsteps for a time with a
career in the navy. In 1752 he too served as *kapudan paşa*.
He was dismissed in 1755, and then embarked on a career as
provincial governor. In 1765 he married Zeynep Sultan,
the sister of Mustafa III, and became a royal brother-in-law.
Prior to his service in Hotin he acted as *kaimakam*, and
afterward, from 1792 to 1794, he was grand vezir in his
own right. He died in 1802.

Mir-i mirân. A rank conferred on a *sancak beyi*, the official in
charge of a *sancak*. They were given the title of pasha. Some
authorities claim that the rank of *mir-i mirân* was equivalent
to that of *beylerbeyi*, but that does not appear to be the
case here.

Mubadele. The formal ceremony of exchange when a visiting

ambassador and an Ottoman ambassador change places
across the frontier.

Mustafa III. He was born in 1717, the son of Ahmet III. In 1757
he succeeded to the throne as the twenty-sixth Ottoman
sultan. Mustafa brought back to the throne the line of
Ahmet III that had been interrupted by the revolt of 1730.
He attempted to reintroduce the policies and style of his
father. The war with Russia commenced in his reign, and
he died in 1774, a most unpopular ruler.

Mutasarrıf. An administrative term used to designate an official
who administered a region smaller than a province, but
larger than a single subdivision of a *sancak*.

Müteferrika ağası. Like the *çavuş* corps, the *müteferrika* corps was
attached to the service of the grand vezir. They acted as
messengers, and also formed an elite guard for the sultan.
They were highly paid and often came from well-placed
families. In the eighteenth century they numbered about
two hundred. When they subsisted by means of feudal
grants large enough to be in the *zeamet* category, they were
known as *gedikli zaims*. The chief of the *gedikli zaims* was
called the *müteferrika başı*, a possible alternate title for the
official identified in the text as the *müteferrika ağası*.

Mütesellim. A deputy appointed by provincial governors or
beylerbeyis and approved by the central administration, to
administer their provinces or *sancaks* in their absence.

Naip. A deputy. Here the *naip* is the representative of the kadi in
one of the subdistricts (*nahiye*) of his jurisdiction.

Neledinskii-Meletskii, Iurii Alexsandrovich. He was born in
1752. At the age of thirteen he moved to Saint Petersburg
to live with his grandmother, Princess A. I. Kurakina.
Repnin married the princess's daughter, and is, therefore,
related to Neledinskii-Meletskii by marriage. Princess
Kurakina was the sister of Count N. I. Panin who had been
the tutor of the future tsar Paul. It is likely that Paul and
Neledinskii-Meletskii were childhood acquaintances.

After studying in Strasbourg in 1769, he returned to
Russia and asked for duty with the army, where he first
served under Petr Panin. He fought at Bender as a sergeant,
and then in the Crimea as an officer in the jäger corps.
When his unit was disbanded after those early campaigns,

he volunteered for duty in the principalities. He took part
in several battles and he was eventually attached to the suite
of Prince Repnin and attended the negotiations at Küçük
Kaynarca. He died in 1828.

Although Neledinskii-Meletskii was automatically
registered for military service at the age of six and served
with the military until 1785, he is better known as a man of
letters. His poems have been published along with those of
A. A. Del'vig in a volume by A. Smirdin, *Polnoe sobranie
russkikh avtorov* (Saint Petersburg, 1850). A biography
appears in *RBS*, 11:215–19.

Nişancı. In the early period the *nişancı* was an official of the highest
importance. He was charged with power to affix the sultan's
seal, the *tuğra*, to official documents and to examine and
correct documents. His position in official protocol remained
high, but the power of his office diminished.

Oba. A large, tall tent with several compartments, made of felt.

Odabaşı. Subordinate janissary officer who acted as chief of the
barrack-room.

Okka. *See* **Weights and measures.**

Orta. The janissary corps (*ocak*) was composed of 196 companies
(*orta*) of various sizes. The corps was divided into three
divisions, the *cemaat* with 101 *orta*s, the *bölük* with 61, and
the *sekban* with 34 *orta*s. The *sekban* collectively formed the
sixty-fifth *orta* of the *cemaat*.

Panin, Count Nikita Ivanovich. Panin was born in 1718. He
had served as a diplomat for more than ten years when in
1760 he was appointed tutor to Grand Prince Paul and
thereupon became increasingly involved in state matters at
the capital as one of Catherine's closest advisers. Especially
in the early years of her reign, when Catherine was still not
securely ensconced as head of state, Panin was the only
person who enjoyed the confidence of the empress, according
to S. F. Platonov, *Lektsii po russkoi istorii*, p. 613.

Two of Panin's policies help to explain his importance in
the 1760s, and also his decline during later years. First, he
drew up a plan of governmental reorganization which would
have created an imperial council with powers to limit the
monarchy to some extent. The plan was abandoned; the
imperial council created in 1769 did not have such powers.

The longer Catherine held power, the less she was willing to consider limitations on it. Second, Panin was consistently an advocate of the Northern Accord, which called for a union among Russia, Prussia, and other countries of the north to oppose the Bourbons and the Habsburgs. When the war with the Ottoman Empire broke out in 1768, the idea of a northern union fell into decline, and with it to some extent the position of Panin. Furthermore, he shared certain weaknesses with Repnin that could only harm his position with regard to Catherine. He was a close friend of Paul, and he was a Freemason. Finally, even when Catherine was seeking closer ties with Austria, Panin maintained the opposite view that Prussia was the proper ally for Russia.

In spite of these things, Panin played an important role in Russian foreign affairs, evident in some of the correspondence quoted in this study. His biographer wrote, "for a period of almost an entire twenty years (from 1763) he remained the principal adviser of Catherine and directed the foreign policy of Russia," *RBS*, 13:195. Panin died in 1783.

Pera. The European quarter of the capital city. It was composed of two sections called by the inhabitants Galata and Beyoğlu. Gradually Galata was reserved for the lower part of the town and Beyoğlu for the upper. Foreigners used the term Pera to cover the entire area.

Peterson, Khristofor Ivanovich. The grandson of an immigrant from Holstein, Peterson entered the imperial service in 1744 as a member of the corps of pages and by 1760 held the rank of major. In 1763 he was sent to Constantinople by Prince Dolgorukii as a cavalier of the embassy and was promoted there to the rank of lieutenant colonel.

He served in the field during the Ottoman war, distinguished himself, and was awarded the Order of Saint George, Third Class. Rumiantsev recommended him for promotion to the rank of colonel and in 1772 sent him to the negotiations at Focşani and Bucureşti. Again in 1773 he took part in the campaigns. In 1774 he was an official escort to the Ottoman ambassadors at the negotiations of Küçük Kaynarca, where he kept the journal referred to in the introduction. In September 1774 he was appointed chargé d'affaires in Constantinople and in January 1775 carried out the exchange of ratifications to the treaty. In August 1775 he was promoted to the rank of actual state

councillor, and then served in Danzig and Munich. He died
in the latter city in 1789. A biography appears in *RBS*,
13:624–25.

Pleshcheev, Sergei Ivanovich. Pleshcheev was born in 1752. At
the age of ten was registered with the Izmailovskii Guard
Regiment, but then at thirteen he was transferred to England
for naval duty. For five years he sailed the North American
coast, and when he returned for duty with the Russian fleet
in 1770 he had completely forgotten his native language.
During the next five years he sailed in the Mediterranean and
the Baltic, relearned Russian, and then accompanied Repnin
to Constantinople in 1775. One of the things he undertook
in that and the following year was a description of the
Dardenelles. In domestic politics, he was assigned to the
"Little Court" of Prince Paul in 1781, and after the latter
ascended the throne, Pleshcheev attempted to convert the tsar
to Freemasonry, but he failed and fell into disfavor. Thus,
his career seems to bear certain resemblances to that of
Repnin. He died in 1802. A biography appears in *RBS*,
14:113–15.

Polikarpov, Alexsandr Vasil'evich. Polikarpov was born in 1753.
He was enlisted in a guard regiment and distinguished
himself during the war with the Ottomans. In 1774, at the
age of 21, he was promoted to the rank of premier-major.
He died in 1811. A short biography appears in *RBS*,
14:345–49.

Portar başı. This official served as secretary to the hospodar,
directing correspondence with the Ottoman officials. He
also acted as master of ceremonies when visiting dignitaries
arrived at Bucureşti.

Potemkin, Grigorii Aleksandrovich. Potemkin was born in
1739. He was enrolled as a soldier in the guards in 1755,
commissioned as an officer in 1765, and promoted to general
in the first campaigns of the Ottoman war. Catherine
mentions relying on his advice during the entire war,
1768–74. In 1774 he returned to Saint Petersburg and at
least by the following year was firmly fixed in the empress's
favor. He had received the Saint Anna and Saint George
medals in 1770, at which time Rumiantsev wrote a laudatory
letter about him to Catherine. In 1774 he was made colonel
of the Preobrazhenskii Guard Regiment and received the

order of Saint Alexander Nevsky. From 1775 on the empress
bestowed favors on him one after the other. He died in 1791.
A sympathetic biography in English is that by George
Soloveytchik, *Potemkin: A Picture of Catherine's Russia*
(London, 1938). There is also a biography in *RBS*,
14:649–70.

Quarantine. Quarantine regulations were strictly observed and
insisted on by the empress. Repnin had requested permission
for his couriers to pass the station without delay, so as to
improve communications on the negotiations. Catherine
granted the request as long as Repnin was in Russian
territory, but as soon as he crossed to Ottoman territory his
couriers must spend the required time at the station. "We
regard it as necessary and indispensable," she wrote, "that
all precautions be observed which were instituted before the
beginning of the war and that [they] be observed unchanged.
. . . We refrain from allowing your couriers unrestricted
passage here only because when they are dispatched from
you and travel along the road and find themselves in the
closest contact with Turkish carters, they can extremely
easily and, so to say, in the most unavoidable manner be in
contact not only with the places but with persons who are
infected, if after they leave you there an infection should
suddenly occur, which happens not at all infrequently in
that area" (*SRIO*, 5:188, 211–12).

The quarantine stations predate the reign of Catherine II.
For example, an early law provided that Circassians entering
Moscow province and forcing their way past the stations
be hanged. See "2280.—Iiulia 7 [18 July 1710]. Imennyi.—
Ob uchrezhdenii po dorogam zastav dlia predokhraneniia
ot morovago povetriia," *PSZ*, 4:526.

From the *Polnoe Sobranie Zakonov* it appears that the
Russians' fear was mainly of plague from the south, where
perhaps the greatest number of quarantine stations existed,
in such cities as Azov, Tsaritsyn, along the routes leading
from the Crimea, the Ottoman Empire, and the parts of
Poland bordering the Ottoman Empire. In 1729 an elaborate
set of rules was published for preventing the plague. The
Russian resident in Constantinople, Nepliuev, wrote of the
danger of plague, and in Kiev the border was sealed off.
No one was allowed to enter the empire from Constantinople.
Messages from people on the other side of the station were

to be tied to a long pole and passed through fire to the
receivers, and then washed in vinegar. See "5472.—
Sentiabria 30 [11 October 1729]. Imenny, ob'iavlennyi iz
Verkhovnago Tainago Soveta Senatu.—O usilenii dolzhnykh
mer dlia predostorozhnosti ot poiavivshagosia v Turtsii
morovago povetriia," *PSZ*, 8:231–32.

In succeeding years, quarantine stations with isolation
houses and doctors were maintained along the southern
border for traders and their wares from Turkey. For example,
"10.365.—Fevralia 22 [5 March 1775].—Ob uchrezhdenii
pri pogranichnyh tamozhniakh karantinnykh domov, i ob
opredelenii k nim doktorov," *PSZ*, 14:317–19. The largest
number of laws were passed during the time of war, 1768–75.

Early in 1771 a manifesto was published concerning
measures against the epidemic that was appearing in the
Polish provinces close to Turkey. It indicated that the plague
was transferred in clothing, as well as in bronze, iron, and
leather goods. No one was to enter the empire from areas
of Polish or Turkish contact without stopping in the
quarantine stations. If they did, their goods were to be
committed to the fire and the persons punished for their
offense against the laws of God and the state. See "13.551.
Dekabria 31 [11 January 1771]. Manifest.—O
predostorozhnostiakh ot zarazitel'noi bolezni, poiavivsheisia
v Pol'skikh Provintsiiakh," *PSZ*, 19:203–4.

A few days later a set of directions was published on the
establishment of quarantine measures and houses to be used
in the plague areas. Those are probably the houses described
by Abdülkerim Pasha. First in the directions is a description
of the barriers to be erected around cities, the same as the
barriers around the quarantine stations: "In those places
where it is necessary to allow the citizens of one city to
communicate with those of another, the city inhabitants must
not be allowed into the villages. To this end a city guard
will be established at all entrances to the city, and a market
for edible goods at one gate. At this market the city dwellers
are separated from the country inhabitants by a double
barrier [*pregrada*], one standing eight feet from the other.
Between these barriers stands a guard who is responsible for
observing that there is no communication or even less any
contact between the city and rural inhabitants. Neither the
sold goods nor the money that must be given for them must

be received from hand to hand, but when the price has been agreed on, the seller puts his articles on the ground between the two barriers, while the buyer puts his money in a wooden container filled with water or vinegar . . . [so that] the infection is not transmitted via wood and straw, likewise it does not adhere to metals. Money, however, should be put in water or vinegar before it is received, the more so because money is often covered with filth which comes from sweat or from the uncleanliness of the hands in which it was."

The directions then prescribe a quarantine of twenty-one or forty-two days, depending on the seriousness of the plague. It then describes a quarantine station for those being detained. "The place of quarantine, which is also called a lazaretto, consists of one large or of many houses, standing one next to the other, where everyone spends his time apart, not communicating with the others, for which purpose they will supply each one a guard, who may not go away from him and who is maintained by him. The guard must certify under oath that the person in quarantine followed at all times the rules of the lazaretto, of which the essence is: that he communicated with no one, that he was fumigated according to the regulations that will be mentioned below, etc.; the guard is subject to the very same law and is just as unsafe as the one to whom he is assigned and therefore he may not have any contact with the guards . . . .

"Those arriving on the same day and who are to observe the same quarantine may and should be together, so as not to multiply the separate dwellings. All such persons have one guard in common, to keep down the number of guards.

"At the gates of the lazaretto the sale of edible goods is carried out across a double barrier like the one mentioned above. The person who is being kept in quarantine may not go [out] to buy things or leave his room without the guard assigned to him.

"An officer who is honest, prompt, and thorough should be assigned to supervize the lazaretto. He must not communicate by touch or [other] contact with those in quarantine, or with the guards assigned to it . . . .

"The fumigation used in lazarettos and in places subject to infection must be repeated every day in every house at sunset. Rich people will use incense for this, those of a

middle condition will utilize juniper berries, and the poor
and plain folk will be fumigated with juniper or pitch.

"It is also necessary to have at every lazaretto a doctor and
the necessary apothecary, which goes without saying." The
edict goes on to mention the special danger of paper and
describes the elaborate measures for disinfecting letters
crossing the quarantine cordon. Private letters were to be
opened by a gloved attendant, preferably on a marble table,
and fumigated "in thick smoke." See "13.552.—Genv. 9
[20 January 1771]. Senatskii. O predostorozhnostiakh
protivu zarazitel'noi bolezni, okazavsheisia v Pol'skikh
Provintsiiakh, prilezhashchikh k Turetskim granitsam,"
PSZ, 19:204–9, esp. 207–8.

Couriers coming from the war front were not to be
detained for long periods except in cases of extreme need;
nevertheless, they were to stop for "several hours or days."
Their clothes were to be fumigated, their dispatch cases
washed in vinegar and then dried over a fire, and a
certificate issued to them on leaving, telling how long they
were detained. See "13.556.—Genvaria 12 [23 January
1771]. Senatskii. O priniatii Gubernatoram predostorozhnosti
protivu okazavsheisia v pogranichnykh Guberniiakh
zarazitel'noi bolezni," *PSZ*, 19:211–13.

The ambassador did pass through the quarantine cordon
just a few years after the plague which enveloped Moscow
and threatened to spread throughout the empire. A series of
edicts set up measures for sealing off Moscow. During the
winter of 1771–72, quarantine periods had been set for seven
to twenty-one days. "13.745.—Genvaria 19 [30 January
1772]. Senatskii, po Vysochaishe utverzhdennomu dokladu.
O predostorozhnostiakh pri propuske iz Moskvy v
Peterbrug tovarov i o vyderzhanii semidnevnago karantina,"
PSZ, 19:427–29. In March, in recognition of the greater
danger of the plague in the warm months, the period of
confinement for persons was raised in some cases to a full
six weeks. See *PSZ*, 19:460–63.

The plague in Moscow was killing four hundred to five
hundred persons a day by August 1772 and was said to have
arrived in wool imported from Turkey. Soviet authors point
out that in addition to the dangers of disease, the plague was
one factor leading to popular discontent and rebellion. The
authorities, therefore, had good reason to fear it (*Istoriia*

Moskvy, 2:369–70).

A contemporary account of infectious diseases and measures taken against them in Europe is in John Howard, *An Account of the Principal Lazarettos in Europe.*

The particularly severe and widespread measures taken during the war years were repealed in September 1775. The reasons given were that it was a year since the armies had been in infected areas and there was no longer any danger of the plague in or beyond the empire. Quarantine measures reverted to those enacted before the war (*PSZ*, 20:207).

Rakoviţa. The visit by Gospodin Rakoviţa is a good example of diplomatic practices at this time and is connected with the "reliable channels" of information that Repnin was supposed to establish in Constantinople as one of his assigned tasks.

On 24 May 1775 Repnin reported to the empress that he had visited Rumiantsev at the village of Paraefeevka, near Kiev (*SRIO*, 5:182). On 1 June he wrote that during this visit they had received a representative of the hospodar of Walachia, Gospodin Rakoviţa (Raikovich in the Russian transcription), who asked Repnin to negotiate the following matters in Constantinople on behalf of Walachia: (1) a lifetime appointment for the hospodar of Walachia, following the example of Moldavia, (2) reduction of the Walachian payments to the Porte to what they had been fifty years earlier, (3) return of Walachian prisoners who had been taken beyond the Danube by the Ottomans, (4) cession of the area around Giurgiu, previously held by the Ottomans, to Walachia, (5) appointment of a Walachian chargé d'affaires in Constantinople who would be under the protection of the Russian ambassador, (6) conduct of Walachian affairs in Constantinople without delay and without the considerable expenditure of money for bribes, and (7) permission for the hospodar to again wear a feather in his cap, a privilege taken away forty years earlier.

Repnin replied that he felt that the wishes of the hospodar and the empress coincided, but the hospodar should take steps to demonstrate the loyalty to the empress which he professed by showing Repnin the channels through which he could handle Russians affairs with the Porte. In this way the Russians could utilize one of the best secret channels in the capital, that of an experienced Phanariote, Alexander Ypsilanti.

Rakoviţa then spent three days in Kiev with Repnin,
during which they held further discussions. Rakoviţa then
returned to Bucureşti, promising to see Repnin again in
Focşani. Rumiantsev had a high opinion of Rakoviţa's
knowledge of the situation in Constantinople (*SRIO*,
5:189–90).

Ranks. The following is an abridged version of the Russian Table
of Ranks of 1722, corrected to reflect changes made up to
1775, but limited primarily to titles encountered in the text.
Included also is the structure of a cavalry regiment of this
period.

Table of Ranks

CLASS	LAND FORCES	GUARDS	CIVIL SERVANTS	COURT OFFICIALS
1	General-Fieldmarshal *General-Fel'dmarshal*			
2	General of the Infantry, Cavalry, etc.; Full General *General ot Infanterii, Kavalerii; Polnyi General*		Actual Privy Councillor *Deistvitel'nyi Tainyi Sovetnik*	
3	Lieutenant General *General-Leitenant*			
4	Major General *General-Maior*	Colonel *Polkovnik*	Actual State Councillor *Deistvitel'nyi Statskii Sovetnik*	
5	Captain (naval) *Kapitan*	Lieutenant Colonel *Podpolkovnik*	State Councillor *Statskii Sovetnik*	Master of the Horse *Shtalmeister*
6	Colonel *Polkovnik*	Major *Maior*		Master of the Horse *Shtalmeister*
7	Lieutenant Colonel *Podpolkovnik*	Captain *Kapitan*	Master of Ceremonies *Tseremoniimeister*	
8	Premier Major *Premier-Maior* Second Major *Sekund-Maior* Master of the Horse (artillery) *Shtalmeister*	Lieutenant captain *Kapitan-Leitenant*	Voivode *Voevoda*	

CLASS	LAND FORCES	GUARDS	CIVIL SERVANTS	COURT OFFICIALS
9	Captain *Kapitan*	Lieutenant *Leitenant*		Court Master of Ceremonies *Nadvornyi Tseremonii-meister*
10	Lieutenant Captain *Kapitan-Leitenant*	Second Lieutenant *Unter-Leitenant*	Military interpreter *Perevodchik Voinskoi*	
11				
12	Lieutenant *Poruchik*			
13	Second Lieutenant *Podporuchik*			
14	Ensign *Praporshchik* Cornet (cavalry) *Kornet*		Secretary *Aktuarius*	

This table appeared originally as "3890.—Genvaria 24
[4 February 1722]. Tabel' of rangakh . . .", *PSZ*, 6:486–93.
The assignment of lower military ranks to classes 12, 13,
and 14 has been made in accordance with changes listed in
the reform of 1884. See "2178.—Aprelia 26 [8 May 1884].
Vysochaishee povelenie, ob'iavlennoe Voennym Ministrom
(Sobr. Uzak. 1884g.) Iiulia 6 [18 July], st. 550. O sravnenii
ofitserov armeiskikh voisk v preimushchestvakh po chinam
s ofitserami spetsial'nykh chastei i ob uprazdnenii china
Maiora," in *Polnoe sobranie zakonov Rossiiskoi Imperii*, sobranie
tret'e, 4:263–64, which accounts for some of the differences
found in F. A. Brokhaus, and I. A. Efron, eds.,
Entsiklopedischeskii slovar', 63:439–41.

The text does not usually specify which branch of the
military service the officers were drawn from. Therefore,
attention should be called to the fact that a given rank in
various branches of the service, such as infantry, cavalry,
guards, etc., was assigned to different classes in the Table
of Ranks. It is important to note that officers of the guard
were two grades higher than the same named ranks in other
services.

The Table of Ranks applied only to officers. The following
list of ranks and positions of a cavalry regiment may help to
locate the noncommissioned personnel in the hierarchy.
The list is taken from the weekly report of the regimental
commanding officer from the year 1766.

REGIMENTAL STAFF	POLKOVOI SHTAB
Colonel	Polkovnik
Lieutenant Colonel	Podpolkovnik
Premier-Major	Premier-Maior
Second-Major	Sekund-Maior
SUB-STAFF	UNTER-SHTAB
Regimental Quartermaster	Polkovoi Kvartirmeister'
Adjutant	Ad'iutant
Legal Officer	Auditor
Riding Master	Bereiter
Priest	Pop
Medical Officer	Lekar'
Assistant Medical Officer	Podlekar'
Sergeant Majors:	Vakhmistrskie chiny:
Storekeeper	Provientmeister'
Teamster	Oboznoi
Medical Attendant	Nadziratel' dlia bol'nykh
Regimental Clerk	Polkovoi pisar'
Clerks	Pisari
Trumpeters	Trubachi
Kettledrummer	Litavrshchik
His student	emu uchenik
Chaplain	Tserkovnik
Locksmith	Slesar'
Saddler	Sedel'nik
Veterinarian	Konovalov
Sanitarian	Profos
Regimental artillery:	Polkovaia artilleriia:
Sergeant, Corporal,	Serzhant, Korporal,
Cannoneer and Fusilier	Kanoner i fuzeler
COMPANIES	ROTNYI PRIMOPLAN
Captain	Rotmistr or Kapitan
Lieutenant	Poruchik
Cornet or Ensign	Kornet ili Praporshchik
Sergeant Major	Vakhmistr
Company Quartermaster	Rotnyi Kvartirmeister'
Corporal or Sub-Ensign	Efreit-Korporal ili Podpraporshchik
Corporal	Kaporal
Barber	Tsiriul'nik
Drummer	Barabanshchik
Troopers:	Stroevye:
Cuirassier, Carabineer,	Kirasir, Karabiner,
Dragoon, Hussar	Dragun, Gusar
Smith	Kuznets
Carpenter	Plotnik
Teamster	Izvoshchik
Orderly	Den'shchik

The source is: "12.543.—Genvaria 14 [25 January 1766].
Instruktsiia konnago polka Polkovniku,—sostoiavshaiasia
po dokladu Voinskoi Kommissii," *PSZ*, 17:481–529, esp.

p. 498. A work which is of general interest and one which
has been utilized here to some extent in the translations is
that by the United States military attache to Saint Petersburg
in the 1870s: F. V. Greene, *The Russian Army and Its
Campaigns in Turkey in 1877–1878*. An examination of his
charts in Pt. 1, chap. 2, esp. pp. 25–26, will show that
organizational changes from the eighteenth to the
nineteenth century were not radical.

The following terms call for additional comment.

Jäger (eger'). Detachments of jägers, also translated as
chasseurs, were included in sixty-three regiments in 1769
and underwent various reorganizations later on. The
original legislation is "12.494.—Oktiabria 13 [24 October
1765]. Vysochaishe utverzhdennyi doklad Voinskoi
Kommissii. Ob uchrezhdenii Egerskago korpusa," *PSZ*,
17:562, continued in *PSZ*, 43, Kniga shtatov, chast' pervaia;
107–10. For a discussion of these special troops, see
L. G. Beskrovnyi, *Ocherki po istochnikovedeniiu voennoi istorii
Rossii*, pp. 134–38; and by the same author, *Russkaia armiia i
flot v XVIII veke (Ocherki)*, p. 313.

Junior officer (ober-ofitser). Includes commissioned officers
from the rank of cornet or ensign through captain. See the
Entsiklopedischeskii slovar', 42:503.

Staff officer (shtabs-ofitser). Officers of the regimental staff,
as distinguished from company officers; includes ranks of
major through colonel. See Genrikh A. Leer, *Entsiklopediia
voennykh i morskikh nauk*, 8:381.

Noncommissioned officer (unter-ofitser). Ranks below cornet
or ensign, excluding ordinary soldiers (*riadovye soldaty*). See
Leer, *Entsiklopediia*, 8:48–50.

Secretary (aktuarius). A person in charge of correspondence;
at this time a person of the class 14 in the Table of Ranks.
The position was later abolished. See *Entsiklopedischeskii
slovar'*, 1:312, and "3534.—Fevralia 28 [11 March 1720].
General'nyi Reglament ili Ustav . . . Glava XXXII. O
dolzhnosti aktuariusa," *PSZ*. 6:152–53.

Page (pazh). An exclusive corps of boys trained for duty
primarily at court; boys aged 8–13 or 14 were pages, and
aged 15–19 were chamber pages (*kamer-pazh*). The total
number was forty-nine in 1759 and increased to seventy-
eight in 1786. See *Entsiklopedischeskii slovar'*, 44:590.

Captain, naval. The title of captain in the naval forces was

distributed through four classes of the Table of Ranks,
5 through 8. In addition to the Table of Ranks, see the staff
structure listed in "K No. 12.235.—Sentiabria 5 [16 September
1764]. Vysochaishe utverzhdennyi doklad Morskoi
Rossiiskago flotov i Admiralteiskago Pravleniia Kommissii
s prilozheniem Shtata i rospisaniia mundirnykh materialov
vo flot sluzhashchim chinam," *PSZ*, 44, Kniga shtatov,
chast' pervaia: 118–24.

Medical personnel. The Russian term *doktor* has been
translated as doctor, whereas *lekar'* has been rendered as
medical officer in order to indicate the generally higher
status of the former, as may be seen in "K No. 11.455.—
Fevralia 28 [11 March 1762]. Vysochaishe utverzhdennyi
doklad ot Arkhiatera pervago Leib-Medika i Tainago
Sovetnika Iakova Monsiia. O rangakh dlia Meditsinskago
Fakul'teta," *PSZ*, 44, Kniga shtatov, chast' vtoraia,
otdelenie IV: 56–59.

Actual state councillor (deistvitel'nyi statskii sovetnik). This
rank was added after the publication of the Table of Ranks:
see "4500.—Maia 7 [18 May 1724]. Imennyi.—O
pomeshchenii v klassy china Tainago, Deistvitel'nago
Statskago i Statskago Sovetnikov," *PSZ*, 7:280–81.

The example of a regimental table of organization has
been taken from the first part of Catherine II's reign, at
which time several reorganizations were carried through,
mostly for the purpose of negating innovations introduced
by Peter III. On this subject, see Beskrovnyi, *Russkaia
armiia i flot*, chap. 5, pp. 293–343; and his *Ocherki voennoi
istoriografii Rossii*, pp. 107–47. Other useful tables of
organization may be cited. For the Izmailovskii Guard
Regiment, "5623.—Sentiabria 22 [3 October 1730].
Vysochaishe utverzhdennyi doklad Kniazia Golitsyna.—O
sformirovanii Leib-Gvardii Izmailovskago polka s
prilozheniem shtata liudei i zhalovan'ia," *PSZ*, 8:325–26;
"K No. 5623 . . . Tabel' o soderzhanii Izmailovskago polka,
novouchrezhdaemago iz Landmilits," *PSZ*, 43, Kniga
shtatov, chast' pervaia: 49; "No. 5.902.—Dekabria 9
[20 December 1731]. Shtaty Leib-Gvardii Preobrazhenskago
Semenovskago i Izmailovskago polkov," *PSZ*, 41, Kniga
shtatov, chast' pervaia, otdelenie pervoe: 187–95. A useful
bibliography on all the guard regiments will be found in
Beskrovnyi, *Ocherki voennoi istoriografii Rossii*, pp. 309–11.

For infantry regiments, see "12.289.—Dekabria 8
[19 December 1764]. Instruktsiia pekhotnago polka
Polkovniku s prilozheniem form shtatov i tabelei," *PSZ*,
16:972–99, esp. p. 988. For artillery, see "K No. 11.797.—
Aprelia 17 [28 April 1763]. Ob utverzhdenii shtatov
bombardirskago dvukh kanonirskikh i dvukh fiuzilernykh
polkov; o nedozvolenii nikakomu Pravleniiu ne opredeliat'
v Artilleriiskii Korpus, ni izkliuchat' iz onago bez soglasiia
General-Fel'dtseikhmeistera," *PSZ*, 43, Kniga shtatov,
chast' pervaia: 21–29.

   Illustrations of the uniforms of military ranks and units
at this time may be found in volume 3 of the following
extraordinary collection, Aleksandr Vasil'evich Viskovatov,
*Risunki k istoricheskomu opisaniiu odezhdy i vooruzheniia
Rossiiskikh voisk, sostavlennomu po Vysochaishemu poveleniiu*
(Saint Petersburg, 1841–62), 30 vols.

Reaya. A term meaning, originally, flock or herd. By the eighteenth
   century it designated all the subjects of the sultan who were
   not in the military, that is, the ruling class. More and more,
   it came to be used for the non-Muslim, especially Christian,
   subjects. Depending on the context, the word can be
   translated as subject or peasant.

Reis efendi. Known also as *reis ül-küttâp*, he was the official
   responsible for the work of the chancery, that is, the central
   administrative bureaus of the imperial divan, and he also
   controlled the secretaries of the financial administration.
   Gradually, the *reis efendi* began to control the direction of
   foreign affairs, and in the administrative reorganization that
   took place under Mahmud II his office became the Ministry
   for Foreign Affairs.

Reis ül-küttâp. *See* **Reis efendi.**

Repnin, Prince Nikolai Vasil'evich. Repnin's service to the
   Russian empire alternated between military and diplomatic
   undertakings and, as was the case with so many who served
   under Catherine, between success and failure, reward and
   censure. He was born in 1734, and at fifteen he was serving
   with his father on the Rhine. At the beginning of the Seven
   Years' War he was assigned to duty with the French army
   and was promoted to the rank of colonel at the age of
   twenty-six. At twenty-eight he was a general. Upon the
   death of Elizabeth and the accession of Peter III in 1763,

Russia reversed her policy toward Prussia. One result of this
was the assignment of Repnin to the headquarters of
Frederick the Great, where he began his diplomatic career
in the negotiations of that year. In this he was only partially
successful, and the same can be said of his accomplishments
in Constantinople.

Repnin was appointed minister plenipotentiary to Poland
in 1762. It has been suggested that the post reflected the
protection of Count Panin to whom he was related by
marriage; his wife's mother, Princess Kurakina, was
Panin's sister.

Repnin spent the next six years in Poland, where again he
was unsuccessful in carrying out the plans of the empress
and Panin for preserving Poland in a state of political
confusion and dependence on Saint Petersburg. His use of
Russian troops, bribery, and threats succeeded only in
making him unpopular among the Poles. Thus, when the
Ottoman Empire declared war on Russia in 1768, it became
necessary for the Russians to maintain their position in
Poland with as little expenditure of money and troops as
possible. Since this was easier with Repnin removed, he was
recalled. Again his position was somewhat ambiguous. As
a sign of favor he received the Order of Saint Alexander
Nevsky, the rank of lieutenant general, and 50,000 rubles.
On the other hand, he was ordered directly to the army of
Golitsyn, then besieging Hotin, rather than to Saint
Petersburg—which was a sign of disfavor.

During the Ottoman war, Repnin was both decorated
and reprimanded. In 1770 he was assigned to the Moldavian
corps of General Shtoffel'n, whose death in June of that
year left him in command. That same month he was
decorated with the Order of Saint George, Second Class,
for bravery in the capture of Larga. He fought that year at
Kagul, Izmail, and Kiliia, and spent the winter as a hero
in Saint Petersburg, being cited by the empress for his
victory at Kiliia.

In 1771 Repnin returned to the army, via Warsaw, to take
part in the action at Giurgiu and Vakareşti. The latter
action evoked criticism from Rumiantsev, and in response
to this Repnin asked to be relieved of his command.
Rumiantsev immediately replaced him with General Essen,
and in the fall of 1772 Repnin was given a year's leave by

the War College to "take the waters." He was in serious
financial difficulties when he left for Poland, Germany, and
Holland. In 1773 he borrowed 12,000 rubles from a banker
in The Hague.

He returned to duty with the army in 1774, taking part in
the blockade of Silistra in June. In July, Repnin was
ordered by Rumiantsev to take part in the peace negotiations
at Küçük Kaynarca because the ambassador, Obreskov,
could not reach the village in time. He was present, therefore,
at the conference that lasted from 17 to 21 July 1774.

Repnin had the honor of being ordered to carry news of
the successful negotiations to his court, and he arrived at
Peterhof on 10 August, where he was again honored by
Catherine. Promotion to the rank of general in chief, to
lieutenant colonel of the Izmailovskii Guard Regiment, and
a present of another 50,000 rubles were his.

At this time, Rumiantsev had become ill and Catherine
ordered that Repnin should assume his command in the
event of the field marshal's death. Rumiantsev recovered,
but Repnin was retained in the role of negotiator and was
given the task of leading the embassy to Constantinople.
This was probably a welcome and a needed opportunity to
reestablish himself, both financially and politically. After
spending the winter in Saint Petersburg, he set out on the
long journey in the spring, visiting Rumiantsev in Kiev in
mid-May. His activities in Constantinople are covered in
the text and in other notes.

The rewards Repnin received for his moderately successful
mission to Constantinople appear meager in comparison to
previous honors. He was appointed governor general of
Smolensk. This reflection of coolness in the attitude of the
empress is traced to Repnin's increasing closeness to Prince
Paul, and to his involvement with Freemasonry which
Catherine was probably aware of and to which she was
hostile.

It is less interesting to study Repnin's career after the
embassy to Constantinople, except to note that the
alteration of success and failure continued to the end of
his days. In the next Ottoman war, Repnin took to the field
and was successful at Focşani, Bender, and Izmail, and in the
peace negotiations at Galaţi in 1791, but his accomplishment
earned him the anger of Potemkin. Therefore, Repnin

received the Order of Saint George, First Class, instead of
the rank of field marshal. In 1792 he was involved in the
trial of Novikov, where his association with the Freemasonry
movement earned him the lasting disfavor of the aging
empress.

He later served as governor general in Riga and performed
military service during the Polish uprising of 1794. His
earlier friendship with Prince Paul caused his fortunes to
improve when the latter ascended the throne in 1796. He
received, among other things, the rank of field marshal, and
an estate of six thousand serfs. This too, however, was
shortlived. In 1798 he was removed from the imperial
service, whereupon he retired to Moscow. He died there of
an attack of apoplexy in 1801.

Repnin's one legitimate male child had died in 1774. As a
final mark of imperial favor, Alexander I declared that
Prince Nikolai Volkonskii, Repnin's grandson, should
adopt the illustrious name as his own.

Several works trace the family of Repnin back to the
House of Riurik in Chernigov; Aleksandr A. Bobrinskii,
*Dvorianskie Rody, vnesenie v obshchii gerbovnik Vserossiiskoi
imperii*, 1:48–52.

A biography of Repnin appears in *RBS*, 16:93–118.

Resmi Ahmet Efendi. *See* **Ahmet Resmi Efendi.**

Rumeli beylerbeyi. Governor general of Rumeli. The first
Rumeli beylerbeyi was Lala Şahin, the tutor of Bayezid I, in
the reign of Murad I (1360–89). This official was responsible
for military matters in the conquered areas of Rumeli. A
beylerbeyi was later appointed for Anatolia, and as the
empire expanded in the fifteenth and sixteenth centuries,
new *beylerbeyilik*s were organized, composed of smaller
administrative districts called *sancak*s. Gradually, what had
once been a post became a rank, and was conferred on
people who had no connection at all with the administration
of Rumeli. The rank of *Rumeli beylerbeyi* brought the holder
the title of pasha and the right to three horsetails.

Rumiantsev, Count Petr Aleksandrovich. Rumiantsev's father
Aleksandr Ivanovich, headed the Russian mission to
Constantinople in 1740, following the Peace of Belgrade.
Petr, who was born in 1725, was enrolled in the Cadet Corps
in 1740. In that same year he was appointed as a second

lieutenant and transferred to Finland, where he achieved a
reputation for riotous living. During the Seven Years' War
he distinguished himself, and in 1764 he was appointed
governor general of Malorossiia and president of the College
of Malorossiia. (He is buried in the Kievo-Pecherskaia Lavra.)
In 1768, at the outbreak of the Ottoman war, he was chosen
to head the Ukrainian Second Army, and in 1769 took over
as commander of the First Army when Golitsyn incurred
the displeasure of the empress. In 1770 he achieved fame
through victory at Kagul and was promoted to the rank of
field marshal. He was made commander of all forces in the
south. His disagreement in 1771 over military affairs with
Prince Repnin caused the latter to ask for retirement from
the service. During 1772 and 1773, Rumiantsev was in
charge of the negotiations with the Ottomans. In 1773 and
1774 he renewed the war and brought about the defeat
which led to the negotiations at Küçük Kaynarca. He was
rewarded handsomely by Catherine during the peace
celebrations of July 1775. Among other things, his village
of Troitskoe was renamed Kainardzhi. He died in 1796.

   Rumiantsev is now considered to be one of the great
military figures of Russian history, and a considerable
amount of material about him has been published in the
Soviet Union. See Iu. R. Klokman, *Fel'dmarshal Rumiantsev
v period russko-turetskoi voiny 1768–1774 gg.* and P. A.
Rumiantsev. Sbornik dokumentov (Moscow, 1953–59), 3 vols.
See also the biography in *RBS*, 17:521–73.

Saadabad. *See* **Kağıthane.**

Şahinşah. One of the titles of the Ottoman sultans, borrowed from
   Persian usage, meaning king of kings.

Sancak. The *sancak* was the basic administrative unit in the
   Ottoman Empire. It was under the control of the *sancak
   beyi*. The *beylerbeyi* of a number of *sancak*s grouped together
   as a *vilayet* was himself the head of one of those *sancak*s
   known as the *paşa sancağı*. The feudal cavalry was assigned
   holdings in the *sancak*s and rallied to the sultan's banner
   for campaign under their *sancak beyi*, and through him to
   their *beylerbeyi*.

Şemsiye. A kind of pavilion, open halfway around, capable of
   being moved so as to offer shade.

Serdar. Local janissary commanders were called *serdar*s.

Serdengeçti. A term used for janissaries who volunteered for
   hazardous duty and distinguished themselves by their
   courageous exploits. The term may be translated as
   "head-riskers."

Sherbet. Baron de Tott has left a description of his encounter with
   sherbet in Jassy. "I was obliged to suffer the whole routine
   of Turkish ceremonies. The most important and respectful of
   these is the presenting of Sherbet, which is always followed
   by an aspersion of Rose-water and perfume of Alloes. This
   Sherbet, so much talked of in Europe, and so little known,
   is made of conserved fruits dissolved in water, but with so
   much musk as almost to destroy the taste of the liquor.
   Thus the Vase once filled, suffices for the visits of the week.
   I used it very sparingly, as I likewise did the conserves
   brought with the coffee, and in the serving of which they
   never change the spoon." De Tott, *Memoirs*, 1, pt. 2:35–36.

Silâhdar Katibi, Silahdar Emini, and **Sipahiler Katibi, Sipahiler
   Emini.** These two bureaus issued pay vouchers for these two
   cavalry divisions, and for the *bölükât-i erbâa* cavalry divisions
   as well. The certificates had to be countersigned by the
   head of the *suvari* bureau. The *katib* was the chief of each
   bureau, assisted by the *emin*.

Sipahiler katibi, Sipahiler emini. *See* **Silahdar katibi.**

Spatar. This official was in charge of police matters in Walachia.
   In Moldavia his functions were performed by the hetman.

Stakhiev, Aleksandr Stakhievich. Stakhiev was born in 1724.
   He had served under Count Panin in Stockholm and
   remained in that city until 1775, when he was promoted to
   the rank of state councillor and sent as envoy extraordinary
   and minister plenipotentiary to Constantinople at an annual
   salary of 8,000 rubles (*SRIO*, 135:489–90).
      For his efforts in uniting the Crimea with Russia, and for
   opening the Black Sea to Russian vessels, he received a
   reward of 1,000 serfs in Belorussia and the Order of Saint
   Stanislav from Catherine in 1779. He was replaced in
   Constantinople in 1781 by Ia. I. Bulgakov, and he died
   in 1794. A biography appears in *RBS*, 19:360–61.

Subaşı. A janissary officer who acted as the chief of public
   security for the city of Istanbul. Together with the *asesbaşı*

he made his rounds of inspection and arrested persons
suspected of crimes or caught in the act. He also accompanied
the grand vezir on his inspection tours.

Tersane emini. Chief lieutenant of the grand admiral. He directed
the construction and repair of ships, and saw to their
armament. As commissioner of the admiralty he was a
member of the *hacegân*.

Teşrifatçı. This official was the chief of protocol and kept the
registers concerned with protocol matters, including the
established procedures for the reception of foreign
ambassadors. As can be seen from the translations, he
participated in an official capacity at most ceremonies and
functions. He too was one of the *hacegân*.

Tezkireci. An official of the imperial divan. As the bureaucracy
proliferated there came to be two officials known as the first
and second *tezkireci*s; *tezkireci-i evvel*, and *tezkireci-i sani*. They
were of considerable importance and ranked among the
hacegân. In the meetings of the divan the *tezkireci-i evvel* stood
before the grand vezir and read out the petitions for action.
The *tezkireci*s also handled his correspondence and orders
sent to the numerous governmental departments.

Tophane. A district of the capital below Galata, on the entrance
to the Bosphorus. The imperial cannon works were located
here, and there was a pier, the Tophane pier. The district
was noted for its coffee houses as well.

Turnacı. The *turnacı*s were the sixty-eighth *orta* of the janissary
corps. They trained dogs for the hunt, but were also of
prime importance in the collection of Christian youth for
the *devşirme*. Here they appear as garrison troops. Their
commander was the *turnacıbaşı*, and the local commander
was the *turnacı ağası*.

Turnacı ağası. See **Turnacı.**

Valide Sarayı. Situated in Üsküdar, near Şemsi Pasha mosque
and Ayazma gardens. It is no longer in existence.

Vekilharç ağası. A janissary officer on the *bölük* level (about
one hundred men to a *bölük*), especially concerned with
quartermaster problems.

Vestiar maray. *Vestiar* designated the treasurer, *maray*, meaning great, indicated that this person was actually functioning as treasurer at the time.

Voivode. An agent appointed by a pasha or governor to administer a *kaza* (subdivision of a *sancak*) for a share in the tax revenue. This term is not to be confused with voivode used as a title for the hospodars of Moldavia and Walachia.

Weights and measures.

1 *kıyye/okka*	2.83 lbs.
1 *keyl/kile*	20 *okka*
1 *kantar*	44 *okka*
1 *çekke*	4 *kantar*
1 *habbe*	1 grain

Ypsilanti, Alexander. A member of another leading Phanariote family and born in 1725, he served as hospodar of both Moldavia and Walachia and was put to death in 1825, suspected of furthering Greek national ambitions.

Zagarcı. The *zagarcı*s were the sixty-fourth *orta* of janissaries and along with the *turnacı*s were one of the hunting *orta*s. Composed of some four hundred mounted and thirty-five foot soldiers, they accompanied the sultan on hunts.

Bibliography

Archival and Manuscript Materials

Archives du Ministère des Affaires Étrangères, Paris. Correspondance diplomatique, Russie.

Başvekâlet Arşivi, Istanbul. Cevdet tasnifi, Hatt-ı hümâyun tasnifi, Name-i hümâyun defterleri.

British Museum, London. Additional Manuscripts.

Public Record Office, London. State Papers, Foreign: Russia, Turkey.

Süleymaniye Kütüphanesi, Istanbul. Esat Efendi kısmı.

Topkapı Sarayı, Müze arşivi, Istanbul. Evrak (E) ve Defterler (D).

Printed Works

Ahmet Resmi. *Hülâsat ül-İtibar.* Istanbul, 1286/1869.

Ashurkov, Vadim N. *Gorod masterov; Ocherki po istorii Tuly c XVI veka do ustanovleniia vlasti Sovetov.* Tula, 1958.

Auerbach, Hans. *Die Besiedlung der Südukraine in den Jahren 1774– 1787.* Wiesbaden, 1965.

Ayverdi, Ekrem Hakkı. *19. Asırda İstanbul Haritası.* Istanbul, 1958.

Baedeker, Karl. *Russia.* Leipzig, 1914.

Bantysh-Kamenskii, Dmitrii N. *Istoricheskoe sobranie spiskov Kavaleram chetyrekh rossiiskikh imperatorskikh ordenov.* Moscow, 1814.

Beskrovnyi, Lr. G. *Ocherki po istochnikovedeniiu voennoi istorii Rossii.* Moscow, 1957.

———. *Ocherki voennoi istoriografii Rossii.* Moscow, 1962.

———. *Russkaia armiia i flot v XVIII veke (Ocherki).* Moscow, 1958.

Bil'basov, Vasilii A. *Istoriia Ekateriny Vtoroi.* 2 vols. Berlin, 1889–90.

Bobrinskii, Aleksandr A. *Dvorianskie Rody, vnesenie v Obshchii gerbovnik Vserossiiskoi imperii.* 2 vols. Saint Petersburg, 1890.

Boscovich, R. G. *Giornale di un Viaggio da Constantinopoli in Polonia.* Bassano, 1784.

Brokhaus, F. A., and Efron, I. A. (eds.) *Entsiklopedischeskii slovar'.* 82 vols. Saint Petersburg, 1890–1904.

Bruce, Peter Henry. *Memoirs.* London, 1782.

Burgess, Malcolm. "A Survey of the Stage in Russia from 1741 to 1783, with Special Reference to the Development of the Russian Theater." Ph.D. dissertation, Cambridge University, 1953.

Cevdet Pasha (Ahmet). *Tarih-i Cevdet.* New ed. 10 vols. Constantinople, 1309/1891–92.

Corberon, Marie Daniel Bourée, Baron de. *Un diplomate français à la cour de Catherine II, 1775–1780.* 2 vols. Paris, 1901.

Danişmend, İsmail Hami. *İzahlı Osmanlı Tarihi Kronolojisi.* 4 vols. Istanbul, 1947–55.

Dernschwam, Hans. *Tagebuch einer Reise nach Konstantinopel und Kleinasien* (1553/55). Edited by Franz Babinger. Munich, 1923.

Druzhinina, E. I. *Kiuchuk-Kainardzhiiskii mir 1774 goda.* Moscow, 1955.

Dubrovin, Nikolai F. *Prisoedinenie Kryma k Rossii 1775–1782.* 4 vols. Saint Petersburg, 1885.

Encyclopaedia of Islam. New ed. Leiden, 1960–.

Fekete, L. "Die Geschenke des Sultans Abdulhamid I an Zarin Katharina II im Jahre 1775," *Acta Orientalia,* 2 (1952):1–18.

———. *Die Siyaqat-Schrift in der türkischen Finanzverwaltung.* 2 vols. Budapest, 1955.

Gibb, H. A. R., and Bowen, Harold. *Islamic Society and the West.* Vol. 1, *Islamic Society in the Eighteenth Century,* pt. 1. London, 1950. Pt. 2. London, 1957.

Giterman, Valentin. *Geschichte Russlands.* 2 vols. Zurich, 1945.

Gooch, George P. *Catherine the Great and Other Studies.* London, 1954.

Greene, F. V. *The Russian Army and Its Campaigns in Turkey in 1877–1878.* New York, 1879.

Hapgood, Isabel Florence. *Service Book of the Holy Orthodox-Catholic Apostolic (Greco-Russian) Church. Compiled, Translated, and Arranged from the Old Church-Slavonic Service Books of the Russian Church, and Collated with the Service Books of the Greek Church.* Boston, 1906.

Hasluck, F. W. *Christianity and Islam under the Sultans.* 2 vols. Oxford, 1929.

Howard, John. *An Account of the Principal Lazarettos in Europe.* Warrington, 1789.

Huart, C. *Les calligraphes et les miniaturistes de l'Orient musulman.* Paris, 1908.

Hurewitz, J. C. *Diplomacy in the Near and Middle East.* 2 vols. Princeton, 1956.

Iorga, N. *A History of Roumania.* Translated by Joseph McCabe. London, 1925.

Islam Ansiklopedisi. Istanbul, 1941–.

Itzkowitz, Norman. "Mehmed Raghib Pasha: The Making of an Ottoman Grand Vezir." Ph.D. dissertation, Princeton University, 1959.

Kanitz, Felix P. *Donau-Bulgarien und der Balkan.* 3 vols. Leipzig, 1875–79.

Kaplan, Herbert H. *The First Partition of Poland.* New York, 1962.

Kepeci, Kâmil. *Tarih Lûgati.* Istanbul, 1952.

Kiev, Akademiia nauk, Institut istorii. *Istoriia Kieva.* 2 vols. Kiev, 1960.

Kissling, Hans J. *Beiträge zur Kenntnis Thrakiens im 17. Jahrhundert.* Wiesbaden, 1956.

Kliuchevskii, Vasilii O. *Sochineniia.* 8 vols. Moscow, 1956–59.

Klokman, Iu. R. *Fel'dmarshal Rumiantsev v period russko-turetskoi voiny 1768–1774 gg.* Moscow, 1951.

Lane, Edward W. *An Account of the Manners and Customs of the Modern Egyptians.* 3d. ed. London, 1890.

Lawrence-Archer, James Henry. *The Orders of Chivalry.* London, 1887.

Leer, Genrikh A. *Entsiklopediia voennykh i morskikh nauk.* 8 vols. Saint Petersburg, 1883–95.

Leningrad, Akademiia nauk, Institut istorii. *Istoriia Moskvy.* 6 vols. Moscow, 1952–59.

Lewis, Bernard. *Istanbul and the Civilization of the Ottoman Empire.* Norman, Okla., 1963.

——. *The Middle East and the West.* London, 1964.

Lewis, W. H. *Levantine Adventurer.* New York, 1963.

Macmichael, William, *Journey from Moscow to Constantinople in the Years 1817, 1818.* London, 1819.

Mamboury, Ernest. *The Tourists' Istanbul.* Translated by Malcolm Burr. Istanbul, 1953.

Mantran, Robert. *Istanbul dans la seconde moitié du XVIIe siècle.* Paris, 1962.

Miller, Barnette. *Beyond the Sublime Porte.* London, 1931.

Moscow University. I. Obschestvo istorii i drevnostei rossiiskikh. *Chteniia.* 64 vols. Moscow, 1846–1918.

Nabi Efendi. *Conseils de Nabi Efendi.* Trans. by M. Pavet de Courteille. Paris, 1857.

———. *Tarih-i Kamanice.* Istanbul, 1281/1864.

Naff, Thomas. "Reform and the Conduct of Ottoman Diplomacy in the Reign of Selim III, 1789–1807," *Journal of the American Oriental Society*, 83, no. 3 (Sept. 1963): 295–315.

[Mustafa] Naima Efendi. *Tarih-i Naima.* 3d. ed. 6 vols. Constantinople, 1281–83/1864–66.

Pakalın, Mehmet Zeki. *Osmanlı Tarih Deyimleri ve Terimleri Sözlüğü.* 3 vols. Istanbul, 1946.

Pickthall, Marmaduke. *The Meaning of the Glorious Koran.* London, 1930.

Platonov, S. F. *Lektsii po russkoi istorii.* 6th ed. Petrograd, 1915.

Polnoe sobranie zakonov Rossiiskoi Imperii s 1649 goda. 45 vols. Saint Petersburg, 1830.

Polski Słownik Biograficzny. Cracow, 1935–.

Porter, Sir James. *Observations on the Religion, Law, Government, and Manners of the Turks.* 2 vols. London, 1768.

Pyliaev, Mikhail I. *Staraia Moskva.* Saint Petersburg, 1891.

Redhouse, James W. *A Turkish and English Lexicon.* Constantinople, 1921.

Reychman, Jan. "Une famille de drogmans orientaux en Pologne au XVIIIe siècle," *Rocznik Orientalistyczny*, 25 (1961): 83–99.

Rossiiskoe Posol'stvo v Konstantinopol' 1776 goda. Saint Petersburg, 1777.

Russkii biograficheskii slovar'. 25 vols. Saint Petersburg, 1896–1918.

Sacke, Georg. "Katerina II. im Kampf um Thron und Selbstherrschaft," *Archiv für Kulturgeschichte*, 23, no. 2 (1932): 191–216.

Sbornik imperatorskago Russkago istoricheskago obshchestva. 148 vols. Saint Petersburg, 1867–1916.

Sefaretname-i Adbülkerim Paşa. Istanbul, 1316/1898.

Sertoğlu, Midhat. *Muhteva bakımından Başvekâlet Arşivi.* Ankara, 1955.

Sidorov, A. A., ed. *400 let russkogo knigopechataniia 1564–1964.* 2 vols. Moscow, 1964.

Solov'ev, Sergei M. *Istoriia Rossii s drevneishikh vremen.* 29 vols. Moscow, 1959–1966.

Spasskii, Ivan G. *Russkaia monetnaia sistema.* 3d. ed. Leningrad, 1962.

Spuler, Bertold. "Die europäische Diplomatie in Konstantinopel bis zum Frieden von Belgrad (1739)," *Jahrbücher für Kultur und Geschichte der Slaven,* 11 (1935), Hft. 1, 53–115, Hft. 2, 171–222, Hft. 3–4, 313–66; *Jahrbücher für Geschichte Osteuropas,* 1 (1936), Hft. 2, 229–62, Hft. 3, 383–440.

Stuart, Francis A. *Scottish Influences in Russian History.* Glasgow, 1913.

Sumner, B. H. *Peter the Great and the Ottoman Empire.* Oxford, 1949.

Svodnyi katalog russkoi knigi grazhdanskoi pechati XVIII veka 1725–1800. Moscow, 1962–.

Tooke, William. *The Life of Catharine II. Empress of Russia.* 3 vols. London, 1798.

Tott, François, Baron de. *Memoirs.* 2 vols. London, 1785.

Tournier, J. *Postguide through Russia.* London, 1812.

Tula. *Materialy dlia istorii goroda XVI–XVIII stoletii.* Moscow, 1884.

Turkey. Maarif Vekilliği Kütüphaneler Müdürlüğü Tasnif Komisyonu. *İstanbul Kütüphaneleri Tarih-Coğrafya Yazmaları Katalogları.* Istanbul, 1943–.

Unat, Faik Reşit. *Hicrî Tarihleri Milâdî Tarihe Cevirme Kılavuzu.* Ankara, 1959.

———. "Şehdî Osman Efendi Sefaretnamesi," *Tarih Vesikaları,* 1 (Haziran, 1941): 66–70.

United States Board on Geographic Names. *Bulgaria.* Washington, D.C., 1959.

———. *Rumania.* Washington, D.C., 1960.

———. *Russia.* Washington, D.C., 1959.

———. *Turkey.* Washington, D.C., 1960.

Uzunçarşılı, İsmail Hakkı. *Osmanlı Devletinin Merkez ve Bahriye Teşkilâtı.* Ankara, 1948.

———. *Osmanlı Devleti teşkilâtından Kapukulu Ocakları.* 2 vols. Ankara, 1943–44.

Vorontsov-Dashkov, I. I., compiler. *Istoricheskii ocherk rossiiskikh ordenov i sbornik osnovnykh ordenskikh statutov.* Saint Petersburg, 1891.

Waliszewski, K. *Paul the First of Russia.* London, 1913.

Wittek, Paul. *The Rise of the Ottoman Empire*. London, 1938.
Yazır, Mahmud. *Eski Yazılar Anahtarı*. Istanbul, 1942.
Zinkeisen, Johann W. *Geschichte des osmanischen Reiches in Europa*.
    6 vols. Gotha, 1840–63.

Index

Abbot, George (London banker), 40
Abdülhamit I, Sultan, 55, 108, 209; gifts from Catherine described, 20–21
Abdülhamit Han. See Abdülhamit I
Abdülkerim, 5, 6, 7, 9, 12, 13, 15, 17, 19, 21, 23, 25, 26, 27, 28, 30, 31, 58, 201; appointed, 57; audience with Catherine, 94–96; departs from Istanbul, 58–59; departs from Moscow, 110; on Eastern European politics, 118–20; final letter to Catherine, 111; forwards grand vezir's instructions to Panin, 114; objects to quarantine, 82; presents instrument of ratification, 94–95; presents letters to Panin, 93; on Pugachev, 117; rank and titles, 125; rank assigned, 57; receives reply from Panin, 114; reception for, in Moscow, 97–98; return to Istanbul, 117; on Russian character, 112; sagacity of, 77; speech at sultan's audience, 95; speech on leaving Moscow, 108; visits Rumiantsev at Kaynarca, 109. See also Rumeli beylerbeyi
Abdülkerim Efendi. See Abdülkerim
Abdülkerim Pasha. See Abdülkerim
Abdullah Aga, turnacı of Giurgiu, 144, 145
Abdurrahman, 19, 20; commander of Karnabat, 148, 149
Abode of Islam (dâr ül-islam), 1, 13
Abode of war (dâr ül-harp), 1, 7
Academy of Sciences: and Russian printing, 32

Acek (small boat), 72
Adjutant (kethuda), 56. See also Kâhya
Adjutant general (kapıcılar kâhyası), 170, 179; of kapudan paşa, 179, 181; of Melek Mehmet Pasha, 201; of sultan, 170; title awarded to Ahmet Bey, 191
Administrators. See Mutasarrıf; Mütesellim
Admiralty, 179; commander (tersane emini), 180, 181
Aga, 26, 195; birun aga, 96, 210; Bölükât-ı erbâa aga, 160, 210; kamor aga, 159; müsellim aga, 193; müteferrika aga, 160, 219; vekilharç aga, 198, 239; vezir of agas, 179; yemeklik aga, 158. See also Janissary Aga
Ağa Bahçesi, 58
Ahmet Bey, 147, 148, 149, 174; promoted to adjutant general of sultan, 192
Ahmet Cevdet: publishes sefaretname, 8
Ahmet Han. See Ahmet III
Ahmet Pasha (mutasarrıf of Beyşehir sancak), 66
Ahmet Resmi Efendi, 210, 236; embassy to Prussia (1763), 16
Ahmet III, 55, 108, 209
Ahor kâhyası, 160
Akvalı Mehmet Aga (zagarcıbaşı), 145
Alay çavuşu, 159, 164, 210
Alay kiosk, 59
Alekseev (legal officer), 160
Aleppo, 18
Algeria, 182
Ali Pasha of Chirmen, (quartermaster general of the sultan), 150, 151, 154

All-Russian empire, 171
Altynovka, 86
Ambassadors and diplomats,
European, 11, 41, 163 n; Repnin
meets with, 163; Repnin takes
leave of, 191, 192. *See also*
Braganza, Duc de; Celsing,
Ulric; Gaffron, Herr de;
Gradenigo, Bartolommeo;
Hayes, Anthony; Porter, Sir
James; Saint Priest, Compte de;
Solms, Count Victor F.; Thugut,
Freiherr v.; Weiker (Weiler),
Heer; Zegelin, Herr v.
Ambassadors and diplomats,
Russian: appealed to by Turks
in Bukovina issue, 42. *See also*
Cantacuzene, Prince; Obreskov,
Aleksei M.; Orlov, Count
Grigorii G.; Peterson,
Khristofor I.; Repnin, Prince;
Rumiantsev, Count
Aleksandr I.; Stakhiev,
Aleksandr S.
Ambassadors, Ottoman, 4, 5, 9,
15, 16, 23. *See also* Abdülkerim;
Ahmet Resmi Efendi; Hatti
Efendi; Ümni Pasha
Ambassadress. *See* Repnina,
Princess
Amsterdam: as financial center, 40
Anna, Empress, 36
Arabic language, 9
Arnauts, 131
Arşın (area unit), 78, 84 n
Asesbaşı, 159, 164
Asılbeyli, 193
Aşmon', 88
Attendant of inside service
(*enderun* aga), 59, 73, 92, 93, 214
Augustus III, 3
Austria: occupies Bukovina, 42,
49; and Poland, 118–19
Aynalı Kavak, 177, 210;
convention of, 153 n
Aytos, 193

Bahâriye palace, 184, 210
Bahary, 88
Bahşiş, 96, 102
Balance of power, 38, 41
Balkans, 31; crossing of, 148
Balta, 3
Baş bakı kulu, 186
Baş çuhadar, 145, 146
Baş defterdar. *See* Financial officer,
chief
Baş ezancı efendi of janissaries, 184,
185, 210
Başvekâlet Arşivi (archives), 18
Batardella galley, 174
Battles: Pruth River (1711), 2;
Shumen (1774), 38; Vienna
(1683), 14
Baturin, 86, 87
Bayraktar of janissaries, 148, 210
Bazargıc, 194
Bektir Kioi (Furca), 194
Belgrade, 2
Belopol'ye, 78
Bender. *See* Embassies, Russian;
Embassies, Turkish; *Mubadele*;
Rumiantsev, Count Aleksandr I.;
Ümni Pasha
Berdichev, 78; Russian-Polish
battle at, 80–81
Berg (aide-de-camp), 160
Berg, Ensign, 160
Besh, Cornet, 160
Beylikçi, 183, 187, 210
Bayşehir *sancak*, 66
Bîrlad, 137, 196
Birun aga (aga of the outside
service), 96, 210
Black Sea, 36, 46
Boats. See *Acek*; Batardella
galley; Caique; *Karla*; *Kayik*;
Şeyke; *Zevrak*
Bodisko (interpreter), 159, 168
Bok, Colonel, 160, 202
Bölükât-ı erbâa aga, 160, 210
Borzna, 86
Bostancı, 152, 171

Bostancıbaşı, 152, 153, 211; of Edirne, 151

Boutourlin, Countess: house of, occupied by Abdülkerim, 92 n

Boyars, 132, 136, 137, 139, 141, 195, 197, 198, 211; Polish boyars, 118; of Walachia petition Repnin, 143 n

Braga, 200

Braganza, Duc de, 165, 171

Brăila, 6, 61, 62; archbishop of, visits Repnin, 137

Bread and salt: as sign of welcome, 150, 151

Brink, Cornet Karl, 136 n, 151, 159, 164

Brovary, 86

Bruce, General in Chief Iakov Aleksandrovich, 104, 108, 211

Bruce, William (Polish general), 118

Bucureşti, 139; archbishop of, 139; Congress of, 48; Repnin's stay in, 140–43

Bukhanovskoi (embassy staff member), 164

Bukovina, 42, 43, 49

Bulgakov, Iakov Ivanovich, 129, 130, 149, 151, 152, 153, 158, 165, 167, 168, 171, 177, 178, 181, 184, 185, 186, 189, 202; author of Russian text, 32; marshal of the embassy, 126 n

Bureaucracy, Ottoman, 6, 7, 11, 19, 20, 23, 27, 66; *hacegân*, 7, 145; *seyyid*, 6, 7, 57. *See also* Master of ceremonies, chief; *Tezkireci*

Burgaz (Lüle Burgaz), 59, 154, 193

Bursa, 18

Büyükçekmece, 154, 192

Büyük imrahor. *See* Master of the horse

Buzău, 139

Buzticnu, 78

Caique, 164, 168, 174, 175, 178, 179, 182, 185, 186

Călăraşi, 61, 62

Călugăreni, 143

Calendar, Turkish. *See* Time, Turkish calculation

Camboyluk tribe, Crimea, 46

Cantacuzene, Prince, 139, 140, 141, 142, 143

Casimcea, 195

Catherine the Great. *See* Catherine the Second

Catherine the Second, 5, 10, 15, 16, 17, 18, 19, 20, 33, 34, 36, 37, 40, 50, 171–72; attire, 94; accepts instrument of ratification, 95; audience with Abdülkerim, 94–96; celebrations for guard regiments, 105; as colonel of guard regiments, 105; departs for Saint Petersburg, 109; fear of Cossack revolt, 117; fear of plague, 82; invites Abdülkerim to audience, 91; irritation with Turks, 75 n; jewel collection, 106; journey to Tula, 108; masquerade ball, 103–5; priority of Crimea in foreign policy, 118–19; residence in Moscow, 97

Cavalier of the embassy, 162, 212

Cavalry, imperial, 57. *See also Divanegân; Gönüllüyân; Silâhdar*

Çavuş, 130, 164, 165, 210

Çavuşbaşı, 156–78 passim, 188, 189, 213; Said Efendi appointed as, 157

Çavuşlar emini, 159, 165, 173, 213

Çavuşlar katibi, 159, 165, 173, 213

Celebichioi, 195

Celebrations: cannonades prohibited in Istanbul during pregnancy of Sultana, 175; feast day of Saint Elijah, 80; feast day of Saint Hizir, 64; for guard regiments, 105–6; for holders of the Order of Saint Alexander Nevsky, 142; for

holders of the Order of Saint
Andrew, 106–7; for holders of
the Order of Saint George, 105;
for peace treaty of Küçük
Kaynarca in Moscow, 80, 107,
109; for victory over Pugachev,
109. *See also* Fireworks
Celsing, Ulric, 163
Ceremonies, 15, 16, 17, 83, 114,
132, 133, 142, 144, 146, 149,
154–55, 156, 195; on Dnestr
River, 76–77, 116, 125–28, 199,
200–203; in Istanbul, 158, 162,
165–88; in Moscow, 94–96, 108.
See also Celebrations; *Mubadele*;
Parades and processions
Cerna, 195
Chalik Kavak pass (Karnobatski
Prokhod), 60, 148
Chamberlain (equivalent of
kapıcılar kethuda), 90
Chervena Voda, 146
Chios, 182
Christians, 36, 84; and prisoner of
war issue, 99. *See also* Islam;
Religion
Chuchulya, 64, 65
Chudnov, 78
Chuvardino, 88
Ciz ye baş bakı kulu. See Purser
Commander. See *Müsellim* aga
Confederation of Bar, 3
Constantinople. See Istanbul
Controller of the imperial kitchen
(*matbah-i amire emini*), 23
Çorbacı, 144, 159, 165, 168, 173,
174, 179, 182, 184, 185, 187, 191,
192, 200, 213
Çorbacıbaşı, 167; of the guard, 164
Çorlu, 154, 192, 193
Cossacks, 109; Catherine's fear of,
117
Couci, 44
Council secretary (*divan katibi*), 58,
59, 69, 70, 76, 93, 99, 116, 214
Creața, 139

Crimea, 35, 36, 38, 39, 41, 51;
annexation of, 31; civil war, 46;
diplomatic discussions over,
47–50; Giray dynasty of Crimean
Tatars, 44–46, 47, 49; incorporated into Russia, 44; lacuna in
history of, 43; priority in
Catherine's foreign policy, 118–
19; Russian diplomatic maneuvers
regarding, 43; Russianized, 46;
struggle over, 42–50; tribes, 46
Çuhadar. See Valet

Daia, 143
Dancing, 133, 134, 183; Asiatic and
Greek, 176; criticism of European
dancing, 10, 97
Dandrii (student), 159, 160
Danube River, 61, 144; crossing
of, 195
Dâr ül-harp. See Abode of war
Dâr ül-islam. See Abode of Islam
Davut Pasha, 157, 213
Dcherul, 196
Debasta (*spatar*), 196
Defterdar, 40, 171; luncheon for
Repnin, 185–86
Dekolin, 137, 196
Denmark, 2
Deste, 22, 213
Devlet Giray, 45, 46, 47
Diplomacy: Abdülkerim assesses
Russian and Turkish styles of, 77;
Repnin establishes secret channels
for, 39
Diplomats. *See* Ambassadors and
diplomats
Divan: chamber of, 170; imperial,
59, 72; Moldavian, 197
Divan çavuşlari. See Pursuivant of
the imperial divan
Divan efendi, 130; sends gifts to
Russians, 129
Divanegân (cavalry troops), 58, 75,
213. See also *Gönüllüyân*; *Silâhdar*
Divan katibi. See Council secretary
Dmitrovsk-Orlovsky, 88

Dnepr River, 84, 114
Dnestr River, 27, 33, 34, 66, 68, 115, 125, 198, 199, 200; crossing of, 200; scene of *mubadele*, 67, 201
Dobrol, 148
Doctor, 165, 200
Documents: Ottoman, 4, 7–8, 10, 16, 17, 18, 19, 21, 22, 29 n, 57 n; Russian, 33
Dolzhok, 78
Dönüm (area unit), 84, 85
Dragoman. See Kostaki Muruza
Druzhinina, E. I., 50
Dubrucaova, 116

Edirne, 3, 6, 23, 59, 60, 151, 152, 153, 161
Elchaninov, Capt., 160
Embassies, Russian: to Turkey (1739), 27, 28, 65–66; to Turkey (1793), 29–30. See also Rumiantsev, Count Aleksandr I.
Embassies, Turkish: to Austria (1754), 16; to Prussia (1763), 16; to Russia (1740), 23, 65–71, 75 n, 77, 90–91, 93, 153 n, 158 n, 168 n, 173 n; to Russia (1793), 6, 15, 17, 18, 19, 22, 25–26, 101 n. See also Ahmet Resmi Efendi; *Mubadele*
Enderun aga. See Attendant of the inside service
England: diplomatic position, 42; first Ottoman embassy, 4
Entertainment: at Istanbul ceremonies, 176–77, 180, 183, 184, 185, 186, 187
Equipment: for Turkish embassy, 20, 22, 24–30, 60, 61, 63, 64–65, 66
Erikler, 193
Esat Efendi manuscript collection, 7, 8
Expansion of Russia, 36

Fakiya, 193
Fastov, 78
Fekete, Professor L., 18, 19
*Ferace*s (fur-lined robes), 184

Ferrieri (consular official), 160, 165
Financial officer, chief (*baş defterdar*), 19, 23, 27, 210
Fireworks, 107, 109, 135, 142
Firman, 27, 65, 171
First (Petersburg) Grenadier Regiment, 34
Focşani, 136; Congress of, 48; monastery, 138
Footmen (*şatiran*), 59, 92, 200, 201
France, 3, 41, 42
Frankish: Ottoman term for European, 4, 10, 80, 83, 87, 97, 112
Fruit-server of the sultan (*yemişçibaşt*), 162

Gaffron, Herr de, 50 n
Galata (mountain), 135
Galaţi, 6, 60, 61, 116, 195; war destruction in, 63
Gedik aga. See Household attendant
Gedikli zaim, 187, 214
Genghis Han, 41, 44
Ghika, Prince Gregory II: voivode of Moldavia, 60, 64, 70, 116, 132, 134, 135, 136, 138, 197, 198, 214; hospodar of Moldavia, 131, 133
Gifts: for Russians, 15–16, 17, 18–21, 57, 67, 76, 82, 94, 95–96, 129, 132, 140, 145–46, 149, 151, 158–89 passim; for Turks, 21–22, 91, 129, 168, 192
Giol'bab, 151
Giray dynasty of Crimean Tatars, 44–46, 47, 49
Giterman, V., 36
Giurgiu, 145, 146; sends delegation to Repnin, 144
Glukhov, 86, 87; renamed Kaynarca in honor of victory, 109
Gokhfel'd (medical officer), 161, 165
Gönüllüyân (cavalry troops), 58, 75, 214–15
Gordineshty, 130, 198
Gorodishche, 86

252   Index

Goven, Major, 160
Governor (muhafız), 70
Gradenigo, Bartolommeo, 162,
  163 n
Grand Duchess (wife of Paul):
  death, 114–15; pregnancy, 107
Grand vezir, 3, 15, 17, 34, 35, 37,
  43, 56, 57 n, 58, 59, 109, 155, 156,
  162; appointment of Izzet
  Mehmet Pasha as, 57 n; attends
  luncheon incognito, 187; first
  luncheon for Repnin, 174–79;
  first meeting with Repnin, 163–68;
  instructions to Abdülkerim on
  Tatars and prisoners of war, 114;
  former grand vezir, 6–7; relations
  with Repnin, 169 n, 170 n, 171 n,
  173 n; replies for sultan to Repnin,
  167, 172; rescript to Catherine,
  189; travel instructions of, 116
Greenhouses, 85, 112–13
Guild system, Turkish, 25
Guru-Paraskevului, 137

Hacegân. See Bureaucracy, Ottoman
Hacı Ahmet Aga, 145
Hacıoğlu Pazari, 116
Haiduk, 152
Hakan, 55, 95, 215
Hangerli, Dmitrii (interpreter),
  127, 133, 136, 154, 160
Hanlıyenice, 152
Hanto, 92
Hasan, 147, 149
Haseki aga, 145, 215
Hatti Efendi: embassy to Austria
  (1754), 16
Hayes, Anthony, 20
Hazinedar (treasurer), 94, 215–16
Head of secretaries (reis ül-küttâp),
  56, 233
Hekimoğlu Ali Pasha, 2
Hetman of Moldavia, 132, 133, 136,
  138, 196, 198. See also Spatar
Hibsch and Timoni (bankers), 40
Horsetail (sign of rank), 56, 65 n,
  125 n, 149, 150, 191, 200, 201

Hospodar. See Voivode
Hotin, 6, 26, 33, 35, 60, 63, 64, 66,
  67, 74, 76, 114, 115, 116, 125, 128,
  199, 200. See also Melek Mehmet
  Pasha; Mubadele
Hotin Pasha. See Melek Mehmet
  Pasha
Household attendant (gedik aga),
  59, 94, 95, 214
Household steward. See Kethuda
Hungary, 43
Husayn Pasha, 115, 116, 192;
  appointed as Repnin's first
  mihmandar for return trip, 191

Ialomiţa River, 139
Iaşi. See Jassy
Ibershukov, General, 91, 93, 109
İbrahim Münip Efendi (head of
  secretaries) (reis ül-küttâp), 56
Igel'strom, Lieutenant General, 76,
  86, 91, 97, 104, 109, 127, 161, 192,
  199; promoted from major
  general, 80
Ikdam (newspaper published by
  Ahmet Cevdet), 8
Ikindi (prayer), 177
Imperial Council, 34
Inalcık, Halil, 44
Indemnities, 41
India, 18, 20, 96
Interpreter of the Porte, first
  (Kostaki Muruza), 154–87 passim
Isaccea, 60
Islam, 1, 12, 13, 79
İsmail Bey (sipahiler ağası), 160
Ispravnik, 131, 136, 195, 216
Istanbul, 18, 61 n; Abdülkerim
  departs from, 6; admiralty, 179;
  Ağa Çeşmesi fountain, 161;
  arsenal, 179; Asiatic bank, 186;
  Eyyub, 161, 214; Fener district,
  161, 214; Repnin arrives at,
  157–62; Silivri gate, 59; Süley-
  maniye Library, 7; threatened by
  Russia, 39. See also Pera; Tophane
  pier

Istanbul palaces: Aynalı Kavak,
179, 210; Bahâriye, 184, 210;
Kâğıthane, 185, 216; Küçük
Göksu, 186, 218; Topkapı, 58;
Valide Saray, 182, 239
Istikbal, 64
İvaz-Pashazade Ibrahim Bey
Efendi (sheikh ul Islam), 58 n
Izburuga, 63, 64
Izmailovskii Regiment, 105, 127,
159, 160, 165, 174, 191, 215
İzzet Mehmet Pasha: appointment
as grand vezir, 57 n

Janissaries, 144, 153, 157, 159, 164,
170, 174, 175, 179, 182, 185, 187,
191, 192, 193, 199, 200; *baş
ezancı efendi*, 184, 185, 210;
bayraktar, 148, 210; kamor agas,
159; *kapu kethudası*, 159;
karakullukçu, 59, 217
Janissary Aga, 74, 75, 152, 153,
173, 199, 200, 216; luncheon for
Repnin, 184–85
Jassy (Iaşi; Yaş), 63, 132, 195, 196,
197, 198; Repnin's stay in, 133–
36

Kaçılar kiosk, 153
Kadi, 148, 149, 150, 155, 192, 193,
194, 199, 200
Kâğıthane palace, 185, 216
Kâhya, 130, 133, 136, 217–18; of
Abdülkerim, 200, 203; of grand
vezir, 168, 175, 185, 191; of grand
vezir gives luncheon for Repnin,
182–84; of *defterdar*, 186; of
Hotin pasha, 199, 201, 202. *See
also* Adjutant (*kethuda*)
Kaimakam (deputy of grand vezir),
61, 69, 216
Kalkay, 44, 45
Kamanice (Kamenets-Podolsky),
78; churches converted to
mosques, 79; conquered by Turks,
79; fortress described, 78–79
Kamenskii, General, 38

Kamor agas of janissaries, 159
Kanara, 193
Kapıcıbaşı, 65, 72, 134, 148, 160,
165, 169–89 passim, 194, 195,
217; chief gatekeeper of imperial
palace, 62; of Karnabat, 150;
official escort (second *mihmandar*)
of Repnin, 62. *See also* Kara
Hisarî Ahmet Bey; *Mihmandar*
Kapıcılar kâhyası. See Adjutant
general
Kapıcılar kethuda, 60, 75, 114;
equivalent of chamberlain, 90
Kapudan paşa, 171, 172, 174, 188,
217; luncheon for Repnin, 177–80
Kapu kethudası of janissaries, 159
Kara Ahmet Pasha (first *mihmandar*
of Repnin), 134, 135
Karabunar (Grudovo), 193
Karacı (interpreter), 203
Kara Hisarî Ahmet Bey (*kapıcıbaşı*
and second *mihmandar* of Repnin),
146; appointment, 66
Karakullukçu of janissaries, 59, 217
Karıştıran, 192
Karla (small boat), 62
Karlowitz, Treaty of. *See* Treaties,
Karlowitz
Karnabat (Polyanovgrad), 148, 149
Kayik (small boat), 62
Kaynarca. *See* Glukhov
Kerch', 38, 45; political importance
of, 39
Kerrâke (camlet caftan), 178
Kesedar efendi, 186, 187, 217
Kethuda, 56, 59, 74, 76, 83, 92, 93,
110, 116, 217. See also *Kâhya*;
Kapıcılar kethuda
Kherkheulizev, Prince (master of
the horse), 126, 130, 133, 136, 151,
159
Kiev, 6, 10, 12, 34, 192; Abdül-
kerim's arrival, 83; Abdülkerim's
departure, 86; fortress described,
83–84; gardens, 84; greenhouse,
85; palace, 85; Pechersky
monastery, 84; province of, 81;

quarters for Abdülkerim, 84;
return to, 114
Kievskii Cuirassier Regiment, 34
Kinburn, 38, 45
Kınıklı, 59, 192
Kırım Giray, 45
Kırk Klise, 116
Kırklareli, 193
Kitchen, controller of imperial
(matbah-i amire emini), 23
Kleman, Second Lt., 160
Kliuchevskii, V. O., 36
Komarovka, 86
K'opryu-k'oy, 194
Kostaki Muruza (first interpreter
of the Porte), 154–87 passim
Kosteshty, 131, 198
Kotyudzhen', 65, 66, 67
Kovarna, 194
Kozelets, 86
Kozluduza, 194
Krolevets, 86
Kromy, 88
Kruta (interpreter), 126 n, 160, 203
Küçükçekmece, 17, 59, 154, 155,
192
Küçük Göksu palace, 186, 218
Küçük Kaynarca, 38, 56. See also
Treaty of Küçük Kaynarca
Kuleli, 154
Kurultay (Tatar tribal assembly), 45
Kuruş. See Money

Larga, 130, 198
Lepanto, 61
Lev (levok). See Money
Levant, 4
Levashev, Prince, 159
Levok. See Money
Litkhen, Cornet, 133
"Little Russia," 87, 109
London: first Ottoman embassy to,
4
Loshkarev, 160
Lüle Burgaz, 59, 154, 193
Lupasnya, 88, 90
Lutaev, Ensign, 160

L'vov, Captain, 160, 164, 168, 195

Măcin, 61, 116, 195
Maksud Giray, 45
Mamut-Kuius, 195
Mansurov, Captain, 160
Margineanu, 139
Marklovskoi, Captain, 160
Marklovskoi, Karl (secretary),
126, 159
Markov, Major, 126 n, 151, 159,
164, 196; discusses Crimean issue
with reis efendi, 48–51
Marshal of the embassy. See
Bulgakov, Iakov Ivanovich
Martini (gold craftsman), 168
Masalov, Captain, 160
Masivtsy, 78
Masraf efendi, 158, 218
Master of ceremonies, chief
(teşrifatçı), 155, 156, 165, 239
Master of the horse (imrahor), 171,
178, 189, 216. See also Kherkheuli-
zev, Prince
Matbah-i amire emini (controller of
the imperial kitchen), 23
Mavrocordato, Prince, 131, 132
Mavroyiani (interpreter), 179
Medical officer. See Gokhfel'd
Medzhibozh, 78, 79
Mehmet Pasha. See Melek Mehmet
Pasha
Mehterhane. See Military band
Mehterhane-i amire. See Tent depot,
imperial
Mektupçu. See Secretary
Melek Mehmet Pasha, 63, 64, 65,
67, 70, 83, 129, 198, 199, 201, 202,
218; former deputy (kaimakam) of
grand vezir, 61; governor of
Hotin, 115; "Hotin Pasha," 129;
illness, 199–200; negotiates with
Russians at Hotin, 68–72; takes
part in mubadele, 73–77, 128
Mel'nikov (interpreter?), 160
Memâlik-i mahrusa. See Ottoman
Empire

Mengli Giray, 44
Metropolitan of Bucureşti, 142
Metropolitan of Jassy, 135, 197
Mihmandar, 62, 65, 72, 73, 76, 115,
    116, 128–53 passim, 160, 164, 168,
    172, 174, 175, 179, 182, 187, 192,
    194, 199, 200, 201, 202;
    appointment as official escort to
    Russians, 61; equals rank of
    colonel, 65 n; first *mihmandar*
    (Kara Ahmet Pasha), 134, 135;
    second *mihmandar* (Kara Hisarî
    Ahmet Bey), 146; first *mihmandar*
    for return trip (Husayn Pasha),
    191. See also *Kapıcıbaşı*
Military band (*mehterhane*), 59, 76,
    92, 218
Military intelligence, 11
mir-i mirân, 72, 115, 116, 218;
    official escort assigned rank of, 65
Miropol', 78
*Mirza*s (Tatar aristocracy), 45
Moldavia, 34, 39–40, 43, 198;
    flourishes after war, 116; as
    Ottoman listening post, 11
Monastery of Forty Martyrs, 141,
    142; Repnin visits archimandrite,
    141
Money, 40; Abdülkerim describes
    Russian money, 113; *kuruş*, 23,
    40 n; *lev* (*levok*), 40, 168; *para*, 29 n
Morea, 2
Moscow, 6, 8, 10, 88; Abdül-
    kerim's arrival, 90; Abdulkerim's
    quarters, 92–93; Catherine's
    residence, 97; described, 111;
    fireworks display, 107, 109;
    Foundling Home, 111–12;
    greenhouses, 112–13; military
    careers for foundlings, 112;
    renovated for Catherine's arrival,
    96–97, 102 n; theaters, 102–3;
    trade and manufacture, 111
Motovilovka, 78
Mtsensk, 88
Mubadele, 34, 77, 83, 218–19; at
    Bender (1740), 68, 71 n, 72, 75, 77;

on Dnestr River (1775), 66–76,
    125–28; on Dnestr River (1776),
    115–17, 200, 201–3
Müftü, 148
Muhafız (governor), 70
Muhammad, 2
Mulla, 152. See also *Naip*
Musa Aga (voivode of Giurgiu),
    144, 145
Musabei, 194
Müsellim aga (commander of a city),
    193
Music, 10, 80, 90, 92, 97, 133, 142,
    181, 195, 201. See also Military
    band
Musicians, 34, 183. See also Parades
    and processions
Muslims, 10, 11, 13, 41; and
    prisoner of war issue, 99
Mustafa Efendi, 145
Mustafa Han. See Mustafa III
Mustafa Pasha: former grand vezir,
    6; patron of Abdülkerim, 6, 7
Mustafa Rasih Pasha: embassy to
    Russia (1793), 15, 17, 18, 19, 22,
    25–26, 101 n
Mustafa III, Sultan, 2, 55, 219
Mutasarrıf (administrator of a
    sancak), 66, 219
Müteferrika aga, 160, 219
Mütesellim (provincial
    administrator), 66, 219
Muzhiks, 87

Nadur, 194
Nahifi Mehmet Efendi, 7;
    appointed, 57; author of the
    sefaretname, 6; quarters in
    Moscow, 93
Naima, 1, 4, 14
Naip (deputy of mulla), 152, 219
Nastana Karşi, 78
Negin, 78
Neledinskii-Meletskii, Major, 160,
    219–20
Netherlands: diplomatic position,
    42

Nezhin, 86
Nikol'skoye, 88
Nişancı, 171, 220; nişancı bench, 170, 188
Nogay tribe of Crimea, 46
Northern Accord, 37
Nosovka, 86
Novosil'tsov, Lt., 160
Numan Pasha: at mubadele of Bender (1740), 68, 69
Nuradin, 44

Oba (tent), 73, 220
Obreskov, Aleksei Mikhailovich, 48
Odabaşı, 195, 220
Official escort, 115. See also Igel'strom, General; Mihmandar
Oka River, 89
Olsuf'ev, Cornet, 160
Orël, 6, 88, 114
Orlov, Count Grigorii Grigor'evich, 48
Orta, 220. See also Janissaries
Orthodox church, 5. See also Celebrations; Religion
Osman Pasha, 145
Osterman, Andrei Ivanovich, 36
Ottoman Empire, 1, 4, 12, 55, 171; and Europe, 2, 4, 5, 11, 13, 15, 31; financial difficulties, 26; memâlik-i mahrusa, 4
Ottoman Way, the, 10, 11
Ottomans, 2, 3, 5, 12, 14; defined, 11; pre-Tanzimat, 4; provincialism, 7
Palaces, Kiev, 85. See also Istanbul palaces
Palladoklis, Anton (interpreter), 126, 160
Panaiodoros (secretary of Oriental languages), 127n, 131, 133, 136, 140, 152, 158, 160, 198, 199, 203
Panin, Count Nikita Ivanovich, 34, 39, 50, 90, 110–11, 220–21; gift from Porte, 189; meeting with Abdülkerim, 93; note on

prisoners of war, 100–101; note to grand vezir, 166; receives reply from grand vezir, 189; replies to grand vezir's letter, 109, 114
Para. See Money
Parades and processions, 58–59, 72, 75–77, 83, 91–92, 93–94, 116, 126–27, 130, 132, 133, 136, 138, 151–52, 156, 157–61 164–65, 169, 175, 191, 197, 199, 200–201
Paşa. See Pasha
Pasha, 6, 9, 149; of the galley, 175, 178; rank of, 65n, 125n, 191, 200. See also Horsetail
Paul, Grand Duke, 96; death of wife, 115; departs for Petersburg, 107–8
Pavoloch', 78, 81
Penevul, 196
Pera, 161, 162n, 184, 191, 192, 221
Persian language, 9
Peterson, Khristofor Ivanovich, 34, 38, 42, 165, 221–22; chargé d'affaires in Istanbul, 63, 75n, 158n, 167, 179, 180, 181; meets Repnin at Silivri, 154
Peter the Great, 12, 13, 36; constructs earth fortress at Kiev, 84
Pizani (interpreter), 157, 160, 165, 191
Pleshcheev, Lt. Sergei Ivanovich, 160, 222
Podikuram, 139
Podol (Kiev suburb), 84, 114
Podolia, 3
Poland, 3, 8, 37, 39–40, 77–78, 81; Abdülkerim leaves territory of, 81; partition of, 118; Polish boyars, 118; Polish frontier, 83, 87, 110; Polish lands described, 81; and Repnin, 234; request for Russian military assistance, 118–19; Russian influence in, 119; succession, 3
Polikarpov, Major Alexandr Vasil'evich, 160, 222

Polonnoye, 78, 114, 115; fortress
  described, 80
Pomistraveskului, 137
Poniatowski, Stanislaw, 3
Portar başı. See Protocol officer
Porte, 16, 22, 23, 27, 39, 156, 164,
  165, 168, 169, 174, 175, 186, 189
Porter, Sir James, 22
Potemkin, General in Chief
  Grigorii Aleksandrovich, 96,
  104, 222–23
Prayers: Muslim, 177, 180, 183,
  185, 186
Preobrazhensky Regiment, 105,
  215
Prices: government (*mirî*), 19–20;
  market (*rayiç*), 19
Priests, 159
Printing, in Russia, 32
Prisoners of war, Russian: Repnin
  on Turkish attitude toward, 99 n
Prisoners of war, Turkish, 14;
  Abdülkerim adds to retinue, 102;
  and Abdülkerim's drafts, 98–99;
  Panin's reply on, 100–101; receipt
  of grand vezir's instructions on,
  114; Russian dilatoriness con-
  cerning, 99–100
Prophet, sacred banner of, 150.
  See also Muhammad
Protocol, 17, 22, 57 n, 65 n,
  75–83 passim, 101, 107, 109, 111,
  115–16, 157–85, 170 n, 171 n, 172,
  173, 177, 181, 183, 188, 189, 201,
  202; right hand, left hand, 69,
  73–75, 128, 202. *See also* Master of
  ceremonies, chief; *Mubadele*
Protocol officer (*portar başı*), 62,
  222
Provadiya, 194
Prussia, 2, 3, 42
Pruth River, 60, 61, 64, 198
Pugachev revolt, 37, 109; and
  Catherine, 117; celebrations for
  victory over, 109
Purser (*cizye baş bakı kulu*), 185, 213

Pursuivant of the imperial divan
  (*divan çavuşlari*), 72, 159
Puțeni, 196
Pyatki, 78

Quarantine station, 81–83, 223–27;
  Abdülkerim objects to, 82
Quartermaster, 144. *See also* Ali
  Pasha of Chirmen

Rağıp Mehmet Pasha, 2
Ragusa, 1
Rakovița (Raikovich) (secretary of
  the Hospodar of Walachia), 138,
  227–28
Ramazan, 43, 102
Rank, 58, 65 n, 90, 125 n, 161 n,
  200, 228–33; of *kâhya* and pasha
  of two horsetails, 202; of
  kapıcılar kethuda and chamberlain,
  90. *See also* Horsetail; Parades and
  processions; Pasha
Razgrad, 147
Razumovskoi, Captain, 160
Reaya, 63, 233
Recea, 196
Recruits, levy of, 37
Refreshments, 132, 133, 135, 139–
  40, 152–85 passim, 189, 197, 199,
  202, 236
Regiments. *See* First (Petersburg)
  Grenadier Regiment; Izmailovskii
  Regiment; Kievskii Cuirassier
  Regiment; Preobrazhensky
  Regiment; Semenovskii Regiment; Sumskii Hussar Regiment
Reis efendi, 40, 41, 42, 43, 162, 166,
  168, 170, 175, 176, 177, 178, 191,
  233; discussions on Crimean issue,
  47–48; luncheon for Repnin,
  186–87
Reis ül-küttâp. See Head of
  secretaries
Religion, 14, 41, 48, 49, 79, 135,
  138, 141–42, 197. *See also*
  Celebrations; Islam; Orthodox
  church; Prayers

Reparations, 39, 40
Repnin, Prince Nikolai Vasil'evich,
27, 34, 40, 43, 60, 63, 66, 67, 71n,
72, 74, 114, 233–36; appraisal of,
50; appointed, 33; and Catherine,
235–36; departure from Istanbul,
174, 190, 191–92; displeasure with
Turkish gifts, 162n; diplomatic
tasks, 39–40; entry into Istanbul,
157–62; farewell audience with
grand vezir, 188–89; farewell
audience with sultan, 188–89;
farewell speech to sultan, 188; first
audience with sultan, 168–73;
first luncheon with grand vezir,
174–79; at Küçük Kaynarca, 235;
luncheon with *defterdar*, 185–86;
luncheon with Janissary Aga,
184–85; luncheon with *kâhya* of
grand vezir, 182–84; luncheon
with *kapudan pasha*, 179–82;
luncheon with *reis efendi*, 186–87;
meeting with grand vezir, 163–68;
in Poland, 234; prepares embassy,
33; quarters in Pera, 162n, rank
and titles, 125; recalled, 50;
relations with grand vezir, 169n,
170n, 171n, 173n; takes leave of
European ambassadors, 191, 192;
visits European ambassadors, 163
Repnina, Princess Natal'ia
Aleksandrovna (ambassadress),
132, 133, 134, 136 139, 140, 141,
143, 153, 162, 163, 197; daughters,
129n, 133, 136; pregnancy, 135
Rescript: of Catherine for the
sultan, 165, 166, 169, 170; of the
grand vezir for Catherine, 189;
of the sultan for Catherine, 188.
See also Treaty ratification
Resmi Ahmet Efendi (adjutant
[*kethuda*] of the grand vezir), 56
Rîmna River, 138
Rîmnicu Sărat, 139
Romadan River, 144
Rontsov, Adjutant General, 127,
136, 141, 160, 203

Rozendal, Second Lt., 160
Rumeli beylerbeyi, 125, 236
Rumiantsev, Count Aleksandr
Ivanovich (father of field
marshal): Embassy of (1739), 27,
28, 65–66; and *mubadele* of 1740,
68–69, 153, 158n, 168n, 173n
Rumiantsev, Field Marshal Petr
Aleksandrovich, 34, 36, 38, 56,
60, 63, 90, 105, 236–37; Glukhov
renamed Kaynarca in honor of
his victory, 109; presented
residence at Glukhov, 87; resists
Abdülkerim's initiatives on
prisoners of war, 101
Ruse (Ruščuk), 145, 146. 155
Rusokastro, 193
Russia: expansion to south, 36;
financial problems, 119–20; fur
trade, 120; maneuvers against
Austria in Poland, 118–19;
national character assessed, 112;
priority of military, 120; war aims,
35, 36–37
*Russian Embassy to Constantinople
of 1776, The*, 31, 35; author of, 32;
gap in narrative, 35, 163; publication of, 31, 32; and Repnin's
journal, 32, 163n; value of the
book, 31–32, 35
Russian text. See *Russian Embassy to
Constantinople of 1776, The*
Russo-Turkish War (1768–74),
55; as a commercial war, 37;
declared, 3

Saadabad, 174, 237
Sabar River, 143
Sahin Giray, 45, 46, 49; invited to
Moscow, 45
Şahinşah, 54, 116, 237
Sahip Giray, 45; flees to Istanbul,
45, 47
Said Efendi, 160; appointed as
çavuşbaşt, 157
Saint Petersburg, 96

Saint Priest, Compte de, 41, 153 n,
  162, 163 n; orders welcome for
  Repnin in Edirne, 153
Saints' days. *See* Celebrations
Saltykov (aide-de-camp), 127, 161
Sancak, 66, 237; administrator of
  (*mutasarrıf*), 66, 219
San Stefano (Yeşilköy), 155
Saray (palace), 168, 169, 173, 188,
  189. *See also* Istanbul palaces
Şatiran. See Footmen
Satişchioi, 195
Savino, 88
Şayke (river boat), 62
Schiller, Friedrich, 30
Scînteia, 136, 196
Sculeni, 131, 198
Secretary (mektupçu), 166, 168 n,
  183, 187, 189, 218. *See also* Head
  of secretaries
Secretary of the embassy, 68, 134,
  136. *See also* Bulgakov, Iakov
  Ivanovich; Marklovskoi, Karl
Sefaretname, 5, 6, 7, 8, 9, 10, 12, 14,
  15, 17, 20, 30; defined, 4. *See also*
  Documents, Ottoman
Seim River, 87 n
Selam ağası, 76
Selim Giray, 45
Selim III, Sultan, 26
Semenov, Sgt., 164
Semonovskii Regiment, 105, 215
Semipolki, 86
Şemsiye (awning), 73, 237
Sengul bathhouse, 59
Senovo, 146
Serdar, 194, 238
Serdengeçti, 144, 148; *serdengeçti* aga,
  146
Sergiyevskoye, 88
Seriryovski, 88
Serpukhov, 88
Seven Years' War, 2
Severin, Ivan (interpreter), 127, 160
Sevsk, 88
Seyyid. See Bureaucracy, Ottoman

Shchepot'ev, Semon (interpreter),
  127, 160
Shchorba (embassy staff member),
  164
Sheikh ul Islam, 58
Sherbet. *See* Refreshments
Shirkov, Major General, 127
Shreder, Captain, 160
Shumen (Kolarovgrad), 38, 60,
  147, 149; negotiations at, 37
Shumovtsy, 78
Sikstel', Major, 160
Silâhdar, 57, 200, 201, 203, 238;
  silâhdar ağası, 160; *silâhdar emini*,
  160; *silâhdar katibi*, 160
Silistra, 6, 56, 60, 61, 62
Silivri, 116, 154, 192; Silivri
  Gate of Istanbul, 59
Singing, 10, 80, 90. *See also* Music
Sipahi, 160
Sipahiler ağası, 160. *See also*
  İsmail Bey
Sipahiler emini, 160, 238
Sipahiler katibi, 160, 238
Slobozia, 138
Smirnov, Sgt., 164
Smoking. *See* Refreshments
Smyadovo, 148
Solms, Count Victor Friedrich,
  50 n
Solova, 88
Spatar, 196, 216, 238; of
  Walachia, 138
Staff of Russian embassy, 33, 34,
  159 n. *See also* Parades and
  processions
Staff of Turkish embassy:
  supplemented by Russians in
  Moscow, 90
Stakhiev, Aleksandr Stakhievich,
  34, 50, 186, 188, 228
Stefănesti, 131, 198
Subaşı, 159, 164, 194, 238–39
Sublime State, 55
Sugar, Canary Island, 28 n
Süleymaniye Library, Istanbul, 7
Süleyman the Magnificent, 13

Sultan, 6, 11, 12, 14, 16, 17, 23,
56, 63, 65, 95, 167, 174;
Abdülhamit I, 55, 108, 209;
Ahmet III, 55, 108, 209;
Mustafa III, 2, 55, 219; pavilion,
169, 175; first audience with
Repnin, 168–73
Sumner, B. H., 36
Sumskii Hussar Regiment, 34
Suvorov, General, 38

Tabăra, 131, 198
Tahir (silâhdar ağası), 160
Tamara (interpreter), 49
Tasdikname. See Treaty ratification
Tatar (courier), 66
Tatars, 40, 47, 114; of Crimea,
36, 39, 42; factions, 44; han of,
44; non-Crimean, 49; problem
of definition, 46, 49. See also
Crimea
Tecuci, 137
Tent depot, imperial
(mehterhane-i amire), 19, 26
Tersane emini (admiralty
commander), 180, 181, 239
Teşrifatçı. See Master of
ceremonies, chief
Teşrifatçı efendi, 160, 175, 177,
180, 182, 183, 184, 185, 186,
187, 189
Tezkireci, 183, 187, 239
Tezkireci efendi, 176
Thugut, Freiherr v., 163
Timarabad, 60
Time, Turkish calculation, 17, 26,
58, 73, 97, 103, 107; error in,
93n
Titles. See Parades and
Processions; Rank
Tokay Timur, 44
Tolstodubovo, 88
Tooke, Richard: on Catherine's
Turkish policy, 36
Tophane pier, 164, 168, 174, 179,
182, 185, 187, 188, 239

Topkapı Palace: archives, 17–18,
19
Topliceni, 138
Trashchinskii (secretary), 160, 168
Travel conditions, 110, 114,
146–47, 148, 196
Travel route of Abdülkerim,
204–5; Hotin to Kiev, 78; Kiev
to Russian frontier, 85; Russian
frontier to Moscow, 88
Travel route of Repnin, 205–6
Treasurer: hazinedar, 94, 215–16;
vestiar maray, 131, 239–40
Treasury, Turkish state, 24
Treaties: Belgrade (1739), 2;
Hudaybiyah (A.D. 627), 2;
Karlowitz (1699), 1, 14
Treaty of Küçük Kaynarca (1774),
3, 4, 5, 14, 32, 35, 37–42, 48,
166, 172; Catherine's attitude
toward, 38; celebrated in
Moscow, 107; difficulty of
maintaining, 48; and exchange
of ambassadors, 5–6, 21, 33,
188; preliminary negotiations
for, 37–38, 56; prisoner of war
clauses, 99; revision attempted,
41, 43, 47, 48; Turkish attitude
toward, 40–41
Treaty ratification, 38;
Catherine's insistence on, 39,
48, 50, 108; ceremony of,
Istanbul, 38, 168–73; ceremony
of, Moscow, 94–95; instrument
of (tasdikname), 17, 58, 59, 93,
108. See also Rescript
Trifeşti, 131, 198
Tsar' Grad, 144, 168, 182, 191,
192, 197. See also Istanbul
Tula, 6, 88, 113; armament
industry, 12, 89, 118; described,
89; skill of craftsmen, 89
Tuligolovo, 86
Turkish language, 9, 11
Turkish text. See Sefaretname

Turnacı, 144, 147, 148, 159, 193,
  239; of Giurgiu (Abdullah Aga)
  144, 145
Turnacı ağası, 144, 145; Abdullah
  Baki, 144; Çadırcıoğlu Mehmet,
  144; Hasan, 147, 149
Turnovo, 63
Tutol'min, Major, 130, 133, 136,
  161
Tutora, 62, 64
Tynna, 78, 79

Uchevlar, 198
Ukhtomskoi, Prince, 159
Ukraine, 3
Ulema, 47, 49; religious
  fanaticism of, 49
Ümni Pasha: embassy to Russia
  (1740), 23, 90–91, 93. *See also*
  Embassies, Turkish
Unat, Professor Faik Reşit, 4n, 15
Unceşti, 137, 196
Utaşrahina, 78
Uzunlar [Dlŭzhko], 147

Vakareshti Monastery, 143
Valet (*çuhadar*), 59, 63, 92, 151,
  160, 164, 201
Valide Sarayı, 182, 239
Valts, Ivan (interpreter), 127
Varlaam (archimandrite of
  Focşani Monastery), 138
Vashana, 88
Vasil'kov, 81
Vaslui, 137, 196
Vekilharç aga of Hotin, 198, 239
Verderovskoi, Lt., 159
Vestiar maray (treasurer), 131,
  239–40
Vezir, 49, 69; of the agas, 179;
  veziral pomp, 70
Viazemskii, Prince, 40
Vienna, 2
Vild (secretary), 162, 200
Vilkens (interpreter), 127, 160

Vîrteşcoiu, 138
Voeikov, General in Chief Fedor
  Matveevich (governor general
  of Kiev), 72, 74, 76, 83, 125,
  126, 127, 128; negotiates
  mubadele, 71
Voivode (hospodar), 11, 240;
  of Giurgiu, 144, 145; of
  Kırklareli, 193. *See also* Ghika,
  Prince Gregory II; Ypsilanti,
  Alexander

Walachia, 2, 34, 39–40, 43, 61;
  as Ottoman listening post, 11;
  petition of boyars to Repnin,
  143n; *spatar* of (Rakoviţa), 138,
  145
Weights and measures, 240;
  arşin, 84n; *arşun*, 78; *dönüm*, 84,
  85; *zira*, 85
Weiker (Weiler), Heer, 162, 163n

Yambol, 60
Yarmolintsy, 78
Yaş. *See* Jassy
Yediçkul tribe of Crimea, 46
Yedisan tribe of Crimea, 46
Yemeklik aga, 158
Yemişçibaşı (fruit server of the
  sultan), 162
Yenikale, 38, 45; political
  importance of, 39
Yesman, 87
Ypsilanti, Alexander (voivode of
  Walachia), 61, 62n, 141, 142,
  143, 235; title of hospodar, 140

Zagarcıbaşı, 145, 240
Zegelin, Herr v., 163; Porte's
  displeasure with, 155n
Zevrak (boat), 90
Zhvanets, 27, 67, 72, 115
Zinkeisen, J. W., 43, 50
Zira (linear unit), 85

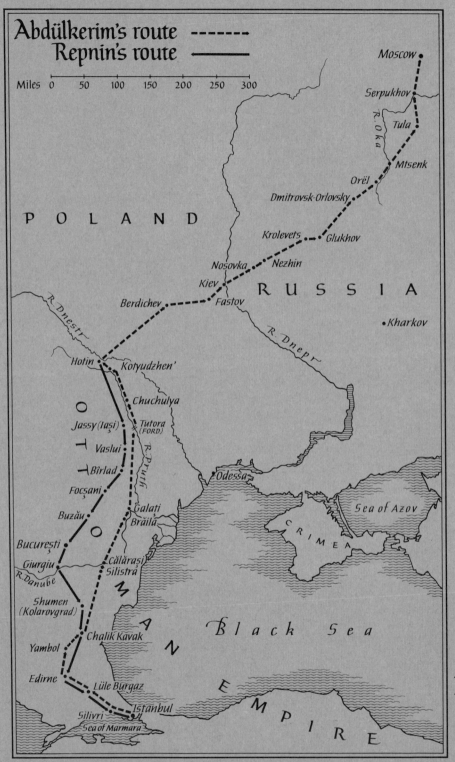

Abdülkerim's route ----------
Repnin's route ——————

Miles 0   50   100 150 200 250 300

POLAND

RUSSIA

Moscow
Serpukhov
Tula
R. Oka
Mtsenk
Orël
Dmitrovsk-Orlovsky
Kharkov
Glukhov
Krolevets
Nezhin
Nosovka
Kiev
Fastov
Berdichev
R. Dnestr
R. Dnepr

Hotin
Kotyudzhen'
Chuchulya
Jassy (Iaşi)
Tutora (FORD)
Vaslui
R. Pruth
Bîrlad
Focşani
Galaţi
Buzău
Brăila
Bucureşti
Odessa
Giurgiu
Călăraşi
R. Danube
Silistra
CRIMEA
Sea of Azov
Shumen (Kolarovgrad)
Chalik Kavak
Black Sea
Yambol
Edirne
Lüle Burgaz
Istanbul
Silivri
Sea of Marmara
OTTOMAN EMPIRE

Map by Leo Vernon